Philosophy on Tap

To anyone who has ever lifted a pint in philosophical contemplation, and to the brewers who make it possible.

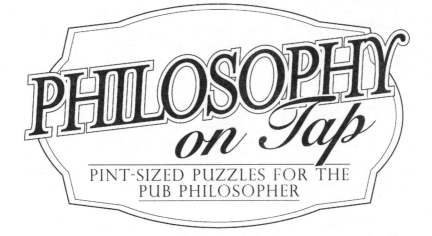

PHILOSOPHY on Tap

PINT-SIZED PUZZLES FOR THE PUB PHILOSOPHER

MATT LAWRENCE

WILEY-BLACKWELL

A John Wiley & Sons, Ltd., Publication

This edition first published 2011
© 2011 Matt Lawrence

Blackwell Publishing was acquired by John Wiley & Sons in February 2007. Blackwell's publishing program has been merged with Wiley's global Scientific, Technical, and Medical business to form Wiley-Blackwell.

Registered Office
John Wiley & Sons Ltd, The Atrium, Southern Gate, Chichester, West Sussex, PO19 8SQ, United Kingdom

Editorial Offices
350 Main Street, Malden, MA 02148-5020, USA
9600 Garsington Road, Oxford, OX4 2DQ, UK
The Atrium, Southern Gate, Chichester, West Sussex, PO19 8SQ, UK

For details of our global editorial offices, for customer services, and for information about how to apply for permission to reuse the copyright material in this book please see our website at www.wiley.com/wiley-blackwell.

The right of Matt Lawrence to be identified as the author of this work has been asserted in accordance with the UK Copyright, Designs and Patents Act 1988.

Wiley also publishes its books in a variety of electronic formats. Some content that appears in print may not be available in electronic books.

Designations used by companies to distinguish their products are often claimed as trademarks. All brand names and product names used in this book are trade names, service marks, trademarks or registered trademarks of their respective owners. The publisher is not associated with any product or vendor mentioned in this book. This publication is designed to provide accurate and authoritative information in regard to the subject matter covered. It is sold on the understanding that the publisher is not engaged in rendering professional services. If professional advice or other expert assistance is required, the services of a competent professional should be sought.

Library of Congress Cataloging-in-Publication Data is available on request.

ISBN 978-1-4443-3640-5

A catalogue record for this book is available from the British Library.

This book is published in the following electronic formats: eBook 9781444397000; ePub 9781444397017

Set in 10/12pt Meridian by Thomson Digital, Noida, India
Printed in Malaysia by Ho Printing (M) Sdn Bhd

01   2011

Contents

Preface   xi
A funny thing happened on the way to the monastery

Personal Acknowledgments   xvii

Acknowledgments   xviii

● ● ●

1 Transporter Troubles   1
   Shall we beam up another round?
   Pint of the Puzzle: Guinness *Extra Stout*

2 Zeno's Hand to Mouth Paradox   5
   How does the glass ever reach your mouth?
   Pint of the Puzzle: Weihenstephan *Original Lager*

3 If a Pint Spills in the Forest...   10
   If no one is there to hear it, would it still make a sound?
   Pint of the Puzzle: Sierra Nevada *Pale Ale*

4 The Beer Goggles Paradox   14
   Is beauty in the eye of the beerholder?
   Pint of the Puzzle: Flying Dog *Horn Dog Barleywine*

5 Pascal's Wager   19
   Would you dare bet against God?
   Pint of the Puzzle: Harp *Irish Lager*

6 The Experience Machine   23
   Would you choose the ultimate life of pleasure?
   Pint of the Puzzle: Young's *Double Chocolate Stout*

● ● ●

7 Lucretius' Spear   28
   Is there a pub at the end of the universe?
   Pint of the Puzzle: Unibroue *La Fin du Monde*

8   The Omnipotence Dilemma   33
     Can God make a keg so big that He himself can't lift it?
     Pint of the Puzzle: Belhaven *Wee Heavy Scotch Ale*

9   What Mary Didn't Know About Lager   36
     Can she know its taste without having a sense of taste?
     Pint of the Puzzle: Foster's *Lager*

10   Malcolm X and the Whites Only Bar   40
     What is race?
     Pint of the Puzzle: Avery's *White Rascal Ale*

11   Untangling Taste   44
     Are some beers truly better than others?
     Pint of the Puzzle: Big Sky *Moose Drool Brown Ale*

12   The Foreknowledge Paradox   50
     If God always knew which beer you'd order, are you still free?
     Pint of the Puzzle: Aktien's *Hell Lager*

● ● ●

13   The Buddha's Missing Self   54
     Are you the same person now as when you took your first sip?
     Pint of the Puzzle: Kingfisher *Premium Lager*

14   The Blind Men and the Black and Tan   59
     Could all the major religions be true?
     Pint of the Puzzle: Bass *Ale*

15   Liar's Paradox   65
     Can you discern the truth?
     Pint of the Puzzle: Roy Pitz *Truly Honest Ale*

16   Paley's Cask   69
     Is there an intelligent designer?
     Pint of the Puzzle: Newcastle *Brown Ale*

17   Chuang Tzu's Butterfly   74
     Could you be dreaming at this very moment?
     Pint of the Puzzle: Great Divide *Espresso Oak Aged Yeti*

18   Descartes' Doubt   78
     What do you know with absolute certainty?
     Pint of the Puzzle: Dogfish Head *Raison D'Etre*

● ● ●

19   God's Command   83
     Can saying make it so?
     Pint of the Puzzle: Shmaltz *He'brew Origin Pomegranate Ale*

20 Mill's Drunkard   87
    Are intellectual pleasures better than bodily pleasures?
    Pint of the Puzzle: Samuel Smith's *Oatmeal Stout*

21 The Myth of Gyges   91
    Who finished the pitcher?! Are we all just selfish?
    Pint of the Puzzle: Mythos *Greek Lager*

22 Laplace's Superscientist   95
    Is your next round totally predictable?
    Pint of the Puzzle: Surprise Me

23 Gaunilo's Perfect Ale   99
    If it were truly perfect, wouldn't it have to exist?
    Pint of the Puzzle: Chimay *Bleue "Grande Réserve"*

24 The Problem of Moral Truth   103
    Are moral beliefs ever true?
    Pint of the Puzzle: Wasatch *Polygamy Porter*

● ● ●

25 How to Sew on a Soul   107
    Where do I attach my inner taster?
    Pint of the Puzzle: Rogue *Dead Guy Ale*

26 Plato's Forms   112
    Are you tapping into a perfect world?
    Pint of the Puzzle: High and Mighty *Purity of Essence Lager*

27 Realizing Nirvana   116
    Are you ready to be enlightened?
    Pint of the Puzzle: Lhasa *Beer of Tibet*

28 The Problem of Evil   121
    If God exists, then why are there bad beers?
    Pint of the Puzzle: Victory *HopDevil IPA*

29 Time's Conundrum   125
    Does time exist? What about happy hour?
    Pint of the Puzzle: La Trappe *Quadrupel*

30 Time Travel Paradoxes   130
    *Is time travel possible? And if so,
    can I brew the world's first beer?*
    Pint of the Puzzle: Kronenbourg *1664*

● ● ●

31   Hitler's Hefeweizen   136
     Would you poison Hitler's pint?
     Pint of the Puzzle: Hofbräu *Hefeweizen*

32   The Zen *Kōan*   141
     What is the sound of one glass clinking?
     Pint of the Puzzle: Sapporo *Premium Lager*

33   Sex and Sensibility   146
     Are men and women from different morality planets?
     Pint of the Puzzle: His: Anchor *Steam;* Hers: Chardonnay

34   Socrates' Virtue   150
     Can you knowingly do wrong?
     Pint of the Puzzle: Blue Point *Hoptical Illusion*

35   Nature Calls   154
     Are human beings inherently good or evil?
     Pint of the Puzzle: Stone *Sublimely Self-Righteous Ale*
     OR *Arrogant Bastard Ale*

36   Nietzsche's Eternal Recurrence   159
     Would you choose that beer all over again? And again? And ...
     Pint of the Puzzle: North Coast *Brother Thelonious Abbey Ale*

37   The Most Interesting Man and the Firing Line   164
     Does it matter who pulls the trigger?
     Pint of the Puzzle: Dos Equis *Ambar*

38   Turing's Tasting Machine   169
     Could a computer judge beer?
     Pint of the Puzzle: Fuller's *London Pride*

39   Singer's Pond   174
     What do we owe to others? Should we buy them a round?
     Pint of the Puzzle: Yuengling *Traditional Lager*

40   The Wisest One of All   179
     Can ignorance be wisdom?
     Pint of the Puzzle: Elysian *The Wise ESB*

41   Enter the Matrix   182
     Is your pilsner merely electrical signals in your brain?
     Pint of the Puzzle: Moonlight Brewing *Reality Czech Pilsner*

42   A Case of Bad Faith   187
     Are you responsible for everything you do?
     Pint of the Puzzle: Fantôme *Pissenlit Saison*

43 Cask and Cleaver   191
    Are you a speciesist?
    Pint of the Puzzle: Laughing Dog *Alpha Dog Imperial IPA*

44 Flirting with Disaster   195
    When does flirtation become harassment?
    Pint of the Puzzle: St. Pauli Girl *Lager*

45 Fear of Zombies   200
    Are you tasting what I'm tasting?
    Are you tasting anything at all?
    Pint of the Puzzle: Alesmith *Old Numbskull Barleywine*

46 Lao Tzu's Empty Mug   204
    What good is emptiness?
    Pint of the Puzzle: Tsingtao *Lager*

47 Beer and the Meaning of Life   209
    Does life have meaning? Does it mean that
    I should have another beer?
    Pint of the Puzzle: Deschutes *The Abyss Imperial Stout*

48 The Case for Temperance   213
    To drink or not to drink? That is the question.
    Pint of the Puzzle: O'Doul's *Original Premium Non-alcoholic Beer*

Notes   218

Glossary of Beer and Philosophical Terms   229

Preface

A *funny thing happened on the way to the monastery*

I was driving down the southern California coast on my way to a meditation retreat, and thinking about the book of philosophical puzzles that I had been writing. My editor was enthusiastic about the project, but I still wasn't set on a title. Since it was a book of very short philosophical puzzles designed to whet the reader's appetite for philosophy, I tried to brainstorm titles based around small things, quick things, short things, wet things. Five-Minute Philosophical Puzzles? Bite-Sized Philosophical Puzzles? Forty-Eight Quick Conundrums? Obviously, I had to keep thinking. And then, out of nowhere, it hit me: Pint-Sized Philosophical Puzzles! After all, what goes better with a philosophical puzzle than a pint of good beer? And who loves philosophical puzzles more than beer drinkers? Like beer and football, or beer and pizza, beer and philosophy is a match ordained by the gods. One never knows quite how or why inspiration strikes, but, in retrospect, I realize that the idea came to me when I was just a couple of miles downwind of the Stone Brewery in Escondido, California. Surely the smell of fresh hops must have breezed through my open window. In any case, *Philosophy on Tap* was born – the first book ever to pair 48 great beers (two full cases) with 48 philosophical puzzles.

The basic idea of the book is to explain and examine each philosophical conundrum in no more time than it takes to drink the pint that accompanies it, and each pint has been selected expressly for its particular puzzle. For example, "Zeno's Paradox" is the oldest puzzle in the book from the Western philosophical tradition, so I've paired it with a beer from the oldest brewery in the Western world, Weihenstephan Original Lager. Plato's "Myth of Gyges" has been paired with a Greek lager that is quite appropriately called Mythos. And what would go better with the "Beer Goggles Paradox" than a Horn Dog Barleywine from the Flying Dog Brewery? In this manner you can explore 48 puzzles over

48 pints – preferably not all in one night. By the end of the book you'll be well versed in philosophy and in the great beers of the world.

About the Puzzles

In choosing the puzzles for the book, I have tried to cover the most central and perplexing questions of philosophy. Most are what can be fittingly called "life's biggest questions," but several were included because of their relevance to the beer-loving philosopher. "Untangling Taste" is a good example here, as is "The Case for Temperance." My aim throughout the book has been to "set up" the puzzles rather than to solve them. After all, half the fun of philosophy is to figure things out for oneself. So while I often suggest some possible solutions or relevant points to consider, the reader is generally left to reach his or her own conclusion, or, better still, to discuss it with friends at the pub.

About the Truth

You should be warned that I follow the well-established pub tradition of embellishing my stories. Occasionally I'll stretch the truth, and once in a while I'll tell a bald-faced lie. Of course this is all for your reading (and drinking) enjoyment. If you have a penchant for the truth, I suggest that you look for the "Truth be told" section that follows some of the puzzles. If there was a lie or "pub-stretch" somewhere in the puzzle, it is there that I will set the record straight.

About the Beer

In choosing the 48 beers that would become the "pints of the puzzles," my primary aim was to find beers that fit the particular puzzles in interesting or amusing ways. As you'll soon see, there are all sorts of ways that beer and philosophy intersect. Another key concern was quality. I have tried to avoid bad beers – though this can be a bit of a gray area given that people's tastes differ. Generally you'll find that the majority of the beers that I've included are award-winning brews that stand among the very best in the world. But because they cover a wide range of styles, it is doubtful that you will be crazy about them all. Yet anyone who drinks all 48 will be sure to encounter a number of their old favorites and to discover many new ones.

Since we've got two full cases to work with, we can break them down into four 12-packs.

American craft beers (lighter brews)

| Sierra Nevada *Pale Ale* | Avery's *White Rascal Wheat Ale* | Roy Pitz *Honest Ale* | Shmaltz *He'brew Origin Pomegranate Ale* | Rogue *Dead Guy Ale* | High & Mighty *Purity of Essence Lager* |

| Victory *HopDevil IPA* | Anchor Brewing *Anchor Steam* | Blue Point *Hoptical Illusion IPA* | Yuengling *Traditional Lager* | Moonlight *Reality Czeck Pilsner* | O'Doul's *Original Lager* (To be explained) |

American craft beers (darker/stronger brews)

| Flying Dog *Horn Dog Barley Wine* | Big Sky *Moose Drool Brown Ale* | Great Divide *Espresso Oak Aged Yeti* | Dogfish Head *Raison d'Etre Extreme Ale* | This Beer to be Determined by the Laws of Physics | Wasatch *Polygamy Porter* |

| Stone *Arrogant Bastard Ale* | North Coast *Brother Thelonius Abbey Ale* | Elysian *The Wise ESB* | Laughing Dog *Alpha Dog Imperial IPA* | Alesmith *Old Numbskull Barleywine* | Deschutes *The Abyss Imperial Stout* |

Beers of the world (lighter brews)

Weihenstephan	Harp	Foster's	Aktien	Kingfisher	Mythos
Original Lager	*Irish Lager*	*Lager*	*Hell Lager*	*Premium Lager*	*Greek Lager*

Lhasa	Kronenbourg	Hofbrau	Sapporo	St. Pauli Girl	Tsingtao
Beer of Tibet	*1664 Lager*	*Hefeweizen*	*Premium Lager*	*Lager*	*Lager*

Beers of the world (darker/stronger brews)

Guinness	Young's	Unibroue	Belhaven	Bass	Newcastle
Extra Stout	*Double*	*La Fin du*	*Wee Heavy*	*Pale Ale*	*Brown Ale*
Irish Stout	*Chocolate*	*Monde*	*Scotch Ale*	*(Black & Tan)*	
	Stout	*Tripel*			

Samuel Smith's	Chimay	La Trappe	Dos Equis	Fuller's	Fantôme
Oatmeal Stout	*Bleue*	*Quadrupel*	*Ambar*	*London Pride*	*Pissenlit*
	Trappist Ale	*Trappist Ale*			*Saison*

As you might imagine, some of the amber beers and strong ales resist classification in terms of simply light or dark, so please don't take their designation here too seriously. But I hope you'll appreciate the fact that I've tried to give you a rather balanced beer drinking experience through a wide range of beer styles from a number of different countries. Since half of them are American brews, only an American could find this assortment to be geographically "balanced" by any stretch of the imagination. But since American craft brewing has undergone such a revolution over the past 20 years, and has produced so many great and interesting beers, I hope you'll enjoy their prevalence nonetheless. I've also tried to create a balance between well-known beers and the more esoteric beers. Some of the latter may be tricky to find. Searching them out might strike you as a worthy and challenging quest – perhaps something to put on your "bucket-list" (beers to drink before you "kick the bucket"). But if you'd like to minimize the search, I've arranged several "Philosophy on Tap" beer packages with *Hi-Time Cellars*. They have one of the largest selections of bottled beer on the planet, and can ship them to your doorstep. You can order online at www.hitimewine.net/. Just select the tab for "beer" and search alphabetically for "Philosophy on Tap." At the end of each puzzle, you'll also find a space for your tasting notes, so that you can keep track of your new-found favorites. You can also visually document the flavors using the spider-web graph. Mark low-flavor values closest to the center, and high-flavor values toward the outside. The sample shown here is from a Belgian Dark Ale.

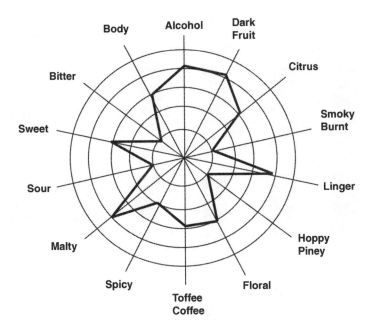

With your beer and book in hand, you're ready to begin. But please remember:

Drink in moderation. Think in excess.

Cheers,
Matt Lawrence
www.philosophyontap.com

Personal Acknowledgments

I'd like to offer a toast to all the people who made this book possible or helped with its fermentation. First and foremost, I want to thank my family: my wife Lisa and sons Jacoby, Jeremy, and Keenan, for their unwavering support despite the sacrifices that writing a book inevitably entails. If they hadn't each helped out in their innumerable ways, this book would never have come to be. An extra thanks to Jeremy for the use of his artistic talents on some of the illustrations, and to Jacoby for his helpful feedback and for proofreading the entire manuscript two times over. Randy Firestone's comments on early drafts were invaluable, and his enthusiasm for the project really helped to keep me going. Randy, I'm sure I owe you a few pints more. Thanks to Matt Sanders and Will Heusser for their aid (and good taste) during several beer tasting expeditions (I'll always keep a couple of craft brews cold for you guys), and to Will and Eric Cave for their thoughtful comments on the initial manuscript, as well as to Peter Lange for his proofreading and editing feedback.

Many of the ideas in the book, along with the manner of their presentation, were developed (sans beer) in the classroom, so I owe a huge debt of gratitude to my students at Long Beach City College. Their questions, comments, enthusiasm (and occasional boredom) have had a dramatic effect on my approach to philosophy, teaching, and writing. And thanks to members of the Long Beach City College Philosophy Club, who read and discussed a number of the chapters, and especially to Danny Wilson and Joe Shumsky, who not only had great ideas about the puzzles, but also laughed in all the right places. And to Randy Firestone's Philosophy Club at El Camino College, where a number of these puzzles were also put to the test.

Thanks to the team at Wiley-Blackwell. To Nick Bellorini who brought me on board (again), to Jeff Dean who saw the project through to its completion, to Sarah Dancy for her careful editing, and to everyone else who worked behind the scenes to bring it all together.

And finally, thanks to my mom. She inspired my love of philosophy long before I even knew what philosophy was. She will be missed.

Acknowledgments

The editors and publisher gratefully acknowledge the permissions granted to reproduce the following images in this book:

Chapter 7	Potential shapes of the universe. Used with permission from NASA/WAMP Science Team
Chapter 11	Flavor wheel. Used with permission from the American Society of Brewing Chemists
Chapter 12	Thinking about beer. Used with permission from Jeremy Lawrence
Chapter 14	Duck-rabbit. Used with permission from the Duck-Rabbit Craft Brewery, Inc.
Chapter 14	Maps. Used with permission from Jeremy Lawrence
Chapter 21	Skeleton with ring. Used with permission from Jeremy Lawrence
Chapter 25	Pineal gland. © Raúl González III
Chapter 30	Faces. © Raúl González III

Transporter Troubles

Shall we beam up another round?

Pint of the Puzzle: Guinness *Extra Stout*

Incredibly dark and rich, with hints of smokiness and coffee, Guinness Extra Stout is a perennial favorite among pub philosophers. In fact, a 2057 AD Gallup Poll will show that philosophers tend to beam up a pint of Guinness Extra Stout more frequently than any other beer.

If you have ever seen the classic television show *Star Trek*, you are surely familiar with Captain Kirk's famous line, "Beam me up, Scotty." As the Chief Engineer aboard the *Starship Enterprise*, Mr Scott would use the ship's transporter to make crew members disappear in one location and reappear in another. Since *Star Trek*'s debut in 1966, "teleportation" has become a staple of science fiction films.

Although teleportation is strictly science fiction today, it may one day become possible – perhaps in our lifetimes. If so, would you use this technology? Of course it sounds great. Who wouldn't want to have a fresh Guinness Stout transported straight to their easy chair from the St. James Gate

Philosophy on Tap: Pint-Sized Puzzles for the Pub Philosopher, First Edition. Matt Lawrence
© 2011 Matt Lawrence. Published 2011 by Blackwell Publishing Ltd.

Brewery in Dublin, Ireland? Or, better yet, why not transport yourself over to Dublin to take the brewery tour? (FYI: Everyone who takes the tour gets a complimentary pint of Guinness at its conclusion.) Well, before "beaming" yourself across the globe, perhaps you should first consider how these teleportation devices might work.

According to *Star Trek: Next Generation Technical Manual*, the *Star Trek*'s transporter works by scanning and recording the state of all of the subatomic particles within your body. The scan destroys the atomic bonds that hold the particles together and then sends the particles to your chosen location by way of a subatomically de-bonded matter stream. Upon arrival, your subatomic particles are reassembled using the atomic blueprint that was recorded by the scan. Suppose that 20 years from now a transporter is invented using this type of process. Thousands of people have now tried it out and there have never been any injuries. Everyone who has been transported agrees that they look and feel totally normal when they reach their destination. Would you give it a try? One possible reason for hesitation is the fact that the transporter is going to KILL YOU! By tearing apart all your subatomic particles, the transporter will quite literally *blow you to bits*. On the upside, of course, it will put you back together again, as good as new. Death and resurrection all within a few microseconds.

There are some other ways in which a transporter might work. Suppose that instead of sending your subatomic particles to your chosen destination, the transporter simply destroys them. What it sends is just the recorded scan of your atomic blueprint. Then, at your destination, the transporter reassembles your body using all new subatomic particles. In this case, you awaken at your destination with a *completely new body* – although it will look and feel exactly like your old one.

Consider one more possibility inspired by the Oxford philosopher Derek Parfit. Suppose that you are beaming from Los Angeles to Dublin. You've used transporters many times before, so you're not the least bit nervous. You step onto the pad and give the engineer the "ready" signal. You watch as she flips the switch and the blue light of the scanner moves down your body. You expect the usual "flicker" of unconsciousness before finding yourself in Dublin's St. James Gate Brewery Transport Center, but it never happens.

You look at your engineer inquisitively, and she says "Okay, you're all set. Please step off the pad and down the stairs on your left."

Puzzled, you reply, "But I'm supposed to be in Dublin – this is LA!"

"Oh, but you are in Dublin," she says. "Just look at the monitor."

To your amazement, you look up at the monitor and see yourself in the St. James Gate Brewery Transport Center stepping off the "arrivals" platform. The engineer explains: "You must not have known that this is the new ST101 Transporting System. As with many of the older systems, we send only your body scan to your chosen destination. In Dublin you were reassembled using entirely new particles. Of course, things went perfectly, and you are feeling quite yourself in Dublin." See, look again at the monitor. You're lining up for the Guinness tour.

"Yes, but I'm still here," you protest.

"That's the difference with the ST101," she continues. "While some of the older machines would destroy your body right here in order to use its atomic energy to deliver your body scan at light speed, the ST101 doesn't require that much energy. So instead, what I need you to do is to follow the yellow line to the elevator. Once inside, the red button will take you down to the power-plant level. When the door opens, your body will be instantly obliterated for you. Sorry about the extra wait, but this will allow us to use your atomic energy for Los Angeles's ever-increasing energy needs."

Slowly you walk to the elevator. Inside there is only one button, the red one. You know that by pushing it you will be delivered to your death. You know that the obliteration will be painless, and try to take comfort in the fact that your "new self" is already in Dublin soaking up the sights and sounds of the Guinness Storehouse. Nevertheless, it seems pretty obvious that "you" are still here, and are about to die.

Will you push the red button?

What do you think?

- The ST101 requires you to walk voluntarily to your own death, but isn't that true of the first two examples as well? Is the ST101 any "worse" than the other methods of teleportation?
- Would you push the red button?
- If you were to push the red button, would that be *your* death? Suppose that your friends were waiting for you in Dublin. What would they think?
- If your body is reassembled using all new particles, is that body still "yours?"
- Do you have a soul? If so, how is it related to your body? Would your soul travel to Dublin, or would it be "reborn" there? Or, would only some kind of mindless zombie arrive at the Guinness Storehouse?

Did you know?

- In June 2002 a team of scientists at the Australian National University successfully teleported the photons of a laser beam. Using a process called *quantum entanglement*, the team effectively teleported a radio signal contained in the laser beam from its location to a location one meter away. While this was the teleportation of *photons,* as of yet no one has been able to teleport a material object.

- David Page Mitchell's 1877 story "The Man Without A Body" may be the earliest use of the concept of teleportation in science fiction. His story told of a scientist who discovered a way to disassemble a cat's atoms, transmit them over a telegraph wire, and then reassemble them at a new location. When the scientist tried transporting himself, however, the telegraph's battery died when only his head had been transmitted.

- The Bible tells a story of what might be called the "miraculous teleportation" of Philip from Gaza to Azotus. In *Acts* 8:36–40 we find the following: "Then both Philip and the eunuch went down into the water and Philip baptized him. When they came up out of the water, the Spirit of the Lord suddenly took Philip away, and the eunuch did not see him again, but went on his way rejoicing. Philip, however, appeared at Azotus and traveled about, preaching the gospel in all the towns until he reached Caesarea."

- The Guinness Storehouse is located inside the St. James Gate Brewery, and its architecture is that of a giant pint glass. It has seven floors, the top of which is The Gravity Bar. (This is where you pick up your complimentary Guinness at the end of the tour.) If filled, this giant pint glass would hold 14.3 million pints of Guinness.

- Guinness Extra Stout can be used to make great cocktails. The classic Guinness cocktail is half champagne and half Guinness Extra Stout, served in a flute glass.

Recommended reading

- Derek Parfit, *Reasons and Persons* (Oxford: Clarendon Press, 1984).
- Richard Hanley, *The Metaphysics of Star Trek* (New York: Basic Books, 1997).

Tasting Notes: Guinness *Extra Stout*

Style: Irish Dry Stout   **Rating:** 1 2 3 4 5

| Appearance: |
| Nose: |
| Mouthfeel: |
| Flavors: |

Body   Alcohol   Dark Fruits
Bitter   Citrus
                          Smoky
Sweet   Burnt
Sour   Linger
Toffee   Hoppy
Coffee   Piney
Spicy   Floral
        Malty

Zeno's Hand to Mouth Paradox

How does the glass ever reach your mouth?

Pint of the Puzzle: Weihenstephan *Original Lager*

Since Zeno's Paradox is the oldest puzzle of the book from the Western philosophical tradition, it seems fitting to pair it up with a beer from the oldest brewery in the Western world. The Weihenstephan Brewery of Bavaria was founded in 1040 AD, making it not only the oldest brewery in the West, but the oldest on the planet. Original Lager is one of their classic recipes. It is clear, sparkling, and (thankfully) fresh. With a mild malt presence and light bitterness, it is the sort of beer that makes you want another – if you ever get the first up to your lips.

Before you take a sip of this historic brew, think about this. In order to take that sip, the pint must first be hoisted up to your lips. Suppose that this distance is a mere 12 inches. That should be simple enough. But notice that before it gets to your lips, your pint must pass through the halfway point between its resting spot on the bar or table and your mouth.

But once it reaches that halfway point, there is another halfway point between *it* and your lips. You cannot drink your beer until the pint passes through *that* point also.

Philosophy on Tap: Pint-Sized Puzzles for the Pub Philosopher, First Edition. Matt Lawrence
© 2011 Matt Lawrence. Published 2011 by Blackwell Publishing Ltd.

And, once the pint reaches *that* halfway point, it must pass through another halfway point between that former point and your lips. And, once it arrives *there* it must pass through another halfway point, and so on.

The problem, you now realize, is that in order to drink this pint, you are going to need to lift it through an infinite number of halfway points (since any distance can always be divided in half). And since it is impossible to pass through an infinite number of points in a finite amount of time, you will never get to taste this beer!

The Ancient Greek philosopher Zeno of Elea came up with this paradox (sometimes called the paradox of bisection) in the fifth century BC. Now, I know what you are thinking. Something has got to be wrong here. We know for a fact that the pint does reach your lips. In fact, I expect you have already proven that Zeno is wrong. (Refutation tastes pretty good, don't you think?) But Zeno would be unimpressed by the fact that you are currently sipping your beer. He thought that since reason shows us that the pint *cannot* reach your lips in a finite time (much less in a few seconds) our senses must deceive us. In a showdown between reason and the senses, he believed that we ought to choose reason. Zeno's conclusion: motion is impossible – no one ever drinks anything!

As you sit there drinking in the clean hop bitterness and light malty sweetness of your Original Lager, I expect that you believe that reason is on *your* side. But can you articulate those reasons? If Zeno is mistaken, where did he go wrong?

If you need a little help, here are a couple of ideas that you might do well to consider. First, must the beer really move through an infinite number of points in a finite amount of time? After all, can't we do the same sort of bisection concerning time? The two seconds that you took lifting the glass to your mouth can be divided at its midpoint, as can the next half of the journey, and the next, and so on. So we are left to suppose that while your pint passed through an infinite number of spatial points, it had an infinite number of temporal points in which to do so. No hurries – no worries. This reply may still leave us a bit uncomfortable (and Zeno smiling in his grave), because we are left wondering how the pint moved through infinite points (special *or* temporal) in only two seconds.

Another possibility, radical as it may seem, is to conclude that Zeno is right. Maybe objects don't really move at all. Some contemporary theories of space–time seem to support this idea. According to tenseless theories of time, all of time is "laid out" in both directions. It is inaccurate to say that the past is "gone" and that the future is "yet to be." Rather, both exist, just at different points within the space–time continuum. (For more on this, see chapter 29, "Time's Conundrum"). According to this theory, objects don't really move through space–time. Instead, your pint simply *exists* at a variety of points in the space–time continuum. For instance, the pint is sitting on the bar at one point in time, it is halfway to your mouth at another, it touches your lips at another, etc. The pint doesn't move from one point to the next. Instead, it simply exists at all these place-times. In this case, the *appearance* of motion would be just an illusion of your experience caused by the fact that you are unable to see the string of your pint's past and future place-times as a single whole.

Truth be told

Zeno's original paradox didn't really examine the case of lifting a pint to one's lips. Instead, his main example involved Achilles' attempt to catch a tortoise that had been given a head start in a foot race.

What do you think?

- Can you solve Zeno's paradox? Do you find either of the proposed solutions to be satisfactory?
- Is Zeno correct to think that a moving object would have to cross an infinite number of points in a finite amount of time in order to arrive at its destination?
- When push comes to shove, should we follow reason, or go with our sense experience?

Did you know?

- Zeno was a student of Parmenides who taught that both plurality and change are illusions. Zeno used his paradox of bisection to support Parmenides' view that reality is an unchanging, indivisible unity which he called "Being."
- Zeno is sometimes referred to as "Zeno of Elea" so not to be confused with "Zeno of Citium," the founder of Stoicism. (The name "Zeno" has obviously declined in popularity over the years.)
- Established in 1040 AD, the Weihenstephan Brewery predates the Christian Crusades, the first of which was preached in 1095 AD.
- Beer is one of the world's oldest prepared beverages and may date back as far as 9000 BCE. Many cultures learned to make beer before they knew how to bake bread.
- The Dogfish Head Brewery boasts the oldest beer recipe. Their Midas Touch is a recreation of the roughly 2,700-year-old residue found in a Goblet from King Midas's tomb. It contains barley, honey, grapes, and saffron. While not your standard ale, I found it rather tasty.

Recommended reading

- Joseph Mazur, *Zeno's Paradox: Unraveling the Ancient Mystery Behind the Science of Space and Time* (New York: Plume, 2008).
- Nicholas Fern, *Zeno and the Tortoise: How to Think Like a Philosopher* (New York: Grove Press, 2001).

Tasting Notes: Weihenstephan *Original Lager*

Style: Munich Helles Lager   **Rating:** 1 2 3 4 5

Appearance:

Nose:

Mouthfeel:

Flavors:

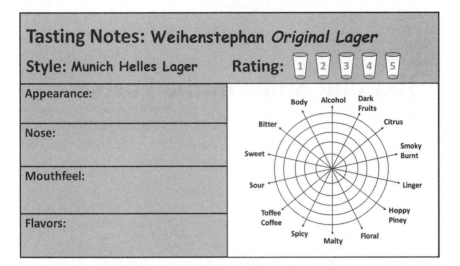

If a Pint Spills in the Forest ...

If no one is there to hear it, would it still make a sound?

Pint of the Puzzle: Sierra Nevada *Pale Ale*

What's a beer doing in the forest all by itself? Well obviously it must be one of those great brews of the Pacific Northwest like Sierra Nevada Pale Ale. Brewed in Chico California, with generous quantities of premium Cascade hops, this is the perfect beer to drink after a long hike in the wilderness – just be careful not to spill!

Here's a classic philosophical question that you may have heard before:

If a pint spills in the forest and no one is there to hear it, would it still make a sound?

This question often gets pulled out at parties and pubs when someone wants to "wax philosophical." Although most of us are inclined to think that *of course* it would make a sound, the point of the question is that we cannot really be sure. If no one was there to hear it, then we have no evidence either way.

Philosophy on Tap: Pint-Sized Puzzles for the Pub Philosopher, First Edition. Matt Lawrence
© 2011 Matt Lawrence. Published 2011 by Blackwell Publishing Ltd.

Before you start trying to invent ways to settle the issue (e.g., hidden recording, devices, sign-language adept chipmunks, etc.), let's consider what the Irish philosopher and bishop, George Berkeley (1685–1753), had to say on the matter. Bishop Berkeley's philosophy can be summed up by his famous dictum: "*To be is to be perceived.*" By this, he meant that objects (such as spilling pints of ale) exist only in the minds of those who perceive them. This is a pretty radical thesis. If correct, it entails that if no one was there to perceive it, not only would the spilling pint fail to make a sound, it would fail to exist at all!

Berkeley's metaphysical view denies the existence of *matter*, insofar as we mean "stuff that exists outside of and independently of our minds." All that truly exists in Berkeley's metaphysics are minds and the ideas, perceptions, or sensations of minds. This, of course, flies in the face of what almost everyone takes to be true – the existence of a material world outside our minds with which our senses interact. We might therefore suppose that a strong burden of proof falls on Berkeley to justify his view. But he maintained that it is those who believe in matter who need to justify their position. It is *their* position that contradicts our experience. As Berkeley put it:

> It is indeed an opinion strangely prevailing amongst men, that houses, moun-
> tains, rivers and in a word all sensible objects, have an existence natural or real
> distinct from them being perceived by the understanding. . . . For, what are the
> aforementioned objects but the things we perceive by sense? and what do we
> perceive besides our own ideas or sensations? and is it not plainly repugnant that
> any one of these, or any combination of them, should exist unperceived?

In order to understand Berkeley's point better, let's take a specific example. Consider, for a moment, what you know about the Sierra Nevada Pale Ale that sits before you. You know, for instance, that it has a beautiful golden hue that lies somewhere between a summer straw and a Malibu sunset. You know that its temperature is cool, that it is wet to the touch with a gently bubbly texture, and, when you put your ear to it, you can hear the ever so slight sound of those bubbles popping. But if you think carefully about this, you will realize that all you are really noticing are your own perceptions or sensations. When you perceive your beer's color, you are having a *sensation* of gold. When you perceive its temperature, you are having a *sensation* of coolness. And, when you perceive the bubbles on your tongue, or by putting your ear up to the glass, you are having certain tactile or auditory *sensations*. In fact, all that you know about this beer (or any beer) is limited to your sensations. But *where* are these sensations? In your mind, of course. *You* are having the sensations of golden, cool, wet, bubbly, etc. Certainly these sensations are not *in* the beer. They are simply a part of *your* awareness. Nevertheless we tend to insist that the pint of ale exists *outside* our minds. But on what grounds? Do sensations *inside* our minds really tell us what is going on *outside* our minds?

When we take a materialistic view of the world, we are asserting that we know what is outside our minds. For instance, that there are pints of beer "out there" shimmering in tones of gold, amber, or brown, wet and bubbly, and which make splashing sounds when they fall. But have you ever been "outside" your mind? Of course not. Wherever you go, you take your mind with you. So, why do you think that you know what is out there? And, what reason do you have for thinking that there is any beer "out there" at all?

Truth be told

As you probably know, the traditional question is: If a *tree* falls in the forest and no one is there to hear it, would it still make a sound?

What do you think?

- If a Sierra Nevada Pale Ale spills in the forest and no one is there to hear it, would it still make a sound?
- If no one was there to taste it, would it still have a taste?
- Suppose that you intentionally place a pint of ale in the forest in such a way that it will inevitably tip and spill. You place a tape recorder next to the pint. The next day you return to see that the pint has spilled (and no one was there to hear it). You play the tape and sure enough you hear the pint tip over and splash onto the forest floor. Does this disprove Berkeley's thesis? Why/why not?
- What is the strongest argument for the existence of matter? Does the fact that everyone seems to perceive beer the same way prove that beer exists outside of our minds?
- Even if we suppose that beers *are* "out there," should we believe that they are *really* golden, wet, bitter, and delicious? Or is this just how *we* perceive them to be? Do you suppose that all creatures perceive beer in exactly the same way?

Did you know?

- *Metaphysical idealism* is the name given to views such as Berkeley's, which maintain that only minds and ideas exist.
- Berkeley maintained that objects do not cease to exist when *we* stop perceiving them. This is because God (infinite mind) still perceives them.

● In 1734 Berkeley was made Anglican bishop of Cloyne, Ireland, where he served for most of the remainder of his life. He was so popular among the townspeople that even today, more than 250 years after his death; he is still affectionately referred to as "the bishop."

● Pale Ale is the flagship beer of the Sierra Nevada Brewing Co. It has won repeated gold medals at the Great American Beer Festival.

Recommended reading

- George Berkeley, *A Treatise Concerning the Principles of Human Knowledge.* Available online through Oregon State University: http://oregonstate.edu/instruct/ phl302/texts/berkeley/principles_contents.html
- George Berkeley, *Three Dialogues Between Hylas and Philonous* (Indianapolis, IN: Hackett, 1979).

Tasting Notes: Sierra Nevada *Pale Ale*

Style: American Pale Ale   **Rating:** 1 2 3 4 5

Appearance:	
Nose:	
Mouthfeel:	
Flavors:	

Body · Alcohol · Dark Fruits · Bitter · Citrus · Sweet · Smoky Burnt · Sour · Linger · Toffee Coffee · Hoppy Piney · Spicy · Malty · Floral

The Beer Goggles Paradox

Is beauty in the eye of the beerholder?

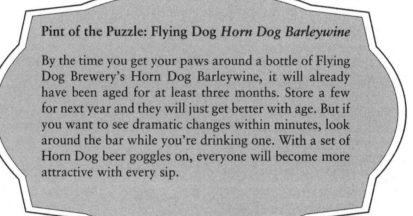

Pint of the Puzzle: Flying Dog *Horn Dog Barleywine*

By the time you get your paws around a bottle of Flying Dog Brewery's Horn Dog Barleywine, it will already have been aged for at least three months. Store a few for next year and they will just get better with age. But if you want to see dramatic changes within minutes, look around the bar while you're drinking one. With a set of Horn Dog beer goggles on, everyone will become more attractive with every sip.

We've all seen it. In fact, I'm sure that many of you have lived it. You know what I'm talking about. "Your friend" goes into a bar – let's call him Joe – and he complains all night: "There are just no good-looking women here. We might as well go home." Knowing that Joe hasn't had a date in a while, you suggest some possibilities. "Ugh! Not a chance!" is his reply. But the evening wears on, you have a few more beers, and, by the end of the night, Joe's whole perspective seems to have changed. The same woman, let's call her Joanne, whom he (quite insensitively) referred to as "butt-ugly" just a few hours ago, is now (apparently) quite attractive to him. He's saying that

Philosophy on Tap: Pint-Sized Puzzles for the Pub Philosopher, First Edition. Matt Lawrence © 2011 Matt Lawrence. Published 2011 by Blackwell Publishing Ltd.

she's "pretty hot" and the next thing you know Joe and Joanne head out the door together.

This phenomenon regarding a person's changing perception of beauty is widely known as "the beer goggles paradox" or the "10@2 paradox." How does a person who was a "2" at 10.00 p.m. become a "10" at 2.00 a.m.? One thing is obvious: when Joe left the bar with her he must have had his "beer goggles" on. But physically and phenomenologically, what exactly has happened? One explanation is that Joe has simply "lowered his standards." While this certainly can, and often does, happen, it is not the kind of case I have in mind with Joe. He's not thinking, "Well, she's ugly, but I'm not leaving here alone." Rather, he's excited about her now. He really seems to think that she is rather attractive (at the moment). He doesn't need to lower his standards. If she had stirred this sort of mental state in him at his very first glance, it might have been love at first sight.

In order to better sort out Joe's case, let's consider another case of changing perceptions and attitudes. In *Consciousness Explained*, Daniel Dennett describes a similar phenomenon regarding the taste of beer. Beer is an acquired taste, Dennett observes. People don't generally like it straight off; they train themselves, or somehow simply come to enjoy the flavor. But *what* flavor? The flavor of the first sip? Dennett imagines a couple of ways that the beer drinker might explain it:

> No one could like *that* flavor [an experienced beer drinker might retort]. Beer tastes different to the experienced beer drinker. If beer went on tasting to me the way the first sip tasted, I would never have gone on drinking beer! Or, to put the same point the other way around, if my first sip of beer had tasted to me the way my most recent sip tasted, I would never have had to acquire the taste in the first place! I would have loved the first sip as much as the one I just enjoyed.

> Other beer drinkers might insist that, no, beer *did* taste to them now the way it always did, only now they like *that very taste*.

We can raise the same question regarding Joe's experience. Does Joanne look rather different to him now (e.g., her hair more lustrous and face more delicate), as illustrated on the next page? Or, does he *see* essentially the same image that he first set eyes on, but somehow arrives at a different set of judgments about what he sees? That is, does she *look* the same, but now he likes that very look?

Which of these is the better explanation of Joe's experience may be tough to sort out, and I'll leave you to puzzle over it yourself. But let me first offer a third alternative so that you can be more thoroughly informed (and much more confused). Dennett contends that there is something

Before four Horn Dog Barleywines.   After four Horn Dog Barleywines.

altogether misguided in questions of the sort: *Was it how she looked that changed* or *was it what he liked?* The problem, according to Dennett, is that there is no such thing either as "how she looked at 10.00 p.m." or as "how she looked at 2.00 a.m." And, there is no "image" or "representation" that is separate and distinct from Joe's judgments about what he likes.

Dennett's theory of consciousness is what he calls a *multiple drafts model.* It denies that there is some center of experience or "Cartesian Theater" where the final stream of conscious experience unfolds under "our" gaze. "We don't directly experience what happens on our retinas, in our ears, on the surface of our skin," he argues. Instead, any experience, from "tasting a beer" to "gazing into Joanne's big dark eyes," is accomplished in the brain by "parallel, multi-track processes of interpretation and elaboration of sensory inputs" and is under continuous "editorial revision." There is no "final edit," and no "ghost in the machine" to view some mythical final product that might be called "how she looked at 10.00 p.m." or "how she struck him at 2.00 a.m." Instead, there are simply many independent streams of data and habits of reaction.

Dennett's theory of consciousness is admittedly anti-intuitive. He believes that most of us are too entrenched in a Cartesian Theater type of view of the mind to comprehend this alternative easily, and it would certainly take more than one pint of beer to treat it adequately here. You might conclude, "Well, I'll just drink four or five Horn Dogs and carefully observe the experience for myself." But Dennett would argue that this won't cut it either. The very problem with understanding the mind through subjective reflection is that appearances are deceiving. It is as if you were trying to understand a film projector by reflecting on how it seems when you watch a movie on the silver screen. Your experience would lead you to believe that the projector is emitting a single fluid moving picture. It is only by studying the projector and film that you would come to realize that the movie is just a series of still pictures flickered in succession. By the same token, Dennett contends that you cannot understand conscious experience just by examining your lived experience. You've got to look at how the brain, senses, and central nervous system work. And unfortunately, four or five Horndog Barleywines are not going to help you engage in that sort of investigation.

What do you think?

- What is the best explanation for Joe's attitude change toward Joanne? With his beer goggles on, does he see her differently, judge her differently, or both (or neither)?
- Do you agree with Dennett that there is no such thing as "how Joanne appears to Joe at 10.00 p.m.?"
- Are there any important differences between the case of Joe's perception of Joanne and the case of the beer drinker's acquired taste for beer?
- Consider the fact that a person may seem more beautiful to you after you get to know them – when their "inner beauty" shines through. (Or, conversely, when their personality may make them seem less attractive.) How should our analysis of this sort of case differ from the beer goggles case?

Did you know?

- One difference we should note between Joe's change of heart and the experienced beer drinker's change of taste is that, for the beer drinker, the change turns out to be rather permanent. Joe, on the other hand, is likely to revert back to his original attitudes toward Joanne tomorrow morning when his beer goggles have come off.
- Our introspections about consciousness seem to suggest that when we look at a person, we see a rather steady image of their face or body. But studies have shown that a person's eyes actually dart about rapidly, making about five fixations every second. The steadiness of the visual field that we seem to experience is due to editing in the brain.
- Horn Dog Barleywine was a Gold Medal Winner at the 2009 Great American Beer Festival. In addition, the Flying Dog Brewing Company won the "Mid-Sized Brewery of the Year" award.
- If the artwork on Flying Dog bottles looks vaguely familiar, that is because it is done by Ralph Steadman, who provided illustrations for Hunter S. Thompson's *Fear and Loathing in Las Vegas*. It was Thompson who introduced Steadman to Flying Dog Brewing's co-owner George Stranahan.

Recommended reading

- Daniel Dennett, *Consciousness Explained* (Boston: Little Brown, 1991).
- Nancy Etcoff, *Survival of the Prettiest: The Science of Beauty* (New York: Anchor Books, 1999).

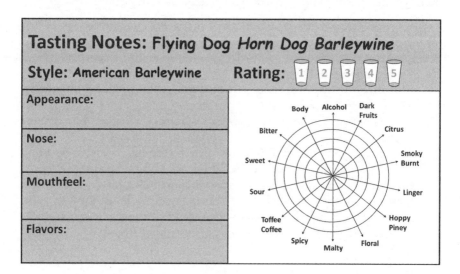

Pascal's Wager

Would you dare bet against God?

Plenty of philosophers have attempted to prove God's existence. But the French philosopher and mathematician Blaise Pascal (1623–1662) denied that such a feat was possible. He compared the likelihood of God's existence to a coin toss. Maybe it will land "heads" (God exists) and maybe it will land "tails" (God does not exist), but we simply cannot know the outcome beforehand. Despite his pessimism in this regard, Pascal counted himself among the "believers," and he developed an argument that he thought ought to make a believer out of you – if you are not one already.

Rather than attempting to prove God's existence, Pascal focused on the question of whether it was more *rational to believe* that God exists than to

Philosophy on Tap: Pint-Sized Puzzles for the Pub Philosopher, First Edition. Matt Lawrence
© 2011 Matt Lawrence. Published 2011 by Blackwell Publishing Ltd.

disbelieve it. His argument rests on the idea that some choices can be more reasonable than others even when one is operating under conditions of uncertainty.

This is an idea that gamblers have long known to be true. Suppose, for example, that you are sitting in an Irish pub with a friend who is an incessant gambler. He'll bet on just about anything, and tonight he wants to wager on what beer will be ordered most frequently over the next 15 minutes. Since you are in an Irish pub, the contenders are pretty clear. You've been keeping an eye on the taps, and so far tonight it has been a dead heat between Harp and Guinness. Nevertheless, you have no idea which of the two would win. And since you prefer to bet only when the odds are in your favor, you tell him that you'll pass on this wager. So he sweetens the pot by saying:

> Choose either beer you'd like. But if you choose Harp and you're right, then I'll buy all the food and drinks tonight, plus I'll spring for the cab ride home. And if you choose Harp and you're wrong, then you only owe me a pint. However, if you choose Guinness and you're right, then I'll buy you a pint. Choose Guinness and you're wrong, and you buy all the food and drinks for the night plus the cab ride home.

If you think about it, so long as he doesn't have any inside information, or is rigging the outcome in some way, this is a pretty sweet bet – so long as you go with Harp Lager. Bet on Harp and you stand to lose very little and to gain quite a lot. Conversely, if you were to bet on Guinness you would stand to lose quite a lot and to gain very little. The choice of Harp is a "no-brainer."

Pascal thought that the choice of whether or not to believe in God is a similar sort of wager taken to the *absolute extreme*. We might put it like this:

> Choose either outcome you like. You can wager that God exists, or that He doesn't. But if you believe that God exists and you're right, then eternal life in paradise will be yours. And, if you believe in God and you're wrong, then you will have wasted a few Sundays in church. However, if you believe that God does not exist and you're right, what do you get? Little more than those few Sundays to watch football, drink beer, etc. But if you don't believe in God and you're wrong, then eternal damnation awaits!

Pascal thought that this was the ultimate no-brainer. Why would anyone wager against God's existence when it means risking so much to gain so little – especially when, by wagering on God, they could risk very little and stand to gain so much? No rational gambler would wager against God's existence under this risk/reward scheme. Yet we are all forced to wager. Each of us will die as a believer or a non-believer. So we must make a choice. And for Pascal's money, there is only one reasonable choice to make, the choice of God.

How strong is this argument? That will depend upon the reasonableness of Pascal's initial assumptions. So here are a couple of points that you might want to consider. First, Pascal is assuming that if God exists, it is the God of Christianity, who gives out rewards and punishments that are in some way tied to one's belief in Him. If you make that assumption, then the argument is fairly effective. But without it, the argument hits a serious snag. For what if there is indeed a God, but it is not the Christian God? Suppose it is Zeus, or Voltar, or some other God who hates nothing more than those who believe in other gods. In this case, the very act of believing in the Christian God could be the very thing that lands you in hell.

Another concern is that Pascal's argument "commercializes" religious belief. The whole argument is based on the individual's selfish desire to do whatever will bring them the greatest personal benefit. We have to wonder, is God going to be impressed with such selfishness? Is He really going to reward you with heaven for having such a self-centered outlook? But keep in mind that nothing that Pascal said commits him to the idea that God will reward you merely for believing. Belief in God may not be sufficient for attaining salvation, but Pascal thought that it was certainly necessary. It is a starting place on the religious path, and Pascal's goal is to get you started.

What do you think?

- Does Pascal succeed in proving that it is more rational to believe in God than not to believe?
- If God exists, what do you suppose is necessary and sufficient for one's salvation? Is believing in God enough?
- Suppose that you currently believe that God's existence is rather unlikely. However, you are convinced by Pascal's argument that it is a better wager to believe in God than not to believe. So now you *want* to believe. Is it in your power simply to choose to believe right here and now? Can you become a believer at this very moment? Or, would you have first to acquire some kind of evidence or experience that would change your mind about the likelihood of God's existence?

Did you know?

- The Vikings had their own ideas about heaven. According to Norse mythology, Valhalla would include a giant goat whose udders would provide them with an endless supply of beer. Who'd bet against that?
- Pascal thought that it was impossible to simply *choose* to believe that God exists just because you see that it "pays" to believe in God. However,

he thought that you could perform actions that would, over time, cause you to believe. He felt that by simply "acting" like believers (by going to mass, taking the holy water, etc.) people often do become true believers. This is, after all, how small children enter the faith.

🍺 Pascal invented one of the world's first calculating machines called "the pascaline." It could enable one person to do the work of six accountants. The computer programming language *Pascal* was named after him, as was *Pascal's Triangle*. The latter is not a three-sided geometrical figure, but a geometrical arrangement of numbers (binomial coefficients) in a triangle shape.

🍺 Harp Lager was first produced in 1960 by The Great Northern Brewery in Dundalk in response to the growing trend among beer drinkers in Ireland and Britain toward continental style lagers.

Recommended reading

- Blaise Pascal, *Pensées*. Available online through Project Gutenberg: http://www. gutenberg.org/etext/18269.
- James Connor, *Pascal's Wager: The Man Who Played Dice With God* (New York: HarperOne, 2009).

Tasting Notes: Harp *Irish Lager*

Style: Irish Lager   **Rating:** 1 2 3 4 5

Appearance:	
Nose:	
Mouthfeel:	
Flavors:	

The Experience Machine

Would you choose the ultimate life of pleasure?

Pint of the Puzzle: Young's *Double Chocolate Stout*

Since this puzzle is about pleasure, let's serve up a really decadent beer. Young's Double Chocolate Stout is a full-flavored English stout brewed with chocolate malt, real dark chocolate, and chocolate essence. It's sure to bring out the hedonist in you.

What do you want out of your beer? The obvious answer would be pleasure. But consider your light beer drinkers. Like anyone else, they want their beer to taste good. But obviously they are willing to sacrifice some flavor for fewer calories. Then there is your bargain hunter who simply chooses whatever 12-pack happens to be on sale. So it would seem that a person might be after any number of things – a smaller waistline, a fatter wallet, great taste, or the "image" that has been marketed for that particular beer. But some philosophers, called hedonists, would argue that such appearances are deceiving. All any of us really want is just one thing – pleasure.

Philosophy on Tap: Pint-Sized Puzzles for the Pub Philosopher, First Edition. Matt Lawrence
© 2011 Matt Lawrence. Published 2011 by Blackwell Publishing Ltd.

According to hedonists, pleasure or happiness (these are the same as far as they are concerned) is the only thing that anyone ever wants – including the light beer and bargain beer drinkers of the world. Despite the short-term loss of pleasure, they obviously believe that they'll be happier in the long run if they keep off the extra pounds and/or keep their wallets fat.

Are the hedonists right? Is pleasure or happiness the only thing that we really care about? Harvard Philosopher Robert Nozick (1938–2002) offered a futuristic thought experiment designed to illustrate that the hedonist's view of human nature is false:

> Suppose that there were an experience machine that would give you any experience you desired. Superduper neuropyschologists could stimulate your brain so that you would think and feel you were writing a great novel, or making a friend, or drinking the best chocolate stout of your entire life. All the time you would be floating in a tank, with electrodes attached to your brain.

If you allow yourself to be hooked up to the experience machine, you are virtually guaranteed considerably more pleasure than you would experience in your "normal" life. After all, the experience machine can be programmed so that you live out your wildest dreams. You could be a basketball star and break all of Michael Jordan's records, date supermodels, and drink double chocolate stouts all night without waking up with a headache. The only catch, of course, is that it would not be "real."

Suppose that The Experience Machine Store in your local mall is offering a two-hour free trial. Would you take them up on their offer? If you're uncertain, consider *EMS*'s responses to some frequently asked questions:

Q: *Is the Experience Machine safe?*

A: The Experience Machine is completely safe. Studies have shown that it is actually much safer than living in the "real world." Since you will be floating calmly in your own individual tank, you are not subject to everyday risks such as contagious diseases, auto accidents, or morning after hangovers. In fact, "lifetime members" have an average life expectancy of over 95 years!

Q: *If I know that the experience isn't real, won't that take the fun out of it?*

A: The great thing about the Experience Machine is that you won't know that the experience isn't real. Using our patented technology, we erase all of your memories concerning our company and this technology. We then weave your machine induced experiences directly into your past memories, giving you an experience that seems completely authentic.

Q: *Won't I miss my friends and family?*

A: Absolutely not. We can program your experience to include anyone you choose – friends, family, even famous celebrities! (Of course these people won't "really" be interacting with you, but it will seem exactly as if they were.)

Q: *Won't my friends and family miss me?*

A: If you choose a lengthy experience package, your friends and family will undoubtedly miss you. If this is a concern, we recommend the "Friends and Family Plan." With this package your friends and family can all connect to the machine on the same day. Although you will each embark on your own individually programmed experience, you will continue to believe that you are all living out your lives together. Thus, no hard feelings!

Q: *Will I still make my own choices?*

A: Certainly not. For example, if you choose to experience the life of a world champion chess player, we obviously cannot allow you to make your own choices – you'd lose terribly. What would be the point? The beauty of the Experience Machine is that it will allow you to experience better choices than those you would ordinarily make, yet it will feel just like you are choosing for yourself.

Q: *How long does the experience last?*

A: You can sign up for any length of time. You can choose a day, a month, a year. But, of course, our most popular item is the lifetime plan. After all, when it comes to pleasurable experiences, more is always better!

Ready to sign up? If you are like me, you'd probably like to try out the experience machine for at least a few hours. Why not experience a few of the things that you will otherwise never get the opportunity to try? The more interesting question is whether you would hook up to the experience machine for an extended period of time – for several years, or even for life. Notice that if the hedonist is correct, this should not be a difficult choice. Since a lifetime in the experience machine would offer much more pleasure than "real life" (and also more pleasure than any shorter experience package), then *of course* you should sign up for a lifetime. But Nozick created this thought experiment precisely because he thinks that most people would choose their "normal" life, with all its frustrations, boredom, loneliness etc., over the life of maximum pleasure that the experience machine would provide. Is he right? Or would you choose to live your life in the artificial paradise of the experience machine?

Truth be told

The quoted passage from Robert Nozick's book, *Anarchy, State, and Utopia,* did not originally contain any mention of chocolate stout. In its place he had said that one might choose to "read an interesting book." But seriously, Robert, who would use an experience machine to read books? Give me a great chocolate stout!

What do you think?

- Is Nozick correct to think that you would choose your "normal" life over a lifetime in the experience machine? And if so, does this prove that pleasure is not our only desire?
- Would you choose the experience machine for a day? What about for a year?
- If you wouldn't choose the experience machine for a lifetime despite the fact that it offers more pleasure, then what other goods does it lack? Consider the following: (a) Would you be able to form real friendships or love relationships? (b) Would you be able to accomplish anything significant? (c) Do you want to make your own choices or merely feel like you are making them?

Did you know?

- According to an Ancient Egyptian proverb, "The mouth of a perfectly contented man is filled with beer."
- With just one exception, Robert Nozick never taught the same course twice during his 33 years as a Harvard University professor, He was interested in most areas of philosophy, and made major contributions in political philosophy, epistemology, rational choice theory, philosophy of mind, and ethics.
- A University of Michigan study found that chocolate causes the brain to release opioids, a chemical that produces pleasurable feelings. (Morphine and heroin are opioids.) Thus chocolate has a slight capacity to dull pain, and to give us a bit of a euphoric feeling, which, I believe, is greatly enhanced when blended with English stout.

According to scientists at Georgetown University Medical Center, chocolate (especially dark chocolate as used in Young's Double Chocolate Stout) has definite health benefits. Their research indicates that chocolate slowed the growth of colon cancer by 50 percent.

Recommended reading

- Steven M. Chan and Christine Vitrano, eds., *Happiness: Classic and Contemporary Readings in Philosophy* (Oxford: Oxford University Press, 2007).
- Nicholas White, *A Brief History of Happiness* (Oxford: Blackwell, 2006).

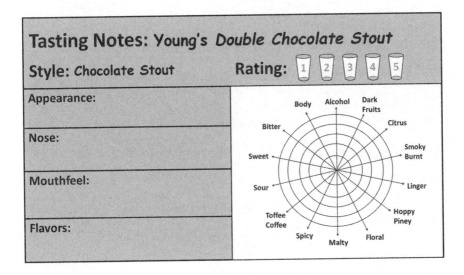

Tasting Notes: Young's *Double Chocolate Stout*

Style: Chocolate Stout **Rating:** 1 2 3 4 5

Appearance:

Nose:

Mouthfeel:

Flavors:

Body Alcohol Dark Fruits
Bitter Citrus
Sweet Smoky Burnt
Sour Linger
Toffee Hoppy Piney
Coffee
Spicy Malty Floral

7

Lucretius' Spear

Is there a pub at the end of the universe?

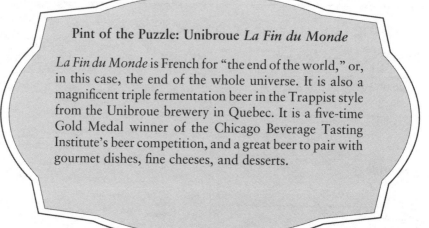

Pint of the Puzzle: Unibroue *La Fin du Monde*

La Fin du Monde is French for "the end of the world," or, in this case, the end of the whole universe. It is also a magnificent triple fermentation beer in the Trappist style from the Unibroue brewery in Quebec. It is a five-time Gold Medal winner of the Chicago Beverage Tasting Institute's beer competition, and a great beer to pair with gourmet dishes, fine cheeses, and desserts.

This is one of the first philosophical mind-benders that I ever encountered. I must have been about 6 or 7 when a friend of my parents said to me, "Imagine that you are in a rocket traveling into the far reaches of space. Do you think that you would ever hit the end?" The answer, I thought, was rather obvious. The universe *had* to go on forever, because if it stopped, what would be outside? More universe of course!

This puzzle was explored by an Ancient Roman philosopher named Lucretius (*c.* 99 BCE – *c.* 55 CE). He put it something like this. If there is an end to the universe, one could toss a spear at it. If the spear sails through, then this wasn't the end after all. If, on the other hand, the spear bounces back,

Philosophy on Tap: Pint-Sized Puzzles for the Pub Philosopher, First Edition. Matt Lawrence
© 2011 Matt Lawrence. Published 2011 by Blackwell Publishing Ltd.

then it must have been stopped by something – a kind of "cosmic wall" or boundary. This wall or boundary would have to have some thickness to it (i.e., it must extend further into space), thus the surface upon which the spear bounced back was not the end of the universe at all. Wherever you mark the end of the universe, Lucretius suggests, one can always ask, "What would happen if I threw my spear at it?" In this manner he concluded that there can be no end to the universe. It must be infinite.

It is kind of nice to know that my boyhood self arrived at the same conclusion as a great philosopher like Lucretius. But these days I realize that while I *may* have been right, the matter is a bit more complicated. Today, the question of the size and shape of the universe has been largely taken over by science. And cosmologists have hypothesized a variety of scenarios.

Here's one hypothesis that averts Lucretius' conclusions. Ever since Einstein's theories of relativity were introduced in the early twentieth century, scientists have understood gravity to be, not an "invisible pulling force," but rather the "bending of space–time." The basic idea is that the moon, for example, doesn't orbit the earth because it is being "pulled" toward us. Instead, it is moving in what would be a straight line (objects always take the path of least resistance), except that the space it moves through is curved. If that is hard to imagine, think of this. Have you ever seen those big steel drums (typically used for donations at museums) where you roll your spare coins into the top, which is shaped like a very large funnel? The coin rolls along the high edge and slowly works its way down the funnel, circling faster and faster until it finally drops into the hole at the center. The coin goes round and round only because the space on which it is rolling is

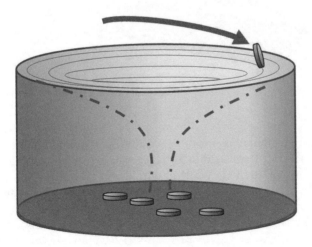

Donation drum.

curved. It is a similar phenomenon with the moon and other satellites that orbit the earth. The difference is that they are not moving across a metal surface. Rather it is the space–time continuum itself that is bent around the mass of our earth.

Einstein's hypothesis that space itself can be curved was rather astounding, yet it was experimentally verified in May 1919 and many times since. If we apply this insight to Lucretius' thought experiment, we can suppose that when he throws the spear, the spear will not move straight outward so long as gravity has caused the space of our universe to be essentially curved. Throw the spear hard enough, and all he will achieve is to send it orbiting around the outskirts of the universe!

For years the available data could not tell us the overall shape of the universe, but cosmologists had narrowed it down to three possibilities – as illustrated here.

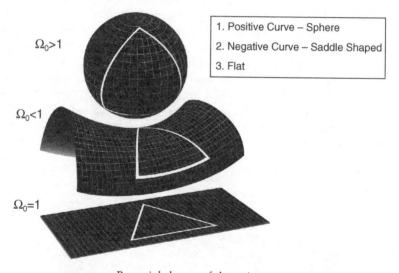

$\Omega_0 > 1$

1. Positive Curve – Sphere
2. Negative Curve – Saddle Shaped
3. Flat

$\Omega_0 < 1$

$\Omega_0 = 1$

Potential shapes of the universe.

Today, with measurements of the cosmic background radiation from the WMAP spacecraft (launched in 2001), cosmologists are confident that the universe is essentially flat. While gravity does curve space locally (around stars, planets, etc.), the universe as a whole has an essentially flat architecture. Throw your spear hard enough, and it will never return.

This still leaves us to wonder about where it will go. Will it ever hit the end? According to physicist Lawrence Krauss, a flat universe will be infinite in spatial extent, so Lucretius' spear would just keep sailing forever into endless space. So by today's best evidence, it would seem that Lucretius was right – the universe has no end.

While Lucretius successfully anticipated the conclusion of modern physics, an infinite universe is still rather puzzling. Infinity is an incredibly difficult concept to wrap your mind around. For example, we know with certainty that the universe is expanding. But if the universe is already infinite, where is it going? Doesn't the idea of expansion presume that there is something beyond our universe? And, if so, what would happen if we threw a spear at it?

What do you think?

- Must the universe be infinite as Lucretius supposed?
- If the universe has a limit, should we say that it is surrounded by "nothingness?" Can we even make sense of that idea?
- Is it illegitimate or somehow self-contradictory to imagine a spear being thrown into absolute nothingness?
- If the universe is truly infinite in size, would it therefore contain an infinite number of pubs?

Did you know?

- Some scientists have suggested that what may be "outside" our universe (if it is bounded at all) is other bounded universes. You might imagine our universe as existing like a soap bubble in an endless sea of foam. Everything that exists (for us) is inside our bubble. However, our bubble could be surrounded by more bubbles (more discrete universes). But again we can ask, does the foam go on forever, or does it reach an end?
- Einstein's eclipse experiment of 1919 showed that the mass of the sun caused the bending of space–time such that the light of a star that is seen during a solar eclipse would appear at a point in the sky where we do not regularly find it at night, when the sun does not affect our view.
- Gravity not only shapes space–time, it also shapes your beer. "Terminal gravity" or "final gravity" refers to a measurement taken by beer brewers regarding the ratio of the density of a sample to the density of water. The "original gravity" is this density prior to fermentation, and the "terminal gravity" is the density after fermentation.
- There is, in fact, a "Pub at the End of the Universe." You can find it at 4107 SE 26th Street, Portland, Oregon 97202.

Recommended reading

- Lucretius, *On the Nature of Things*. Available online through the Internet Classics Archive: http://classics.mit.edu/Carus/nature_things.
- Brian Greene, *The Fabric of the Cosmos* (New York: Random House, 2004).

Tasting Notes: Unibroue *La Fin du Monde*

Style: Belgian Style Tripel   **Rating:** 1 2 3 4 5

Appearance:	
Nose:	
Mouthfeel:	
Flavors:	

Body Alcohol Dark Fruits
Bitter   Citrus
Sweet   Smoky Burnt
Sour   Linger
Toffee Coffee   Hoppy Piney
Spicy   Malty   Floral

8

The Omnipotence Dilemma

Can God make a keg so big that He himself can't lift it?

Pint of the Puzzle: Belhaven *Wee Heavy Scotch Ale*

Is there anything more exhausting than a long night of lifting pints – especially when they are pints of Belhaven Wee Heavy Scotch Ale? Well, I suppose that there are more laborious tasks, but rarely is such hard work so worthwhile. It makes you wonder how much ale God could put down in an evening – if he were so inclined.

People tend to disagree about what exactly God is like. Some, for instance, maintain that God would never drink beer. Others cannot fathom the idea that He would spare himself such a luxury, and think that He must be enjoying some truly heavenly brews. But there's one point on which most everyone seems to agree: if God exists, He must be *omnipotent* or "all-powerful." He can do whatever He sets his mind to. But this idea seems to run one into some philosophical snags. Can God do absolutely anything? If you think so, then how would you respond to the following question:

Can Almighty God make a keg of scotch ale so big that not even He can lift it?

Philosophy on Tap: Pint-Sized Puzzles for the Pub Philosopher, First Edition. Matt Lawrence
© 2011 Matt Lawrence. Published 2011 by Blackwell Publishing Ltd.

Do you see the problem? If you maintain that God truly is "all-powerful," then it seems that you must suppose that He surely could make such a keg. After all, He can do anything. But the moment that you say that God can make this keg, then you are forced to admit that He cannot do *anything* – because He cannot lift that keg. And, conversely, if you say that God cannot make such a keg, then again you have admitted that there is something He cannot do. Your reasoning leaves you stuck between "a keg and a hard place."

This problem is called *the omnipotence dilemma*. There seem to be only two possibilities and both lead us to the conclusion that God cannot be omnipotent.

Is there any way to escape the omnipotence dilemma? One of the most promising routes is to argue that the dilemma arises from a misunderstanding of the concept of omnipotence. We got ourselves into this predicament because we had supposed a particular conception of omnipotence:

Omnipotence[1]: The ability to do anything

when perhaps we should have understood omnipotence as:

Omnipotence[2]: The ability to do anything that is *do-able*.

If we understand omnipotence in this latter sense, then, although God can do anything that is do-able, some things may not be do-able (that is, they are downright impossible). Take, for instance, a round-square. If a figure is round (i.e., perfectly curved and without corners), then it cannot simultaneously be square (i.e., possess four corners). And if it is square, it cannot be round. The idea of a round-square is self-contradictory, and hence impossible to create – even for God. In the same fashion, one can maintain that God cannot create a keg so big that He cannot lift it. The very idea of a keg that is so big that an omnipotent being cannot lift it is self-contradictory, and hence "not do-able" – even for God. Yet God remains omnipotent in the latter sense. Although He can't make that keg, He can still create any keg that is "creatable."

Some people find this solution quite satisfying, while others think that it puts an inappropriate (and even blasphemous) limit on God's power. But you have to wonder, is it reasonable for us to expect, or even want, anything more?

What do you think?

- Do you think that God can do absolutely anything?
- Does understanding "omnipotence" in the sense of omnipotence[2] adequately resolve the dilemma? Why or why not?
- Can you think of any other (or better) ways to resolve the dilemma?

Did you know?

- St. Augustine's solution to the dilemma essentially states that God cannot do anything that would cease to make God "God." That is, God cannot contradict His own nature.
- Averroes (1126–1198) was one of the early Muslim scholars to address the omnipotence dilemma.
- Another version of the omnipotence dilemma arises from the question: Can God make a beer so bitter that not even He can drink it?
- Established in 1719, Belhaven is the oldest and largest brewery in Scotland. It boasts its Belhaven Best as "the pint of pints."

Recommended reading

- George Mavrodes, "God's Omnipotence," *The Philosophical Review* 73 (1964). Reprinted in Steven Cahn, ed., *Exploring Philosophy of Religion* (Oxford: Oxford University Press, 2009).
- Alvin Plantinga, *Does God Have a Nature?* (Milwaukee, WI: Marquette University Press, 1980).

Tasting Notes: Belhaven *Wee Heavy Scotch Ale*

Style: Scotch Ale   **Rating:** 1 2 3 4 5

Appearance:	
Nose:	
Mouthfeel:	
Flavors:	

Body · Alcohol · Dark Fruits · Citrus · Bitter · Smoky Burnt · Sweet · Linger · Sour · Hoppy Piney · Toffee Coffee · Floral · Spicy · Malty

9

What Mary Didn't Know About Lager

Can she know its taste without having a sense of taste?

Pint of the Puzzle: Foster's *Lager*

This puzzle comes from the Australian philosopher Frank Jackson. That seems like excuse enough to pop open a Foster's Lager – the "amber nectar" from Down Under. And while you're at it, take a moment to appreciate the little things – like your taste buds.

Imagine the case of Mary the Neuroscientist. To say that Mary is the leading expert on the physiology of taste is an understatement. Mary, quite frankly, knows *everything* there is to know about the physiology of taste. She knows all the physical facts about people and food, in a wide sense of "physical" which includes everything in *completed* physics, chemistry, and neurophysiology. She even knows all there is to know about the causal relationships that occur when a person tastes a particular food or drink. However, Mary was born with a bizarre genetic disorder that left her without taste buds or even

Philosophy on Tap: Pint-Sized Puzzles for the Pub Philosopher, First Edition. Matt Lawrence © 2011 Matt Lawrence. Published 2011 by Blackwell Publishing Ltd.

olfactory receptors. In her entire life, Mary has never tasted or smelled anything.

Suppose that Mary is watching you drink that nice cold pint of Foster's Lager. She knows exactly what is going on (physiologically) in your mouth, through your nerves, and in your brain. But despite all her physical and physiological knowledge, isn't there something that she doesn't know? Isn't she still oblivious to the most important thing of all – the taste of Foster's Lager?

The Australian philosopher Frank Jackson developed this sort of case as an attempt to refute *materialism*, the view that the world is entirely material and that to understand everything material is to understand absolutely everything that there is. While Mary knows all about brains and beer and the physical connections between them, Jackson contended that Mary didn't understand *everything* that goes on when someone drinks a Foster's. Mary's problem seems all the more evident when we imagine that doctors have now success-fully grafted taste buds onto her tongue and olfactory receptors into her nostrils. For her first taste experience, Mary's friends bring her a big blue and gold can of Foster's Lager. She pops it open and takes her first sip. According to Jackson, Mary now *learns* something new – what Foster's tastes like. She will not say, "Ho-hum, I always knew it tastes just like this." Instead, Jackson maintained that she has suddenly gained new knowledge of the world and therefore materialism must be false.

To most people this may all seem rather obvious. If Mary has never tasted anything, then *of course* she lacks a certain kind of knowledge. But then most people have never taken seriously the idea that materialism is true. Among professional philosophers who work on these sorts of issues however, materialism is by far the dominant view. Does the case of Mary the Neuro-scientist prove them wrong? One thing is certain – the materialists are not ready to admit defeat. Numerous challenges have been raised to the Mary case.

Some have denied that what Mary gains is rightfully called "knowledge." David Lewis (1941–2001) argued that Mary gains a new "ability" (the ability to taste Foster's Lager), but she doesn't "know" any new fact. But Jackson disagrees. If we are correct to believe, as most people do (though we cannot prove it), that the taste of Foster's is roughly the same for you as it is for me, then Mary not only gains an ability, she has gained factual knowledge about the experience of others.

Daniel Dennett has suggested that Jackson's analysis of the Mary case begs the question. That is, it assumes, rather than proves, that materialism is false. For if Mary really understands *all* the material properties and processes involved in drinking a Foster's, *and if* materialism is true, then she would know what Foster's tastes like even prior to her operation. For if materialism is true, then the taste of Foster's is just a "higher order property" of its material composition (much the way that wetness is a higher order property of H_2O), and someone who knows everything about matter and its relationships would be able to "read off" the higher order properties from the lower level properties. According to Dennett, the main obstacle is one of imagination. We have trouble imagining what it would be like to have the kind of *complete* knowledge that Mary is supposed to have. And because we can't fully imagine it, we wrongly suppose that Mary cannot know about the subjective experiences attached to tasting beer.

One way to test Dennett's hypothesis would be to try to trick Mary. Suppose, for example, that when she goes to taste her very first beer ever, we fill a can of Foster's with champagne. If Dennett is right, she wouldn't be fooled any more than you would. But if Jackson is right, she'd have no way to know about our little trick by using taste alone. However, since Mary doesn't actually exist, such a test is impossible to implement.

Truth be told

In Frank Jackson's original "Mary the Neuroscientist" case, Mary was physically normal, but she was imprisoned in a black-and-white room and never had contact with colored objects. Mary had never seen the color red. So in his case, what she didn't know was what the experience of "red" was like. And while Daniel Dennett did come up with the idea of trying to trick Mary, since it was color sensations that Mary didn't know in Jackson's original case, Dennett suggested that one might try to trick her with a blue banana (rather than with a Foster's can filled with champagne).

What do you think?

- Does the case of Mary the Neuroscientist succeed in showing that materialism is false?
- Is taste merely an ability? Or, should we think it also provides us with significant knowledge about the world?
- If we were to try to trick Mary with champagne, do you think she would know the difference?

Did you know?

- Many years after the publication of "What Mary Didn't Know," Frank Jackson ceded the "knowledge argument" to the materialists. In 2003 he wrote: "Most contemporary philosophers given a choice between going with science and going with intuitions, go with science. Although I once dissented from the majority, I have capitulated and now see the interesting issue as being where the arguments from the intuitions against physicalism – the arguments that seem so compelling – go wrong."

- While Foster's Lager is quite popular worldwide, it has limited appeal and availability within Australia. It is brewed primarily for export, or brewed under license in other countries.
- The best-selling beers in Australia include: Coopers, Tooheys, KB Lager, Victoria Bitter, and Carlton Draft.
- The average person has about 10,000 taste buds and each is replaced within approximately two weeks. We lose some as we age, and by the age of 80 you are likely to have only half the taste buds that you once had.

Recommended reading

- Frank Jackson, "What Mary Didn't Know," *Journal of Philosophy* 83 (1986): 291–295.
- Peter Ludlow, Yujin Nagasawa, and Daniel Stoljar, eds., *There's Something About Mary: Essays on Phenomenal Consciousness and Frank Jackson's Knowledge Argument* (Cambridge, MA: MIT Press, 2004).

Tasting Notes: Foster's *Lager*

Style: Australian Lager   **Rating:** 1 2 3 4 5

Appearance:	
Nose:	
Mouthfeel:	
Flavors:	

Body, Alcohol, Dark Fruits, Bitter, Citrus, Sweet, Smoky Burnt, Sour, Linger, Toffee Coffee, Hoppy Piney, Spicy, Malty, Floral

10

Malcolm X and the Whites Only Bar

What is race?

> **Pint of the Puzzle: Avery's *White Rascal Ale***
>
> White Rascal Ale is an authentic Belgian style wheat or "white" ale. It is unfiltered, so you'll find yeast at the bottom. It is lightly spiced with coriander and curaçao orange peel. And given the themes of this puzzle, it shouldn't take a rocket scientist to figure out why White Rascal was chosen for this puzzle.

What is race? Many people tend to think of race in purely biological terms. Just as some people are tall and others short, some people are black, others are Asian, white, Latino, etc. Race, as they see it, is simply a matter of genetics. But some philosophers have questioned the idea that race is a purely factual and biological matter. In contrast, they argue that race is a "social construction." This is to say that, although there are natural genetic differences between people, "race" is a creation of the society or culture. In their view, race is invented rather than discovered.

Philosophy on Tap: Pint-Sized Puzzles for the Pub Philosopher, First Edition. Matt Lawrence
© 2011 Matt Lawrence. Published 2011 by Blackwell Publishing Ltd.

An example that sheds some light on this "constructivist" view of race comes from Malcolm X, the civil rights leader of the 1950s and '60s. In his famous "The Ballot or the Bullet" speech, X told about one of his black friends who tried to "pass" as an African:

> A friend of mine who's very dark put a turban on his head and went into an all white bar in Atlanta before they called themselves desegregated. He went in, he sat down at the bar, ordered a beer, and they served him. And he said, "What would happen if a Negro came in here?" And there he's sitting, black as night, but because he had his head wrapped up the bartender looked back at him and says, "Why, there wouldn't be no nigger dare come in here."

This story is pertinent because, on the one hand, it demonstrates the intense prejudice prevalent in the American South at the time, but, on the other, it shows that this prejudice had little to do with biology. With the turban on his head, Malcolm's friend appeared to be an African, and as an African he could eat anywhere he chose. But without the turban he magically becomes a "Negro," the object of racial scorn and discrimination – despite the fact that he is of African descent in either case.

Malcolm X used this story to show just how crazy the "white rascal" could be. But the social constructivist contends that examples such as this illustrate their thesis that conceptions of race have never been a purely biological matter.

How many races are there, anyway? If race were simply a biological fact, then you would expect this question to have a rather straightforward answer. But when I ask this question to classes of college students, I usually get a variety of responses. Some will confidently say "three," others will just as confidently say "five," others will insist that there are many more than that. Rather than haggle about who is right, I pose a simpler question: "How many eye-colors are there?" Again, someone will usually say "three" and someone else will insist that it is four or five. Eventually someone will point out that there are probably as many eye-colors as there are people. This is not to say that there is not a "natural fact" about the color of a person's eyes. But when we reduce eye-color to a couple of types – say, brown, blue, and green – we have made a decision. For instance, we've decided that gray doesn't count in its own right, so people with grayish eyes must be pushed into one of the other categories. The constructivist believes that the same holds for race. We "decide" how many races we are going to recognize and how they are going to be delineated. In doing so, we essentially decide what is going to count as "the same" and "different." In Malcom X's example, the African and the black American were regarded as different, when they could just as easily have been regarded the same. Somewhere along the line a decision had to be made as to who counts as a "Negro."

This issue was especially important in the American slave trade. Since "whites" were regarded as free and "Negroes" as property, a decision had to be made about "mixed-race" children. If a child had a "white" father and a "Negro" mother, a decision had to be made about the racial status of the child. Would it be a free white, or a Negro slave? From a purely biological perspective, there is no way to settle the issue. Instead, a variety of social and political factors led to the "one-drop rule." If a child had just one drop of "negro blood," then they were deemed a Negro and deprived of their human rights.

For reasons such as these, the Stanford University philosopher Charles Lawrence III has argued that we should rethink the idea of "race" right down to its role in our language. On a biological view of race, the term "race" tends to be regarded as a noun. For example, we might say, "There is tension between the races," or "Race was not a factor in the court's decision," etc. Here race is a regarded as a *thing* out in the world. But Lawrence contends that we should instead think of race as a verb. In this way of seeing it "race" is an *action*. It is something that is done *to* you. "You are raced," Lawrence says. To be "raced" is to be categorized into one of the boxes that society has created. And in virtue of those created categories, some have benefited, and others have suffered.

Truth be told

In his "Ballot or the Bullet" speech, Malcom X's story actually involved a whites-only diner, rather than a whites-only bar.

What do you think?

- Is race purely biological, purely a social construction, or is it somewhere in between?
- Can you come up with an example (besides race) of something that is a social construction?
- Are social constructions necessarily negative and harmful? Why or why not?
- Should "race" play a role in our personal decisions (e.g., friendships, marriage, etc.)? Why or why not?
- Should "race" ever play a role in our governmental policies? And, if so, how?

Did you know?

- Malcolm X was born in 1925 as Malcolm Little. He changed his name because "Little" was the name given to his family under slavery. He chose "X" because in mathematical language "X" is the unknown, like his original African surname.
- It was not until 1968 that all forms of segregation in the United States were declared unconstitutional by the Supreme Court.
- The United States census for the year 2000 compiled data for 63 racial categories.
- White Rascal Ale's logo is a "white devil" – coincidentally, a phrase that Malcolm X sometimes used for those whites who perpetuated racial oppression and segregation.

Recommended reading

- Malcolm X, "The Ballot or the Bullet." Available online at: http://www. historicaldocuments.com/BallotortheBulletMalcolmX.htm.
- James Davis, "Who is Black? One Nation's Definition." Available online at: http://www.pbs.org/wgbh/pages/frontline/shows/jefferson/mixed/onedrop.html.

Tasting Notes: Avery's *White Rascal Ale*

Style: Belgian Style Wheat Ale   **Rating:** 1 2 3 4 5

Appearance:	
Nose:	
Mouthfeel:	
Flavors:	

Body   Alcohol   Dark Fruits
Bitter   Citrus
Sweet   Smoky Burnt
Sour   Linger
Toffee Coffee   Hoppy Piney
Spicy   Malty   Floral

Untangling Taste

Are some beers truly better than others?

If you appreciate beer, then I probably don't have to convince you that while some beers are amazing, others are pure crap. But when you say, "This is a great beer," are you really saying something about the beer itself – or are you merely describing your own preferences? To put it another way, are some beers *objectively* better than others, or is it all a matter of one's *subjective taste?*

Philosophers have had all sorts of opinions on this issue. The Ancient Greek philosopher Protagoras was famous for saying that "Man is the

---

Philosophy on Tap: Pint-Sized Puzzles for the Pub Philosopher, First Edition. Matt Lawrence
© 2011 Matt Lawrence. Published 2011 by Blackwell Publishing Ltd.

measure of all things." Nothing, he believed, was simply large or small, hot or cold, or near or far. Rather, we describe objects in these ways because of their relation to us. Similarly, he would say that no beer is simply delicious, great, or amazing, except in relation to our own taste buds. We wouldn't expect a moose to know the difference between a fine brown ale and a mediocre one, and he shouldn't expect us to be able to discern good dandelions from bad. All things, Protagoras thought, are relative. Sometimes they are relative to a species, and other times they are relative to one's own particular judgments of taste.

Many philosophers have followed Protagoras' footsteps by holding a *subjectivist* outlook about beer. According to this view, to say "This is great beer," is really no different from saying, "I really like this beer." It all comes down to your own personal, subjective mental state. This was the position of Virgil Aldrich, a twentieth-century American philosopher in aesthetics:

> The airy radiance of a great beer is much akin to, if not identical with, the *feeling* of him whom it enthralls. . . . To him it seems as if he consummates his emotional self in the beer. He swathes it with his own feelings, and thereby lends to it a good part of its appeal.

Most people, I expect, are inclined to go along with the subjectivist view. Without a doubt, the enjoyment of a beer is crucial to calling it good. Ludwig Wittgenstein seems to have agreed when he remarked, "Would it matter if instead of saying 'This is lovely,' I just said 'Ah!' and smiled, or just rubbed my stomach?"

But when we make judgments about "great beer," surely we often take ourselves to be saying much more than simply "I like it." As the great German philosopher Immanuel Kant (1724–1804) pointed out, our judgments about beer often have a normative quality:

> When [someone] puts a beer on a pedestal and calls it "great," he demands the same delight from others. He judges not merely for himself, but for all men, and then speaks of its greatness as if it were a property of the beer itself. . . . [I]t is not as if he counts on others agreeing with him in his judgment of liking owing to his having found them in a such agreement on a number of occasions, but he *demands* this agreement of them. He blames them if they judge differently, and denies them taste.

Kant took an *objectivist* view about judgments of "beer greatness." He maintained that there is something about these beers themselves that makes them great. Thus their greatness is independent of any particular person's judgment – and it is certainly independent of majority approval.

This analysis has the fortunate consequence of sparing us the conclusion that Bud Light is the greatest beer of all time, just because most people seem to prefer it. Instead, the objectivist would suggest that in beer, as in most other things, you should not listen to the majority. Rather, you should listen to those who *know*.

But who is the authority on beer? The subjectivist maintains that everyone is their own authority. If you like it, then it's good. You can never be wrong. The objectivist, in contrast, acknowledges that there can be experts. For if there is something about certain beers that make them great, then some people might be better able to recognize those "great-making" characteristics. This ability might stem from a natural talent, but in most cases it is learned and developed. The flavor of beer is, after all, an *acquired taste*. Hardly anyone enjoys beer from their very first sip. So it shouldn't come as any surprise that *good taste* in beer must also be acquired. It seems reasonable to suppose that one must sample the wide variety of beers and beer styles, paying close attention to their subtle smells, flavors, and textures. And, quite frankly, most beer drinkers have never explored the world of beer in this way. In America at least, most people stick to a few mass-produced brands of watered down lagers. They may have tried a stout or strong ale on occasion, and didn't like it – end of story. But had they given up on beer this easily, they'd still be sipping sodas.

When we look at the judgments of truly experienced and observant beer drinkers, the objectivist contends that we will find a fairly large pattern of agreement. While agreement among experts definitely adds to the plausibility of "objective greatness" in beers, we should keep in mind that agreement is one thing, and objectivity is quite another. Ultimately, the objectivist needs an account of what makes a beer great – over and above the fact that they happen to like it. Kant's own view on the matter is far too complex to explain adequately here, but we can point in its general direction by saying that a great beer must invoke *the harmonious play of the imagination and understanding*. In this analysis, a great beer doesn't simply invoke pleasant feelings; it engages the intellect. (Contrary to popular opinion, beer is the thinking man's beverage.) To judge one's beer competently, one must first understand it. One should be able to identify a wide array of scents, flavors, and textures as they diverge, blend, and harmonize upon one's tongue. Thus "great beers" will tend to be those that are rather complex and full of subtle nuances. The discerning palate can recognize hundreds of distinct flavors within the various beer styles, and this understanding adds to the pleasure, and alters the very nature of the experience. The most central textures, scents, and flavors are identified in the flavor wheel created by the American Society of Brewing Chemists, illustrated on the next page.

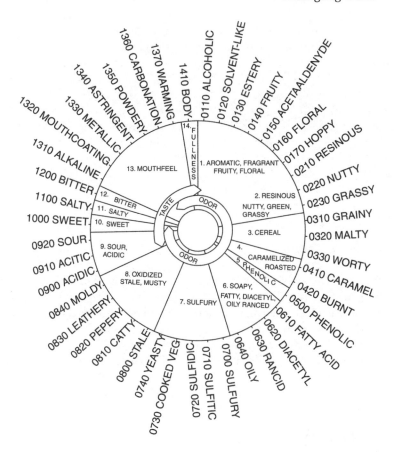

In defense of subjectivism, we might retort that a beer can have all the flavors and complexity in the world, but that doesn't make it good. "Rancid" might be a complex and interesting flavor in its own right, but that doesn't mean we want it in our beer – or anywhere else, for that matter. A beer can only be deemed "great" if we enjoy drinking it, and that, the subjectivist contends, always comes down to the individual's own set of preferences.

Truth be told

I have really stretched the truth on this one. First, the quotes from Aldrich and Kant have been modified. Both statements were originally made in reference to "beautiful objects" rather than beer. Throughout the book I've tried to insure that my little lies and pub-stretches do not significantly affect the philosophers' points, but this one is an exception. Kant, in particular, would be outraged by my treatment of his position. He was very clear that his views about beauty were not intended to be applied to things such as the taste of food or drink, which he believed to be much more (if not completely) subjective. Nevertheless, I think that it is philosophically interesting to consider how a rather Kantian position might be applied to great beer.

What do you think?

- When you describe a beer as "great," are you saying something about the beer, or merely telling us something about yourself?
- If your friend has tried many different beers but still finds the cheap, mass-produced beers to be his favorite, is he making some kind of mistake? If so, is it a cognitive error, or an error of feeling?
- Can a person really judge good beer if they can't discern and identify its various flavors?
- In your opinion, what makes a "great beer" great?

Did you know?

- While Bud Light has been the world's best-selling beer for years, in 2008 it was surpassed by Snow lager of China, which has benefited greatly from the ever-increasing Chinese beer market.
- A central aspect of Kant's theory of aesthetic judgment was that we approach the beautiful with "disinterest." That is, unlike the merely pleasurable, we do not feel the need to possess the beautiful object, but merely wish to apprehend it. (Tell that to some art collectors.) This is one of the reasons why it is problematic to apply Kant's theory of aesthetic judgment to the realm of beer.
- Kant's *Critique of Judgment,* in which he develops his theory of aesthetic judgment, was met with some enthusiasm during the romantic period, but was soon largely ignored until the early twentieth century. Some early critics went so far as to argue that the work was a sign of senility in the aging philosopher. Today it stands as one of the seminal works in aesthetics.

The beer flavor wheel shown above was developed by Morten Meilgaard in the 1970s. It was subsequently adopted by the European Brewery Convention, the American Society of Brewing Chemists, and the Master Brewers Association of the Americas.

Recommended reading

- Immanuel Kant, *Critique of Judgment*, 1790. Available online through the University of Adelaide: http://ebooks.adelaide.edu.au/k/kant/immanuel/k16j/.
- Margaret P. Battin, John Fisher, Ronald Moore, and Anita Silvers, *Puzzles about Art: An Aesthetics Casebook* (New York: St. Martins Press, 1989).

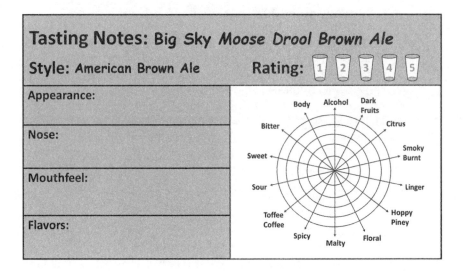

Tasting Notes: Big Sky *Moose Drool Brown Ale*

Style: American Brown Ale   **Rating:** 1 2 3 4 5

Appearance:	
Nose:	
Mouthfeel:	
Flavors:	

12

The Foreknowledge Paradox

If God always knew which beer you'd order, are you still free?

Pint of the Puzzle: Aktien's *Hell Lager*

The recommendation for this puzzle is that you simply choose the beer that God has always known that you will choose. Let's face it, try as you might, you just can't surprise an all-knowing God. If this leads you just to sit there at the bar, stymied like Buridan's ass, then go with a Hell Lager from Germany's Aktien brewery. For if God foresees hell in your future, you'd better hope it comes in the form of a fine German lager.

Many people conceive of God as an *omniscient being*. They believe that God knows *everything*, including the future. But most of these same folk also believe that human beings have free will. They contend that we freely choose our actions. We *decide* to believe in God or not, we *choose* to refrain from sin or not, and we choose our beer one pint or pitcher at a time. The path we take is up to us. The trouble, or so it seems, is that if God knows what you will do before you do it, then it would appear that you *must* perform the action that God had foreknown. And, if you *must* choose the action that God had foreknown, how can it be a *free* choice?

To sort this out, let's consider a specific example. Suppose that you are thinking about which beer to order. The pub has plenty of options, and

Philosophy on Tap: Pint-Sized Puzzles for the Pub Philosopher, First Edition. Matt Lawrence.
© 2011 Matt Lawrence. Published 2011 by Blackwell Publishing Ltd.

eventually you narrow it down to two. You are confident that a New Belgium Fat Tire Amber Ale would hit the spot, but they also have Aktien Hell Lager which you've never tried. At this point you are not sure what to do. Should you go with the sure thing, or the new thing? You feel like you are at a crossroads. There are (or at least there seem to be) two paths open to you, and it is up to you to determine which path to take.

But insofar as we suppose that there exists an omniscient God with the power of foreknowledge, then surely God already knows what you will do. In fact, He's known it since before you were even born. And if *what* God knows is that you are going to order the Hell Lager (and only the Hell Lager) at precisely 7.05 p.m., shouldn't we say that ordering a Fat Tire is not in your power? For, if it were, then it would be in your power to make God wrong, and surely you *can't* make God wrong. (For if God turns out to be mistaken, then God didn't really know, did He?) So it would appear that you are on a one-way track to Hell Lager. You've got the *illusion* of options, the *illusion* of free will, but there is really only one way you can go – the way that God has always known.

On the face of it at least, it would seem that Divine foreknowledge and free will are incompatible. *Either* God has foreknowledge, *or* people have free will, but not both. Many people find the idea of giving up either of these notions totally unacceptable. To suppose that God cannot know the future is to drastically limit God's omniscience. Yet, to suppose that people lack free will would wreak havoc on our beliefs concerning moral responsibility. Imagine the consequences! If you are truly on a one-way track to ordering Hell Lager, then some of us may also be on a one-way track to sinful actions, followed by Hell itself. But if your sinful actions were unavoidable, how can God (or anyone else) blame you for them? After all, as the Creator, God is the one who put you on that track in the first place! And similarly, if you are on a one-way track to righteous actions, then why should God (or anyone else) reward you for it? You simply did the only thing that was possible for you to do.

Is there any way to reconcile God's omniscience and human freedom? One possibility requires modifying our view of omniscience. We landed ourselves in this paradox because we had assumed that God is omniscient in the following sense:

Omniscience[1]: The ability to know absolutely everything.

when perhaps we should have understood God's omniscience to as:

Omniscience[2]: The ability to know everything that is *knowable*.

There may be some things in the universe that are simply unknowable as a matter of principle, such as what a being with free will is going to do next.

Another option is to modify our understanding of God's existence in relation to time. When we think of God "foreknowing" our actions, we are imagining God existing "in" time (e.g., at May 4, 1963), and from there He foreknows those things that have not yet happened. The sixth-century theologian Boethius argued that this is the wrong way to think about God, since He is not "in" time as we are. Rather, as the creator of time itself, He exists outside or beyond time. Boethius maintained that God knows everything as it exists in His "eternal present." Therefore we should regard God as *knowing* all things, but *foreknowing* nothing.

What do you think?

- How would you reconcile Divine foreknowledge and human free will? Can they be reconciled?
- Is it inappropriately limiting to suppose that God cannot foreknow human actions?
- If you had to give up the belief in Divine foreknowledge or the belief in free will, which would you choose? Why?
- Does Boethius provide a satisfactory solution to the problem of Divine foreknowledge? And if not, why not?

Did you know?

- Calvinists are a Christian sect that endorses the idea that everything is preordained by God and hence human beings do not have free will.
- Many philosophers have questioned the idea that we have "free will" regardless of God and foreknowledge. Their concern pertains to the thesis of "causal determinism" which maintains that all events, including human actions, are necessitated by prior causes. For more on this, see chapters 22 and 29 ("Laplace's Superscientist" and "Time's Conundrum").
- At the start of the puzzle I mentioned "Buridan's ass." This refers to a thought experiment in which a mule is placed precisely between a bale of hay and a pale of water. Desiring both equally, he finds himself stuck immobile between them.
- The Aktien brewery in Kaufbeuren, Bavaria was founded in AD 1308, making it one of the oldest breweries in the world. Their *Hell* is brewed in the German Helles style. Helles in German means "light" or "bright." Lager, on the other hand, is the German word for "storage." So while Aktien *Hell* typically refers to a lager in most parts of the world, when in Germany don't ask the bartender for a "lagerbier"; instead ask for a "helles bier" (pale lager) or a "dunkles bier" (dark lager or ale).

Recommended reading

- James Beilby and Paul Eddy, eds., *Divine Foreknowledge: Four Views* (Downers Grove, IL: Intravarsity Press, 2001).
- Boethius, *The Consolation of Philosophy*. Available online through Project Gutenberg: http://www.gutenberg.org/etext/14328.

Tasting Notes: Aktien's *Hell Lager*

Style: Munich Helles Lager   **Rating:** 1 2 3 4 5

Appearance:	
Nose:	
Mouthfeel:	
Flavors:	

Body · Alcohol · Dark Fruits · Citrus · Smoky Burnt · Linger · Hoppy Piney · Floral · Malty · Spicy · Coffee · Toffee · Sour · Sweet · Bitter

13

The Buddha's Missing Self

Are you the same person now as when you took your first sip?

Pint of the Puzzle: Kingfisher *Premium Lager*

Our next puzzle features Siddhartha Gautama (AKA the Buddha), the great Indian sage and founder of Buddhism. In tribute, let's pour a Kingfisher Premium Lager, India's best-selling beer. On the Kingfisher bottle you'll see a depiction of a vibrantly colored kingfisher, a bird best known for two qualities exemplified by the Buddha: razor sharp perception and perfect aim.

Do you remember the first time that you had a Kingfisher Premium Lager? If so, try to recall the sort of person you were at that time. How did you look? What was your style? What were your interests? If you've never had a Kingfisher, then you might instead recall the time that you had your first Indian beer, or at least your first IPA (India Pale Ale). For many readers I'm sure it has been a good while – perhaps months, years, or even decades.

Philosophy on Tap: Pint-Sized Puzzles for the Pub Philosopher, First Edition. Matt Lawrence © 2011 Matt Lawrence. Published 2011 by Blackwell Publishing Ltd.

Suppose, for the sake of argument, that it has been five years or more. Are you the "same" person today as you were then? While undoubtedly you have changed in certain respects, the common conception is that each of us remains essentially the same person throughout our lives. Often this is because we suppose that there is a single, permanent "Self" or "soul" that persists throughout the changes in our life and perhaps even beyond this life.

Siddhartha Gautama (*c.* 563–483 BCE), known as the *Buddha* (a title which means the "enlightened" or "awakened" one), denied the existence of the Self or soul. He maintained that the idea of something permanent, unchanging, and self-sufficient that is the essential "you" is a false notion – a concept that does not correspond to reality. Called *the doctrine of anatta* (the doctrine of no-self), this view is a core component of the Buddha's philosophy. The Buddha maintained that if you look deeply into the nature of things you will find that everything is impermanent and interdependent. Nothing remains the same, and nothing is self-sufficient.

We can easily see his point when it comes to our bodies. Scientists tell you that, every minute, millions of cells within your body are dying and millions more are being born. Within 10 years, most of the cells of your body will have been replaced. Thus, if we were to use a bodily criterion of identity, you are *not* the same person that you were 10 years ago. Your body is almost entirely "new." And where does this new body come from? It is formed out of the food that you eat, the air that you breathe, the sunshine you absorb, and, of course, the pints that you drink. Thus your body *is*, to a certain extent, hops and malted barley; which, in turn, are inseparable from the sunshine, rain, minerals from the earth, etc. So our bodies are by no means permanent, independent, or self-sufficient. Instead, they are constantly changing and interrelated with the rest of the universe.

The Buddha believed that the same point holds for the mind or consciousness. Your state of mind is constantly changing – it is never the same from one moment to the next. A thought arises and then triggers several more. Desires come and go like the tides. New memories are formed and old ones are forgotten. And to regard these states as simply "yours" is very misleading. For example, your thoughts of Kingfisher Lager would never have existed had it not been for the Kingfisher Brewery and the particular brewmasters who developed the recipe for this premium lager. And they might never have come up with such a recipe if it were not for the influence of the great brewmasters of Bavaria. Even the kingfisher that inspired the label helps to shape "your" idea of Kingfisher beer. None of your beliefs, desires, or emotions would be exactly as they are if it were not for your general historical and social situation, your particular family, teachers, and friends, etc. Your beliefs and desires are in many ways a *continuation* of their beliefs and desires, just as your genes are a *continuation* of your parents' genes (and hence a continuation of all of your ancestors' genes). So if we use consciousness as the criterion of identity, again we find nothing permanent, independent, or self-sufficient.

But couldn't there still be something that is beyond all of these changing elements – a "Self" or "soul" that *possesses* this changing body, and is *experiencing* this stream of thoughts and sensations, etc.? While I don't think that we can completely rule out the idea, the Buddha argued that we have no good reason to believe in it. If you reflect upon your experience at any moment, you never seem to find such a Self. You can observe a thought, but never a thinker behind the thought. You can observe your cravings, but never a Self that is having the cravings. From this the Buddha concluded that the idea of Self is just a constructed fiction. In contrast, many philosophers have supposed that a possessor of these mental states is necessary. They contend that *somebody* has to be doing the thinking. But the Buddha saw no reason to make this assumption. Instead, he suggested that it is more in line with our experience to simply suppose that it is "thought" that thinks, "desire" that craves, "realization" that realizes, and so on.

You may begin to wonder whether it really matters whether or not there is a permanent Self. Perhaps it is just idle philosophical speculation either way. But the Buddha maintained that an understanding of *anatta* is crucial for ethical conduct and spiritual enlightenment. The notion of "Self," he argued, is a dangerous idea with disastrous effects. It gives rise to thoughts of selfishness, greed, and conceit, which in turn lead to acts of treachery, theft, murder, and war. The belief in a Self leads to physical and mental attachments and cravings, which, the Buddha maintained, are the source of all suffering and the primary obstacle to liberation or *nirvana*.

For these reasons, the Buddha instructed his disciples to be vigilant against the delusion of Self. As he explained to his son Rahula:

> Whatever body, Rahula, whatever feeling, or perception or mental formation, or consciousness, be it past, future or present, be it your own or be it external to you, be it gross or subtle, mean or noble, remote or near, if you see it all so: – "This is not mine, I am not it, it is not my self" – thus seeing by right insight the thing as it really is, you are liberated, without grasping.

So *anatta* is not simply a theory. What you believe about the Self may very well affect your entire approach to life.

Truth be told

The Buddha would certainly agree that "you" are composed in part of hops and barley. However, he would recommend that you abstain from all intoxicants (including fine Indian lagers), as they tend to be a hindrance to the sort of "one pointed mind" required for attaining enlightenment.

What do you think?

- Is the Self a false notion with no correspondence to reality?
- Is the notion of Self a necessary presupposition? Insofar as there is thought, must we suppose that there is a "thinker"?
- Can you think of anything in your experience of the world that seems to be "Self-sufficient?"

Did you know?

- Buddhists use the term "emptiness" to refer to the idea that all phenomena are without a "Self." The Buddha maintained that nothing whatsoever is permanent or self-sufficient, not even your Indian lager. In this sense, your Kingfisher Lager is empty even when your glass is full.
- David Hume also argued that there is no evidence of a self. In his *A Treatise of Human Nature*, he wrote: "When I enter most intimately into what I call myself, I always stumble on some particular perception or other, of heat or cold, light or shade, love or hatred, pain or pleasure. I never catch myself at any time without a perception, and never can observe anything but the perception."
- Kingfisher's newest endeavor is a premium gravity beer called Kingfisher Red, brewed in the style of the medieval European monks. It has an oaky, woody flavor and can be served chilled or at room temperature.

Recommended reading

- Walpola Rahula, *What the Buddha Taught* (New York: Grove Press, 1974).
- Karen Armstrong, *Buddha* (New York, Viking, 2001).

Tasting Notes: Kingfisher *Premium Lager*

Style: Pale Lager

Rating: 1 2 3 4 5

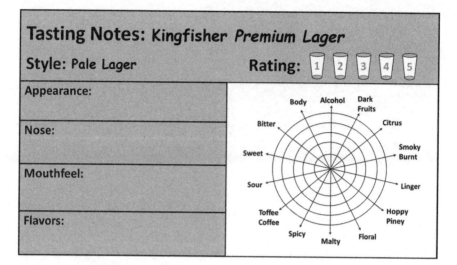

Appearance:

Nose:

Mouthfeel:

Flavors:

The Blind Men and the Black and Tan

Could all the major religions be true?

When most people look at the religions of the world they see conflict. Judaism conflicts with Christianity, which conflicts with Islam. Then you have the Hindus, the Taoists, the Buddhists, and so on – each making a different set of claims about what is real and true. Now generally, when two stories conflict it is safe to say they can't both be right. Somebody must be mistaken. So at first view, it would seem that anyone who thinks critically about religion must make a choice. Either we conclude that all religions are just full of it, or we try to determine which one is the true religion (or at least which one comes closest to the truth).

Philosophy on Tap: Pint-Sized Puzzles for the Pub Philosopher, First Edition. Matt Lawrence
© 2011 Matt Lawrence. Published 2011 by Blackwell Publishing Ltd.

John Hick, a contemporary philosopher of religion has argued for a third position. He maintains that all the world's major religions are true. The interesting thing about Hick's position is that he does not deny that these religions make conflicting and sometimes opposing claims. Rather, he contends that conflicting claims about reality can be equally or incommensurably true.

To support his case, Hick draws on the example of *the three blind men and the Black and Tan.*

> Imagine three blind men sharing a Black and Tan for the first time in their lives. The first man takes a couple of sips and drinks off the foamy head. Never having tasted a beer before, he concludes that a Black and Tan is more or less like a café latte. The second, an experienced beer drinker, sucks down the layer of Guinness. He concludes that, without a doubt, a Black and Tan is a fine Irish stout. The third finishes it off. He concludes that the other men are clearly mistaken. He says, "Certainly this is no coffee drink, nor is it a stout. This is surely an amber ale."

The moral of the story is that while each offers a conflicting report, they are all conveying an experience that was real and true. Hick argues that we might think of religions in much the same way. While any particular religion would be mistaken to think that it has the whole truth and nothing but the truth, each nevertheless speaks truthfully and accurately when conveying its experience of the Divine.

Another set of factors that can contribute to conflicting reports involves variations in culture, experience, and environment. To make this point, Hick offers the example of a "duck-rabbit," shown here in the logo of the Duck-Rabbit Craft Brewery in North Carolina.

Does the label depict a duck (facing left) or a rabbit (facing right)? Your answer is likely to reflect your past experience, education, and cultural traditions. For example, if you live in an area in which there are no rabbits, yet ducks are plentiful (or a traditional food source), you will most likely see this as a duck. And, if you live in an area where there are no ducks, yet rabbits run rampant, then the image will clearly appear to you as a rabbit. So if two people see this image and offer conflicting reports about it, what should we say? Hick contends that they are both right. They both honestly report the truth about what they saw – though neither has the whole truth (which is that both had seen a delicious brown ale).

Hick offers a third analogy for religious experience based on cartography – the science of map-making. Look carefully at the three maps illustrated. All three of these maps are accurate representations of the world. That is, they all represent the three-dimensional (round) earth as well as can be done on a two-dimensional (flat) surface. The Mercator Projection is excellent for uses in navigation, but it radically distorts and enlarges the size of Eurasian and North American countries. (Notice that Greenland appears to be the same size as Africa, yet Africa's land mass is actually 14 times larger.) The Gall-Peters Projection better illustrates the size of South America and Africa, but in doing so it more radically distorts the shape of the Eurasian and North American countries. The Robinson Projection is a bit of a compromise

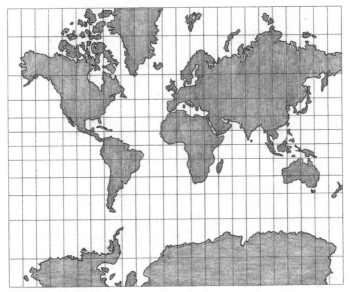

The Mercator Projection

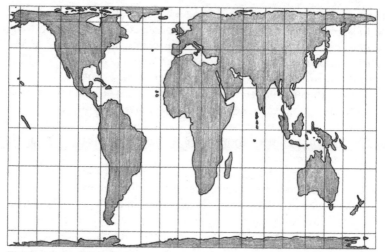

The Gall-Peters Projection

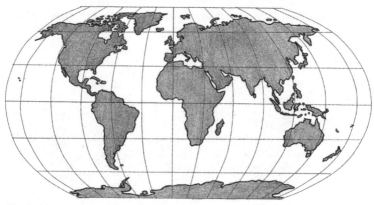

The Robinson Projection

between the other two. The overall look is more globe-like, and the high latitudes are less distorted in size but more so in shape. The point of all this is that while these three maps give conflicting pictures of the two crucial features of continents (their size and shape), they are nonetheless equally (or incommensurably) true. They are each as "true" as true can get when it comes to representing three dimensions onto two. But while each map is true, none should be regarded as completely true, or as any more true than the others.

Hick believes that we should think about the great world religions in much the same way. Just as map-makers base their representations upon real interactions with the surface of the earth, so Hick contends that all the major religions base their conclusions upon real encounters with the Divine, be it the ancient Jewish prophets, Mahavira, the Buddha, Jesus, Muhammad, etc. But, as all the major religions maintain, God (or Absolute Reality) is infinite. God is "multi-dimensional" and therefore cannot be adequately described through our three-dimensional concepts and language. Thus, like the map-maker, we inevitably distort the truth. Each religion describes/distorts the Ultimate in its own unique way, but this is not to be confused with being mistaken (no more than we should say that the Mercator Projection is mistaken). Each is valid in its own right, and can be used to "navigate" the spiritual life.

Truth be told

The story of the three blind men and the Black and Tan is by no means an authentic quote from John Hick. He has never used the example of a Black and Tan to make his argument. However, he does use a similar fable – the classic story of several blind men encountering an elephant for the first time. But Hick *has* used the example of the duck-rabbit – just not in the context of the Duck-Rabbit Craft Brewery (your dark beer specialists).

What do you think?

- Is it possible for all religions to be true? If not, how is religion significantly different from the map-making example?
- What is the relevant difference between the Black and Tan example and the Cartography example? Which one do you think better describes the conflicting reports of the world's religions?
- Suppose that Hick is right and that all the major religions are true. Doesn't this entail that any religion that regards itself as the single true religion is making a fundamental mistake? How big a mistake (or how many) can a religion make before we should no longer regard it as "true?"
- On what points do the major religions agree? On what points do they differ? On what points is it impossible for two religions to differ and yet both be regarded as "true?"

Did you know?

- The view that many different religions can all be true is called "religious pluralism."
- Another example that Hick has used to show how conflicting claims or experiences can both be true pertains to the nature of light. Physicists have found that under some experimental conditions, light behaves as if it were made of particles – tiny bundles of energy. But under other conditions, light behaves as if it were made of waves. So which is it really – waves or particles? The general answer given by physicists today is, "both!"
- Mohandas K. Gandhi was a religious pluralist. Although he was a devout and practicing Hindu, he believed that all the major religions were just different roads to the same spiritual summit.
- The duck-rabbit gained philosophical notoriety from its appearance in Ludwig Wittgenstein's *Philosophical Investigations*.
- There are many variations on the Black and Tan. For instance, you might want to try a Black and Blue (Guinness over Blue Moon Belgian White), a Black and Sam (Guinness over Sam Adams Boston Lager), or a Black Eye (Guinness over Black Eye Ale).

Recommended reading

- John Hick, "The Pluralistic Hypothesis," in David Stewart, ed., *Exploring the Philosophy of Religion*, 7th edn. (Upper Saddle River, NJ: Prentice Hall, 2010).
- David Ray Griffin, ed., *Deep Religious Pluralism*, (Louisville, KY: John Knox Press, 2005).

Tasting Notes: Bass *Ale*

Style: English Pale Ale   **Rating:** ① ② ③ ④ ⑤

Appearance:	
Nose:	
Mouthfeel:	
Flavors:	

Body   Alcohol   Dark Fruits
Bitter   Citrus
Sweet   Smoky Burnt
Sour   Linger
Toffee Coffee   Hoppy Piney
Spicy   Malty   Floral

15

Liar's Paradox

Can you discern the truth?

> **Pint of the Puzzle: Roy Pitz *Truly Honest Ale***
>
> Truth can be a slippery thing, so enjoy this puzzle with a Truly Honest Ale from the Roy Pitz Brewery. They claim to make this beer with four different specialty malts and top-notch ingredients, and I believe them wholeheartedly. But keep in mind that they also claim to be "America's freshest brewery." Hmm . . .

This sentence is false.

How should we understand the sentence above? If you are a trusting reader, you might be inclined to take it as true. But notice that if you take it as true then it must be false, because that's what the sentence asserts. But a simple statement can't be both true *and* false. So which is it?

If you are not so trusting (or if you don't like the outcome above), you might start by supposing that the sentence is false. But if you take it as false, then it turns out to be true, because "false" is precisely what the sentence claims to be. So again we must ask, which is it *really*? True or false?

Philosophy on Tap: Pint-Sized Puzzles for the Pub Philosopher, First Edition. Matt Lawrence
© 2011 Matt Lawrence. Published 2011 by Blackwell Publishing Ltd.

Perhaps the easiest way to escape this paradox is to dismiss the sentence as meaningless (i.e., neither true nor false). But almost as soon as this escape route was discovered, philosophers came up with a way to close it off. For example, how should we understand the following sentence?

This sentence is false, or it is meaningless.

If we regard this sentence as meaningless, then it must be true (because it is true that it is "false *or* meaningless"). But a meaningless sentence *cannot* be true, and hence we again find ourselves in contradiction.

Called the "Liar's Paradox" this sort of puzzle has been boggling minds from antiquity to the present. Here is a new (though somewhat weaker) version that I've constructed around a quote from the actor Mark Ruffalo. Apparently he once told a reporter:

Nothing anyone says in a bar is true.

Let us suppose that Mr. Ruffalo said this while in a bar. If so, then if his claim is true, it would simultaneously have to be false. And if, on the other hand, we take his claim to be false, then this just adds support to the truth of his claim – as it is just another false statement from a person in a bar!

The first appearance of a liar's paradox in philosophical literature can be found in the writings of the Ancient Greek philosopher Eubulides of Miletus in the fourth century BCE. The basic paradox had several variations even in antiquity. One of the more entertaining versions is "The Crocodile Dilemma," which goes as follows:

A crocodile has stolen a child. He then tells the child's father, "I will return your child to you if you guess correctly whether I will do so or not." To this, the father replies, "You will not return my child!"

Let us suppose that the father guessed correctly. The crocodile then, in accordance with the promise, should return the child. However, if the crocodile were to return the child, then that would mean that the father had guessed incorrectly, and therefore, the crocodile is *not* obligated to return the child.

If you are inclined to try to confuse and astound your friends with such paradoxes, then the next time that you are at the pub you might try hitting them with the "Buy a Round Dilemma." When your pints have run dry, tell your friends: "I'll buy us all a pitcher of beer, if and only if you guess correctly whether I'll do so or not." Your friends, hoping to get a pitcher, will probably say, "Yes, you'll buy." In which case, you inform them that unfortunately they guessed incorrectly. And since they guessed incorrectly, being true to your word, you *cannot* buy the next round. Later in the evening, you might try the same stunt again. This time, they'll be on to you, so they'll go with the opposite answer: "No, you're not going to buy us a round!" Your response: "Incorrect! I was going to buy the round, but, being a man of my word, I cannot buy it since you guessed incorrectly. So, who *is* buying?" Either way you escape springing for another round – though let me assure you, your friends will turn out to be much more annoyed than they will be impressed by your logical prowess.

What do you think?

- Can the Liar's Paradox be resolved? If so, how?
- If the crocodile keeps the child, has he kept his promise, broken it, or both?
- A meaningless, or nonsense statement is a statement that is unintelligible and thereby neither true nor false. For example, "Centennial hops ring coldly ambidextrous" is a meaningless statement and hence it is neither true nor false. Is "This sentence is false" also a meaningless statement? Why or why not?

Did you know?

- Eubilides was a contemporary of Aristotle whom he was known to bitterly criticize.
- The Liar's Paradox is good for more than just confusing your friends at the pub. It has helped philosophers to refine our theories of truth.
- The claim that every statement must be true or false is called the "principle of bivalence." Contemporary philosophers who have contributed to discussions of the Liar's Paradox include Saul Kripke, Peter Woodruff, Jon Barwise, and John Etchemendy.
- The prevalence of "dishonest beers" has given rise to many regulations concerning beer selling and brewing over the centuries. Even the oldest set of written laws, the code of Hammurabi, included a section on fixing a fair price for beer. Perhaps the most famous attempt to keep beer honest is the *Reinheitsgebot*, established in 1516 by Wilhelm IV of Bavaria. It stipulated that beer can be made of nothing but barley malt, hops, and water (later provisions were made for yeast and wheat). German brewers generally follow the Reinheitsgebot to this day.

Recommended reading

- Jon Barwise and John Etchemendy, *The Liar* (Oxford: Oxford University Press, 1987).
- Garrett Oliver, "The Beer Matrix: Reality vs. Facsimile in Brewing," in Steven D. Hales, ed., *Beer and Philosophy: The Unexamined Beer isn't Worth Drinking* (Oxford: Blackwell Publishing, 2007).

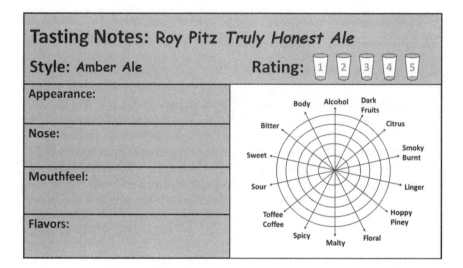

Tasting Notes: Roy Pitz *Truly Honest Ale*

Style: Amber Ale   **Rating:** 1 2 3 4 5

Appearance:
Nose:
Mouthfeel:
Flavors:

16

Paley's Cask

Is there an intelligent designer?

Pint of the Puzzle: Newcastle *Brown Ale*

This puzzle comes to us from William Paley, an English Clergyman of the eighteenth century. So let's toast the British for all they've done for the world of philosophy and the world of beer with a Newcastle Brown Ale. Also known as a "bottle of dog," "mother's milk," and "drink of the Gods," Newcastle is a perennial favorite among barstool philosophers.

William Paley (1743–1805) never purported to have proven God's existence. Instead he offered an argument to show that God was the "best explanation" for the natural world. And, since a rational person should generally believe what they deem to be the best explanation of the phenomena, the rational person, he argued, should believe in God.

His argument essentially goes like this:

Suppose that you are walking along the countryside and you stub your toe on a stone. You may wonder how the stone came to be there, and a natural

Philosophy on Tap: Pint-Sized Puzzles for the Pub Philosopher, First Edition. Matt Lawrence
© 2011 Matt Lawrence. Published 2011 by Blackwell Publishing Ltd.

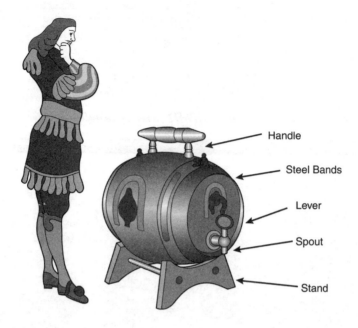

explanation would likely be that, for all you know, the stone might have lain there forever. But suppose that instead you were stumble onto a cask of Newcastle Brown Ale. In this case, the idea that it may have lain there forever is totally implausible. Upon seeing the cask you would undoubtedly surmise that it was manufactured. It must have had a creator who brought it into being in accordance with a specific design or plan.

What is it, Paley wondered, that makes the cask so different from the stone that it calls out for an intelligent designer? The answer, it seems, comes down to two things: complexity and purposefulness. Consider first the complexity of a cask. The barrel itself is architecturally complex, made up of strips of wood bound with iron hoops, and then it is rendered all the more complicated by the handle, stand, and spout apparatus.

Now consider its purposefulness. Even if you had no acquaintance with beer or casks, it wouldn't take you long to figure out that a turn of the lever will release the nut-brown liquid inside. This will undoubtedly lead you to conclude that this device is *for* something – presumably the storage and release of this intriguing liquid.

The complexity of the various parts that are co-adapted to one another in order to perform a specific function leads us to conclude that this "thing" has surely not lain here forever, and it obviously did not come about through the chance operation of natural forces. The best explanation (in fact, the only plausible explanation) is that it is the product of an intelligent being who built it in accordance to a specific design or plan.

If we are inclined to think that there must be an intelligent designer for the cask, then, Paley argued, we should clearly suppose that there is an intelligent designer behind the natural world, for there are many things in nature that are even more complex and purposeful than a cask of beer (though few that are more pleasurable). For example, consider the human heart. Your heart has quite an important purpose – to pump blood throughout your body at just the right pressure to keep you alive for a very long time. If your heart were to stop pumping, or if it were to pump at a significantly higher or lower rate, you would die. And consider its complexity. Imagine, for example, that you are a mechanical engineering major at college. For your senior project you are given the choice to build either a working cask of brown ale or a properly functioning artificial heart. Which would be the easier project? Undoubtedly the cask. So, given its complexity and purposefulness, it would seem that the human heart offers an even stronger case for an intelligent designer than does a cask of Newcastle. And the same would hold true for most things in nature, such as the eyes of an owl, the gills of a fish, or the flower cones of East Kent Goldings hops.

Is an intelligent designer the best explanation for the natural world? Many people think so. Yet, since Charles Darwin's theory of evolution, most biologists have come to believe that the "chance operation of natural forces" provides a better explanation of the complexity and purposefulness of nature. As they see it, there is simply no need for an intelligent designer. The essence of Darwin's theory can be captured in terms of two main mechanisms: *descent with modification* (offspring differ from their parents), and *natural selection* (offspring who are best suited to the environment will live longer and have more offspring). In the case of the eyes of an owl, for instance, descent with modification entails that each baby owlet will have slightly different eyes from one another and from their parents. Therefore some will be able to see farther than others, some will have better night vision, etc. Natural selection entails that if good distance and night vision enable an owl to live longer and thereby have more offspring, then the owls with the better eyesight will have a greater chance of sending their favorable eye genes into future generations. The theory suggests that these mechanisms, operating over hundreds of millions of years, enabled a few simple organisms in distinct environmental niches to evolve into the diversity of complex creatures (with purposeful organs) that we find in nature today.

Truth be told

Paley's original example involved finding a watch in a field rather than a cask of Newcastle Brown Ale. But I am sure that this is only due to the fact that no one would ever leave a cask of Newcastle unattended in an open field.

What do you think?

- What is the best explanation of the complexity of life forms: evolution or an intelligent designer?
- Is Paley correct to believe that complexity and purposefulness are the two key characteristics that call out for an intelligent designer?
- If you do not believe in the theory of evolution, do you believe in "descent with modification" and "natural selection"? (And, if you do acknowledge these mechanisms, where exactly does your disagreement lie?)

Did you know?

- According to a 2005 CBS poll, most Americans do not believe in evolution. Instead, 51 percent say they believe that God created humans in their present form, while an additional 30 percent believe that, while humans did evolve, God guided this process (i.e., evolution occurs through intelligent design).
- Richard Dawkins provides a counter-argument to Paley in his seminal book *The Blind Watchmaker* (New York: Norton, 1996).
- Newcastle's blue star logo was introduced in 1928 – the year after the beer was launched. The five points of the star represent the five founding breweries of Newcastle.
- The origin of Newcastle's nickname of "The Dog" comes from the Englishman's euphemism "I'm going to walk the dog," which really means, "I'm going down to the pub."

Recommended reading

- William Paley, *Natural Theology*, 1809. Repr. in Steven Cahn, ed., *Exploring Philosophy of Religion: An Introductory Anthology* (Oxford: Oxford University Press, 2009), pp. 74–77.

- Charles Darwin, *On the Origin of Species By Means of Natural Selection, or, the Preservation of Favoured Races in the Struggle for Life*, 1859. Available online at: http://www.gutenberg.org/etext/1228.

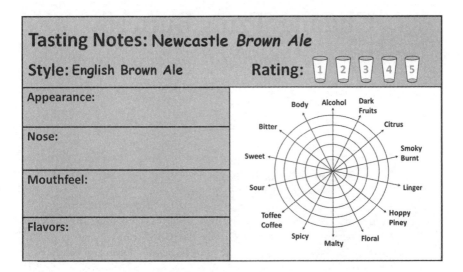

Tasting Notes: Newcastle *Brown Ale*

Style: English Brown Ale **Rating:** 1 2 3 4 5

Appearance:

Nose:

Mouthfeel:

Flavors:

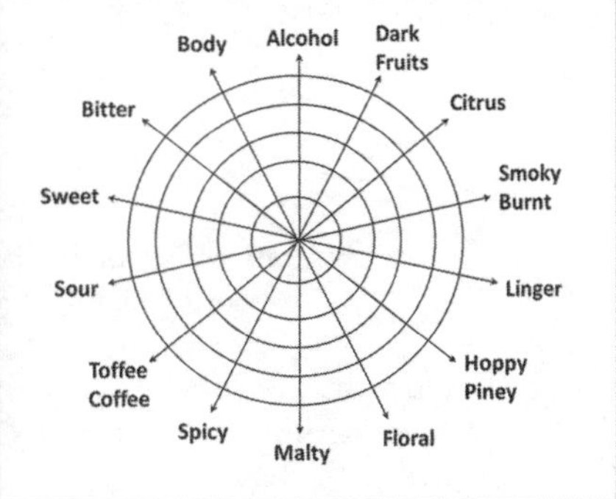
Body
Alcohol
Dark Fruits
Citrus
Smoky Burnt
Linger
Hoppy Piney
Floral
Malty
Spicy
Toffee Coffee
Sour
Sweet
Bitter

Chuang Tzu's Butterfly

Could you be dreaming at this very moment?

Pint of the Puzzle: Great Divide *Espresso Oak Aged Yeti*

Do you ever have doubts about whether you are awake or dreaming? If so, Great Divide Brewing Company of Colorado has the antidote. They infuse their Oak Aged Yeti Imperial Stout with high-octane espresso. It's great for those all-nighters. Or just pour it in a mug and serve it up with waffles for breakfast.

Can you discern the difference between dreaming and waking? Is it possible that your whole life has been a dream? While most people don't seem to take such questions very seriously, the Ancient Chinese philosopher Chuang Tzu (b. 369 BCE) believed that the answers to such questions are not as obvious as they seem. He wrote:

> Once upon a time, I, Chuang Tzu, dreamt I was a butterfly, fluttering hither and thither, through fields of hops and barley. To all intents and purposes I was a butterfly. I was conscious only of following my fancies as a butterfly, breathing in the scent of the hops, licking the barley with my long coiled tongue, and I was

Philosophy on Tap: Pint-Sized Puzzles for the Pub Philosopher, First Edition. Matt Lawrence
© 2011 Matt Lawrence. Published 2011 by Blackwell Publishing Ltd.

unconscious of my life as a man. Suddenly, I awoke, and there I lay, myself again. Now I do not know whether I was then a man dreaming I was a butterfly, or whether I am now a butterfly dreaming I am a man.

Chuang Tzu wasn't sure what to believe. But my guess is that you don't really share his worries. I bet that you feel quite certain that you are wide-awake right now and that the beer in front of you is a *real* beer and not just a figment of your sleeping mind. But what makes you so sure?

You might argue that the fact that you are drinking a highly caffeinated Espresso Yeti guarantees that you are awake. Ah, but there's the rub. Perhaps you are merely dreaming that you are drinking an Espresso Yeti. Perhaps when you awaken, you'll realize that there is no such thing as an Espresso Oak Aged Yeti Imperial Stout. It will then seem so silly to think that you actually believed that someone would put espresso in beer and then name it after an abominable snowman.

Another line of attack is to argue that this experience is just too vivid to be a dream. As you take a swig of Yeti and soak up the coffee and chocolate malt flavors, and feel all those tight little bubbles dancing across your tongue, it is easy to suppose that it all just *has to* be real. But this is to assume that dreams *can't* be this vivid. Are you sure? Chuang Tzu apparently thought that his butterfly dream was quite vivid. And if you think about it, I bet you've had some dreams that seemed so vivid and so real that you were completely fooled by them. So how do you know that your experience during the last few minutes hasn't been one of those particularly vivid dreams?

You might also argue that this experience is too orderly, too predictable, or too long to be a dream. True, sometimes dreams are crazy and unpredictable, but aren't they also sometimes pretty mundane? And can you really be sure about how long this dream (or reality) has actually been going on? Maybe this whole day occurred in just a few minutes of "dreamtime." Or, perhaps only the past couple of minutes have been a dream and the rest of your day was real. (It might be the case that you were so tired that even an Espresso Yeti couldn't keep you awake.)

Another alternative is to pinch yourself. At least that is the "folk wisdom" on the matter. But the reasoning here also seems flawed. The assumption seems to be that you cannot feel pain in a dream (or the pain will inevitably wake you up.) But many people have reported feeling physical sensations during dream states – including pain. So if you pinch yourself and this experience continues, you still don't have sufficient proof that you are awake. You might try asking your friends to vouch for your state of mind, but, for rather obvious reasons, this won't work either. For if you are dreaming, then these aren't *really* your friends. Rather, they are just figments of your imagination. Whatever they tell you has no credibility until you first deter-mine that you really are awake.

I suppose that you could just wait around to see if you wake up. If your experience continues for another six or eight hours, then wouldn't this confirm that you are not dreaming? Well, if Chuang Tzu is right, not even this can help you. For your entire human life could be a dream. Perhaps those times when you experience life as a butterfly (or barfly) are the only times that you are truly awake. Or perhaps both your human experiences and your butterfly experiences are dreams (and dreams within a dream) and you really won't wake up for many years to come!

Truth be told

Chuang Tzu's original telling of this dream oddly omitted the references to fields of hops and barley.

What do you think?

- Is there a reasonable chance that you could be dreaming right now?
- Could you be a Yeti on some mountain in the Himalayas, dreaming that you are a human being?
- Are there any sure signs that we can use to distinguish waking from dreaming?
- Is it a meaningful possibility that your entire life could be a dream?

Did you know?

- Chuang Tzu was a philosopher in the Taoist tradition along with Lao Tzu. For another Taoist puzzle, see chapter 46, "Lao Tzu's Empty Mug."
- When offered the position of prime minister of the state of Ch'u, Chuang Tzu rejected it in order to retain his personal freedom.
- Chuang Tzu was an early environmentalist. He urged people to live in harmony with nature, and he criticized those who attempted to control or conquer nature.
- Great Divide beers have won 16 Great American Beer Festival medals and 4 World Beer Cup awards. Great Divide was also ranked eighth in Ratebeer.com's 2010 "The Best Brewers in the World" and was ranked seventh in Beer Advocate's 2009 "All-Time Top Breweries on Planet Earth."

Recommended reading

- Chuang Tzu, *Basic Writings*, trans. Burton Watson (New York: Columbia University Press, 1996).
- Jeeloo Liu, *An Introduction to Chinese Philosophy: From Ancient Philosophy to Chinese Buddhism* (Oxford: Blackwell Publishing, 2006).

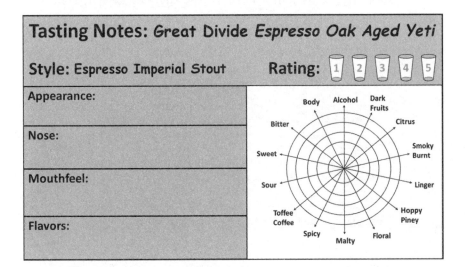

Descartes' Doubt

What do you know with absolute certainty?

Pint of the Puzzle: Dogfish Head *Raison D'Etre*

Raison D'Etre is French for "reason for existing." And the reason why it was chosen for this puzzle will become quite obvious by the time you reach the end. In the meantime, enjoy the unique taste of this deep mahogany ale from the Dogfish Head Brewery of Delaware. It's made with Belgian beet sugars, green raisins, and "a sense of purpose."

Of all the millions of beliefs that you hold, which ones are so completely certain that there is simply no chance that you could be mistaken about them? Take a moment to reflect on this. Create a mental list of your absolutely certain beliefs.

I expect that you probably haven't given it enough time to make a *complete* list, so take another moment to consider how long your complete list might be. Would it contain only a few beliefs, dozens, hundreds, or thousands? I've asked these questions to many people over the years, and most tell me that

Philosophy on Tap: Pint-Sized Puzzles for the Pub Philosopher, First Edition. Matt Lawrence.
© 2011 Matt Lawrence. Published 2011 by Blackwell Publishing Ltd.

their complete list would be quite long – at least in the hundreds or thousands. Their lists of "absolutely certain" beliefs tend to include things such as:

I am in this room.	*Beer is wet.*	*The Earth is round.*
I am drinking a beer.	*My glass is clear.*	*Water is H_2O*
I am male/female.	*Paris is in France.*	*I have two hands.*

If these are the kinds of things that can be known with certainty, then one's list could easily be expanded indefinitely. For, if you are absolutely certain, that you are drinking a beer, then you are probably also certain that the breweries exist and that "Dogfish Head" is a rather odd name for a brewery, and so on.

So now you've probably got a very long mental list. But notice, it is easy to *think* that you are absolutely certain. It is altogether different *really to be* certain – to *know* that there is absolutely no chance that your belief could be false. As philosophers we want to know what *really is* and not what merely *seems to be*. So we must ask, are you *really* certain? Is there absolutely no chance that you are mistaken about these beliefs?

The great French philosopher René Descartes (1596–1650) took up these questions, and he too had supposed that there were quite a few things that he knew with absolute certainty. But then he subjected his beliefs to what is famously known as his "method of doubt." Descartes reasoned that if a belief is absolutely certain, then it should be impervious to doubt. That is, he should not be able to imagine a scenario that would make the belief false, or provide even the slightest reason to doubt it.

We have already seen one potential source of doubt in "Chuang Tzu's Butterfly" (chapter 17) – the possibility that you could be dreaming at this very moment. Descartes was plagued by a similar worry; however, he came to realize that even if he were dreaming, certain beliefs must still remain true. Whether you are awake or asleep, three bottles of beer plus three more bottles make six beers in total. And insofar as the rim of your glass is round, it cannot have corners, etc. Thus, math, logic, and geometry, he realized, are impervious to doubt even if you are dreaming.

But if we try our hardest to doubt even these beliefs, then there is more trouble ahead. For isn't it possible that you could be the victim of an intentional deception? Descartes summed up this idea with a kind of worst-case scenario – "the evil demon."

> I shall then suppose ... some evil demon not less powerful than deceitful, has employed his whole energies in deceiving me; I shall consider that the heavens, the earth, colours, figures, sounds, even the ale I am presently drinking are

nothing but the illusions and dreams of which this demon has availed himself in order to lay traps for my credulity.

To better understand the depth of the evil demon's deceptions, you might imagine him as a "mad scientist" who has hooked you up to a system of electrodes that stimulate your brain. Thereby, he is able to make you see, hear, feel, taste, and smell whatever he wishes. He can implant false memories and erroneous thoughts in your mind, and he can make you go wrong in even the simplest calculations, such as adding bottles of beer, or counting the sides of a square. But it is even worse than this, for you cannot even take it for granted that you have a brain (or even a body for that matter), since these could be part of the deception as well. It is always possible that the evil demon might work his deception through some form of hypnosis or telepathy. You could turn out to be a bodiless spirit who has been deceived into believing in this material world.

If we allow the possibility of such an evil demon (and it seems we have no way to rule him out, as the lack of evidence for him only attests to his ingenuity), then is there nothing at all that can be known with certainty? Ponder this for a moment before reading further.

What about your own existence? Is it possible that you have been deceived into thinking that you exist when in fact you don't? Descartes concluded that he could not be mistaken about his own existence, for one must first exist if one is to be deceived at all. In fact, you must exist if you are to think anything at all. With this realization, Descartes uttered perhaps the most famous line in all of Western philosophy:

"I think therefore I am."

This was Descartes' rock – his immovable point of certainty upon which he built the rest of his philosophy.

> ### Truth be told
>
> Descartes didn't own up to the fact that he was drinking an ale when he wrote the famous "demon" passage above.

What do you think?

⊙ If our goal is absolute certainty, must we allow that there is at least a slight chance that we are being deceived by an evil demon?

- Can you be absolutely certain about your own existence? And if you can, what, if anything, can you know about this "you" that exists?
- Are there other things of which you can be absolutely certain? If so, what are they?
- Was Descartes correct to suppose that whether you are awake or asleep, three beers plus three more make six?

Did you know?

- René Descartes had a lifelong habit of not getting out of bed until noon. (As a student he even convinced his teachers to allow him to "study in bed" in the mornings.) When he was in his fifties, he was invited to tutor Queen Christina of Sweden regarding his philosophy. The Queen liked to take her lessons at five o'clock in the morning, and within a few months of this regimen Descartes caught a bad cold and died.
- Descartes believed that we can ultimately know many things with complete certainty – but only if we first prove God's existence. Later, in his *Meditations on First Philosophy*, he provided an argument that he thought supplied that proof, though most scholars believe that his argument failed.
- Here is a classic Descartes joke. René Descartes is at the pub enjoying a pint of fine ale, when the bartender walks up and asks if he'd like another. Descartes replies, "I think not" and disappears.
- The Dogfish Head Brewery is named after a jut of land off the coast of Maine where Sam Calagione, the brewery's founder, used to vacation as kid. According to local legend, it was named Dogfish Head because the lobster fisherman used to end up trapping more dogfish than lobsters.
- The Dogfish Head Brewery motto is: "Off-centered ales for off-centered people." It specializes in "extreme" beers with ingredients that are off the beaten path. A partial list of the unusual ingredients you can find in their line includes beet sugar, maple syrup, crystallized ginger, juniper berries, vanilla beans, thyme, honey, allspice, chicory, apricots, pumpkins, cinnamon, coffee, blackberries, and nutmeg.

Recommended reading

- René Descartes, *Meditations on First Philosophy*. Available online at: http://oregonstate.edu/instruct/phl302/texts/descartes/meditations/meditations.html.
- Peter Unger, *Ignorance* (Oxford: Oxford University Press, 1975).

Tasting Notes: Dogfish Head *Raison D'Etre*

Style: Belgian Strong Dark Ale   **Rating:** 1 2 3 4 5

Appearance:

Nose:

Mouthfeel:

Flavors:

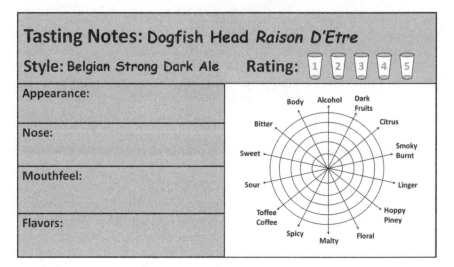

God's Command

Can saying make it so?

**Pint of the Puzzle: Schmaltz *He'brew*
*Origin Pomegranate Ale***

How did morality originate? Did it all begin with a Divine command, or did God merely give us a "heads up" about what was already right and wrong? As you contemplate the source of morality, let's pour a Hebrew Origin pomegranate-infused ale from the Shmaltz Brewery of San Francisco. It's one of "the chosen beers."

What *makes* some actions right and others wrong? According to one popular theory, it is God's *will* or *command* that creates right and wrong. Within this view, actions are right *because* God commands us to perform them, or because He simply wills (prefers) that we perform them. And conversely, actions are wrong because God forbids them, or wills/prefers that we refrain from them. This theory of morality is called the *Divine Command Theory*. If it is correct, then the French philosopher Jean-Paul Sartre was right to have maintained that if God does not exist then everything is permissible. For without God there would simply be no "right" or "wrong."

It is not the purpose of this puzzle to consider whether or not God exists. Rather, it is to examine whether the Divine Command Theory adequately explains the basis of morality. So let's assume (at least for the sake of

Philosophy on Tap: Pint-Sized Puzzles for the Pub Philosopher, First Edition. Matt Lawrence
© 2011 Matt Lawrence. Published 2011 by Blackwell Publishing Ltd.

argument) that God exists. Could God's *saying* that an action is wrong literally *make* it wrong?

Suppose that God were to draw up a new commandment and deliver it to some prophetic brewmaster on a stone tablet that reads:

Thou shall only drink pomegranate infused ales on Thursdays.

The prophet elucidates this decree by saying that it is completely permissible to drink all other sorts of beers on all other days. But on Thursdays, it has to be ale and it has to be infused with the juice of a pomegranate. Some readers may take offense here, saying that God would not make such a silly command. But this is precisely the point in question. Do God's commands *need* to be backed with good reasons in order to make the corresponding act moral or immoral; or is the command sufficient on its own? If God's command is sufficient in its own right, then it need not be a reasonable command.

But let's go ahead and take a more sensible command. Let us suppose that God commands (or at least wills) that pub patrons refrain from stealing the bartender's tips. Despite the fact that this command comes from God, some curious people will surely wonder why on earth God would make such an inconvenient command. We can split the possibilities into two broad categories. Either God commanded this for good reason, or He commanded it for no good reason. Notice that these two categories are mutually exclusive and exhaustive. Either God had good reasons or He didn't – there is no third alternative. This leads us into a problem that is known as the *Divine Command Theory Dilemma*.

A dilemma occurs when you have only two options available and both are bad for you (or in this case, bad for your theory.) The proponent of the Divine Command Theory must pick a side. But do you go left, or do you go right? The critic suggests that whichever route you choose will lead you into trouble.

Most people initially try to avoid the left side or "horn" of the dilemma. Since, if there are *no good reasons* behind God's commands, then these commands would be completely arbitrary – nothing more than capricious whims. God could just have easily commanded us to kill all the French poodles, or to drink pomegranate beers on Thursdays. In that case we might follow God's commands out of fear of punishment, but we wouldn't have any reason to *respect* these commands. For this reason, most people find this alternative to be totally unsatisfactory.

If you go with the right horn, however, morality retains the kind of non-arbitrary importance that we think it should have. The only problem is that the Divine Command Theory (it would seem) is shown to be false. For in this case, the action is not wrong *because* God commanded it. Rather, God commanded it *because* it was wrong (i.e., because there were good reasons against performing the action). Although the Lord works in mysterious ways (or so they say), in this case I think that we *can* comprehend God's reasoning. It seems rather likely that God doesn't want you stealing the bartender's tips because it would be *unfair*. Bartenders work hard for their tips while you have just been sitting around watching the game. By stealing the tips, you are taking unfair advantage of your bartender. Thus it would appear to be the unfairness of the theft that makes it wrong (in God's eyes and our own) and not God's saying so – thus putting the Divine Command Theorist in the proverbial "tight spot."

What do you think?

- Does the dilemma show that the Divine Command Theory is an untenable account of the basis or source of morality? And if not, why not?
- Is this a true dilemma with only two options, or has some third alternative been overlooked?
- Suppose that two societies each believe in God. However, Society A believes that the Divine Command Theory is true, and Society B believes that the Divine Command Theory is false. In what ways would the moral lives of each society's citizens differ?

Did you know?

- Each side or option in a dilemma is called a "horn." This is because a dilemma is like a bull with two very large and sharp horns. You can go left or you can go right, but either way you are going to get skewered.
- The Divine Command Dilemma is similar to an argument made by Plato in *Euthyphro*. In that text, the argument pertains to whether certain things are holy because the Gods love them, or whether the Gods love them *because* they are holy.

- Some of the commands attributed to God in the Torah (or Old Testament) seem to be unsupported by any conceivable "good reason." This inclines some literalists to embrace the left horn of the dilemma. For example in Leviticus 19:19, God commanded: "Thou shall not sow thy field with mingled seed: neither shall a garment mingled of linen and woolen come upon thee." (In other words, thou shall not wear clothes of mixed fibers.)

- Within the Judeo-Christian tradition, God seems to have a penchant for pomegranate. Song of Solomon 7:12 states: "Let us go early to the vineyards to see if the vines have budded, if their blossoms have opened, and if the pomegranates are in bloom – there I will give you my love." And in Deuteronomy 8:8, the "Land of Milk and Honey" is described more precisely as, "a land with wheat and barley, vines and fig trees, pomegranates, olive oil and honey."

- Shmaltz Brewing is America's smallest, biggest, and most award-winning Jewish beer company. Their He'brew brand includes: Genesis Ale, Messiah Bold, Rejuvenator Date Infused Doppelbock, and Jewbelation Bar Mitzvah.

Recommended reading

- Plato, *Euthyphro*. Available at Project Gutenberg: http://www.gutenberg.org/etext/1642.
- John Arthur, "Religion, Morality, and Conscience," in John Arthur, ed., *Morality and Moral Controversies,* 4th edn. (Upper Saddle River, NJ: Prentice Hall, 1996).

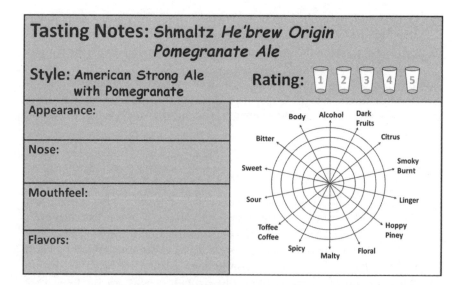

Tasting Notes: Shmaltz *He'brew Origin Pomegranate Ale*

Style: American Strong Ale with Pomegranate

Rating: 1 2 3 4 5

Appearance:

Nose:

Mouthfeel:

Flavors:

Body Alcohol Dark Fruits Bitter Citrus Sweet Smoky Burnt Sour Linger Toffee Coffee Hoppy Piney Spicy Malty Floral

20

Mill's Drunkard

Are intellectual pleasures better than bodily pleasures?

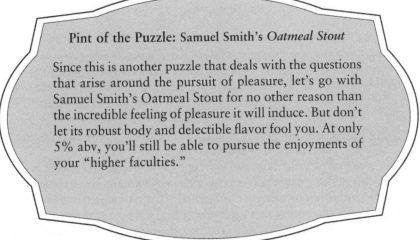

Pint of the Puzzle: Samuel Smith's *Oatmeal Stout*

Since this is another puzzle that deals with the questions that arise around the pursuit of pleasure, let's go with Samuel Smith's Oatmeal Stout for no other reason than the incredible feeling of pleasure it will induce. But don't let its robust body and delectible flavor fool you. At only 5% abv, you'll still be able to pursue the enjoyments of your "higher faculties."

John Stuart Mill maintained that pleasure or happiness was the only true good, and that everything that a person desires is sought either as a means or a part of their happiness. His detractors, arguing that such a hedonistic outlook was degrading, hit him with what has come to be known as "The Swine Objection." The argument goes like this:

> If pleasure is the only thing that is good, then we all might as well live like pigs. After all, pigs are pretty good at pursuing pleasure, and it seems that little else matters to them. Bask in the sun, roll in the mud, eat a lot of food, have a lot of sex, and the piggish life is complete. But such a doctrine puts human beings in a

Philosophy on Tap: Pint-Sized Puzzles for the Pub Philosopher, First Edition. Matt Lawrence
© 2011 Matt Lawrence. Published 2011 by Blackwell Publishing Ltd.

degrading light. We are better than pigs and should not live like them. There is more to a good human life than mere pleasure.

A second parallel argument goes like this:

If pleasure is the only thing that is good, then we all might as well become drunkards. After all, happy drunks (we'll ignore the angry drunks) are pretty good at pursuing pleasure, and it seems that little else matters to them. Drink some beers, hang out at the pub, eat some good food, get lucky on occasion, and the drunkard's life seems to him complete. If we had unlimited funds (and could escape unfortunate side effects, such as hangovers and liver disease), then, by this reasoning, we would all do well to become drunkards. But such a doctrine puts human beings in a degrading light. We are better than drunks and should not live like them. There is more to a good human life than mere drunken pleasures.

Mill agreed that we should not live like drunks or pigs (or drunken pigs). But as a hedonist, he could not say that this is because there is more to life than pleasure. So instead, he argued that our lifestyle should follow a different course because we are capable of enjoying pleasures that drunks and pigs cannot. We can do philosophy, enjoy poetry, have interesting conversations, and develop our talents. In short, there are certain "intellectual pleasures" available to us that are not available to them.

The idea that pleasures come in two types, intellectual and bodily, was not new. Mill's philosophical predecessor, Jeremy Bentham, had also acknowledged this rather obvious point. But Bentham had maintained that one should always choose the option that offers the greatest *amount* of pleasure – be it intellectual or bodily. What mattered was the quantity of pleasure, not the type. But here, Mill disagreed, and added a new chapter to the Utilitarian playbook. He contended that intellectual pleasures are inherently better than bodily ones. He maintained that they are better in *quality* to such an extent as to render quantity of little relative importance.

Mill made his case for the qualitative superiority of intellectual pleasures by invoking a "competent judges" criterion. He argued that we are justified in saying that a pleasure is of a higher quality if all competent judges (those who are thoroughly acquainted with both types of pleasure) would prefer it – irrespective of any feeling of obligation to do so. Furthermore, Mill contended that all or almost all competent judges prefer the intellectual pleasures. And, not only do they prefer them, they prefer them by such a wide margin that they would not trade them for any quantity of the other.

To prove his point Mill asks us to consider a trade. Suppose, for instance, that a magic genie could turn you into a pig, complete with the fullest life of piggish pleasures: all the best pig food, sex, mud pits, and sunny days. Would you be willing to give up your intellectual pleasures for this fullest life of a pig's pleasures? Very few people would make that trade. Of course, this could merely demonstrate our prejudices against pigs, so let's try another example. Suppose that, instead, the genie will turn you into a total drunk, but one who is impervious to hangovers, liver disease, etc. Moreover, you'll get free food, lodging, and drinks at every tavern in town. Would you take that sort of trade? Again Mill thinks that very few among us would. He concludes:

> It is better to be a human being dissatisfied than a pig satisfied; better to be Socrates dissatisfied than a drunkard satisfied. And if the drunkard or the pig are of a different opinion, it is because they only know their own side of the question. The other party to the comparison knows both sides.

Mill believed that these kinds of thought experiments clearly showed the superiority of intellectual pleasures. Such pleasures are so much better, he thought, that the competent judge would not trade them for even the maximum amount of bodily pleasures. But did Mill really prove his point? Notice that he only gave us one side of the comparison. So consider this: imagine that the genie is going to transform you in such a way that you'll have the fullest life of intellectual pleasure. You'll be smarter than Albert Einstein and Bertrand Russell combined. But here's the catch – you'll no longer be able to experience bodily pleasures. To give you this increased intellectual ability, your brain will be removed and put into a vat of nutrient solution that will keep you alive. You'll still be able to converse with others, write papers, do equations, etc., through a computer interface. However you'll never taste another beer again, or witness a beautiful sunset, or have sex, or eat a good meal. Would you trade your bodily pleasures for this fullest life of intellectual pleasures? I didn't think so. And so we are left to wonder: are intellectual pleasures really better than bodily ones?

Truth be told

The original passage from Mill's *Utilitarianism* regarding Socrates compared him to "a fool" rather than "a drunkard."

What do you think?

- Would you take any of the genie's offers? If so, would you choose the pig, the drunkard or the genius?

If you would not take any of the genies offers, what does that mean about the relative importance of intellectual versus bodily pleasures?

Does The Swine Objection succeed in showing that pleasure is not the only good?

Did you know?

John Stuart Mill was educated by his father. He studied Greek as early as age 3, Latin at age 7, and had written nearly 50 articles and reviews by the age of 20.

Samuel Smith's Tadcaster brewery in Yorkshire England was founded in 1758. The brewing water for their ales and stouts is drawn from an 85-foot well that was sunk the same year.

The yeast used in Samuel Smith's fermentation process is one of the oldest unchanged strains in England. It has been used continuously for more than 100 years.

Recommended reading

- John Stuart Mill, *Utilitarianism*, ch. 2 (1879). Available online at Project Gutenberg: http://www.gutenberg.org/etext/11224.
- Henry R. West, *Mill's Utilitarianism: A Reader's Guide* (New York, Continuum, 2007).

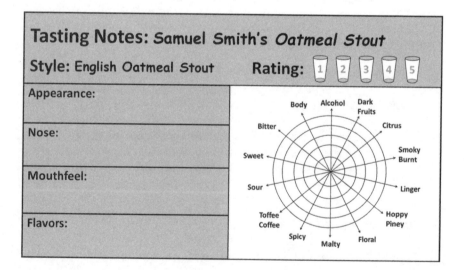

21

The Myth of Gyges

Who finished the pitcher?! Are we all just selfish?

Pint of the Puzzle: Mythos *Greek Lager*

Greece is rich with mythology, in terms of both its abundant array of gods, goddesses, and demi-gods, and its delicious lagers. Mythos Greek Lager is said to be a Divine nectar with the power of invisibility. Put it in a pitcher and watch it disappear before your very eyes!

Don't you hate it when one of your so-called friends drinks far more than their fair share of the pitcher? What happened to common decency? I guess we're lucky that not everyone is so selfish. Or are they? In the *Republic*, Plato (*c.* 428–348 BCE) offers a story that might make you think otherwise. The story, known as the "Myth of Gyges," does not reflect Plato's own position, but that of his older brother Glaucon, who uses it to challenge our common conceptions about the roles that justice and selfishness play in our lives.

Glaucon tells of a shepherd from long ago named Gyges, who tended the king's flocks. One day while he was out on the hillside, there was a huge earthquake and a giant chasm opened up in the earth. Peering down into its

Philosophy on Tap: Pint-Sized Puzzles for the Pub Philosopher, First Edition. Matt Lawrence. © 2011 Matt Lawrence. Published 2011 by Blackwell Publishing Ltd.

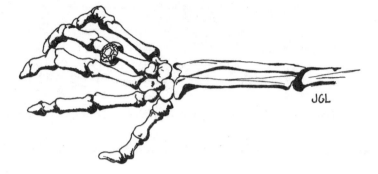

depths, Gyges saw a giant metal horse with windows built into its sides. When he climbed down to get a closer look he saw that at the controls inside this horse was a human skeleton. On its boney finger there was a very unusual ring, so Gyges took it for himself. A few days later, when the shepherds held their monthly meeting to report on the state of the flocks, Gyges sat at the table with the others and began to play with the ring. To his amazement, when he turned the bezel around, he became invisible. He sat and watched as the other shepherds spoke of him as if he were not in the room. When he turned the bezel back to its original position he reappeared. After this discovery, he soon arranged to become a messenger to the king's court. He then used the ring to seduce the queen, murder the king, and seized the throne.

The conclusion that Glaucon draws from this story is that none of us is really so different from Gyges. He suggests that if there were two such rings and one were given to the just person and another to the unjust person, both would act similarly.

> Both would use the ring to their own unfair advantage – fearlessly helping themselves to anything they desired. They'd be snatching free pints from the taverns each night, spitting in their enemies drinks, and performing other deeds far worse and too numerous to mention.

Is Glaucon right? Would everyone take the path of injustice if they knew they could get away with it? I've polled numerous college students about this and for the most part they agree. When I ask, "Who among you can honestly say that you would never use the ring to gain an unfair advantage?" I rarely find more than just a couple who think so. (And generally the other students don't believe them.) A significant number of my students turn out to be "psychological egoists" – that is, they think that people are *always* motivated by selfish interests. Personally, I'm more optimistic. I think that many people really do care about justice, even though they may sometimes succumb to selfish cravings. But it is impossible to prove that the psychological egoist is wrong. For any example that you offer, even the life of Mother Theresa, they'll always point to some hidden selfish motive, saying: "She only does those things because it makes her feel good." Or, "She's just after her eternal reward," and so on. And the bottom line is there is no way to prove it one way or another. You can never be absolutely sure of your own motives, much less another person's. So in the end, you must choose the account that seems most reasonable. Is justice merely a front that we use to hide our selfishness, or is it something that some people value even more than life itself?

Truth be told

The quoted passage is only *loosely* based on Glaucon's speech in the *Republic*.

What do you think?

- If you found a ring of invisibility, would you use it to gain unfair advantages?
- Do you believe that people sometimes care about justice for its own sake?
- If a person gets pleasure from helping others, should this count as selfishness?
- Is there any reason to care about justice for its own sake – apart from its material rewards? If so, what is that reason?

Did you know?

- Plato was the student of Socrates and the teacher of Aristotle.
- Plato's real name was Aristocles. "Plato" was a nickname meaning "broad." Scholars believe that it was given to him either because of the breadth of his shoulders or because of the breadth of his forehead.
- Socrates and Plato both believed that justice *always* benefits a person more than injustice. For more on this, see chapter 34, "Socrates' Virtue."
- The Mythos Brewery of Greece not only makes Mythos Lager; it also produces and distributes the German beers Kaiser and Henninger, as well as a Greek lager called Golden.

Recommended reading

- Plato, *Republic*. Available online at Project Gutenberg: http://www.gutenberg.org/etext/1497.
- Gerald A. Press, *Plato: A Guide for the Perplexed* (New York: Continuum, 2007).

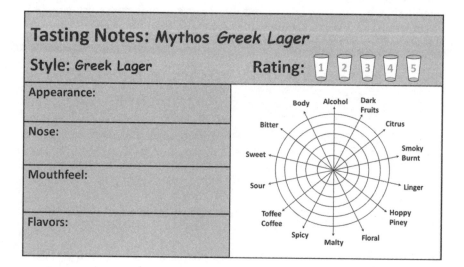

Tasting Notes: Mythos *Greek Lager*

Style: Greek Lager   **Rating:** 1 2 3 4 5

Appearance:

Nose:

Mouthfeel:

Flavors:

Body Alcohol Dark Fruits
Bitter   Citrus
Sweet   Smoky Burnt
Sour   Linger
Toffee Coffee   Hoppy Piney
Spicy Malty Floral

22

Laplace's Superscientist

Is your next round totally predictable?

Pint of the Puzzle: Surprise Me

"Surprise Me" is not the name of some new craft brew. I'm putting down a challenge. Surprise me. Surprise yourself. Try to be completely unpredictable when you choose this beer. Do you think you can? Beware, this puzzle has the very predictable effect of making you rethink your answer.

Is it possible to predict the future? In many ways we already do. Hold a match to a sheet of paper and we know that it will burn. We can accurately predict that the sun will rise at 6.17 a.m. tomorrow and that water will freeze at 32°F while beer will not. Despite our ever-increasing powers of prediction, life is still full of surprises. Some things, it would seem, are just inherently unpredictable.

Many philosophers over the centuries have urged that we should not be fooled by life's apparent unpredictability. Surprising events, they argue, are simply those whose causes we do not yet understand. When fully understood, they too will become as predictable as the tides. Pierre Simone Laplace

---

Philosophy on Tap: Pint-Sized Puzzles for the Pub Philosopher, First Edition. Matt Lawrence.
© 2011 Matt Lawrence. Published 2011 by Blackwell Publishing Ltd.

(1749–1827), a French philosopher, scientist, and mathematician, held this view. In his *Philosophical Essay on Probabilities*, Laplace argued that the right kind of person with the right sort of knowledge could predict anything and everything that will ever happen.

Since one of the chief aims of science is prediction, let's call this hypothetical person with complete predictive abilities a "Superscientist." What would it take to be a Superscientist? Laplace contends that one would need three things:

1. An unlimited ability to calculate.
2. Perfect knowledge of the laws of physics.
3. Complete knowledge of the state of the world at a single moment in time.

Of course, there never has been, and there probably never will be, a bona fide Superscientist. But Laplace's point is that the history of the world is just the "playing out" of the laws of physics. If one knew the state of the world at a given moment, then, with the requisite calculating ability, one could apply the laws of physics to that state in order to deduce the next state, and then the next, and the next, for all eternity.

Laplace's thesis is rather disturbing. Generally, we like to think that at least our own actions are not so predictable. We tend to suppose that human behavior is (unlike the movements of rocks, billiard balls, and amber ales) the result of our own "free will." When you step up to the bar, it certainly seems as if you can freely choose any of the beers on tap, and that which one you choose is not the inevitable result of the laws of physics. But Laplace calls on us to question this assumption. After all, we are physical creatures living in a physical world. Even in Laplace's day it was becoming clear that the movements of the human body are the result of biochemical signals generated in our brains and sent to our arms, legs, torso, etc., through the central nervous system. These are physical processes, and therefore governed by the laws of physics. Human bodies don't get an exemption from the laws that govern all everything else.

Of course, we have beliefs, desires, and motives, but considerable biological research seems to suggest that these mental phenomena are caused by (or are identical to) the activity of our brains – the firing of various neural networks and so forth. And, as physical processes, these too are subject to the laws of physics. Consider, for example, an experiment designed by Benjamin Libet of the University of San Francisco. He hooked up his human subjects to an EEG device in order to monitor their brain activity. He then asked them to watch a clock and report the exact moment that they "decided" to perform a simple motor skill such as moving a finger. He found that their conscious desire or "choice" to move their finger tended to come about 500 milliseconds *after* significant neural activity had occurred in the motor areas of the brain. That is, their conscious decision seems to have occurred only after their brain had already begun to prepare to carry out the action. Experiments of this sort have been taken by many to suggest that our conscious choices don't really cause the action at all; rather they merely "report" what has already occurred.

Even if Libet's experiment does not warrant such a dramatic conclusion, and our conscious decisions *are* the causes of our actions, we must still wonder if there is some further cause for how, why, and when we decided as we did. If, for example, at 8.22 p.m. you decide to surprise me by ordering a pint of Samuel Adams Old Fezziwig Ale, Laplace would argue that there must be a cause of that unusual beer selection. It cannot have occurred outside the bounds of the laws of physics. Surely it is the result of the antecedent states of your brain – including those caused by the ink on this page when you read the "surprises me" challenge at the start of this puzzle. In this case, your beer selection was ultimately as predictable as the motions of the planets (or the flavor of a mass-produced beer), and a bona fide Superscientist would have known it before you were even born.

What do you think?

- Could a Superscientist predict *everything* – including your own actions?
- Are human actions governed entirely by the laws of physics? Why/why not?
- What does the term "free will" mean to you? Do you believe that people have free will?
- Laplace's position involves "causal determinism." Causal determinism is the view that: (a) every event has a cause, and (b) prior causes determine each event in every precise detail (each event unfolds exactly as it must). Do you think that causal determinism is true? Why/why not?

Did you know?

- Pierre Simone Laplace helped to devise the meter and standardized weights and measures as a member of the French Academy of Sciences.
- Laplace's "causal determinist" position is shared by philosophers such as Baron d'Holbach and Robert Blatchford. It has been vigorously rejected by philosophers such as Jean-Paul Sartre and Peter van Inwagen.
- While the macro-sized world of people and planets appears to be totally deterministic, events at the quantum level seem to be merely probabilistic.

Recommended reading

- Pierre Simone Laplace, *Philosophical Essay on Probabilities*, trans. A. Dale (New York: Springer-Verlag, 1995).
- Ted Honderich, *How Free Are You? The Determinism Problem* (Oxford: Oxford University Press, 2002).

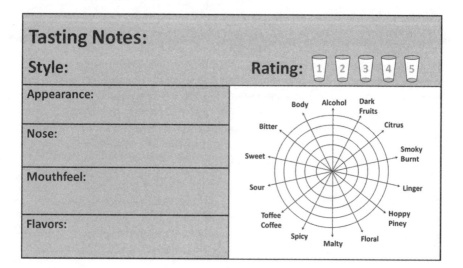

Gaunilo's Perfect Ale

If it were truly perfect, wouldn't it have to exist?

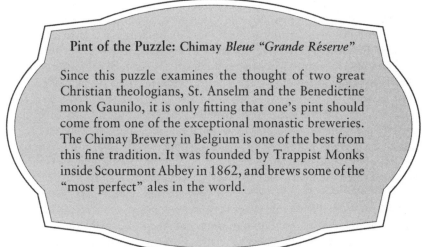

Pint of the Puzzle: Chimay *Bleue "Grande Réserve"*

Since this puzzle examines the thought of two great Christian theologians, St. Anselm and the Benedictine monk Gaunilo, it is only fitting that one's pint should come from one of the exceptional monastic breweries. The Chimay Brewery in Belgium is one of the best from this fine tradition. It was founded by Trappist Monks inside Scourmont Abbey in 1862, and brews some of the "most perfect" ales in the world.

St. Anselm's (1033–1109) famous ontological argument for God's existence is one of the most confounding pieces of reasoning in the history of philosophy. The essence of the argument is that we can know that God exists (in reality) simply by understanding the idea of God that we have in our minds. On the face of it, this seems ludicrous. How can having an idea of something entail that the thing in question exists? Anselm reasoned as follows:

1. God is, by definition, the greatest conceivable being.
2. A being is greater if it exists in reality and not merely in the imagination.

Philosophy on Tap: Pint-Sized Puzzles for the Pub Philosopher, First Edition. Matt Lawrence
© 2011 Matt Lawrence. Published 2011 by Blackwell Publishing Ltd.

3. We can conceive of God existing in reality and not merely in the imagination.
4. Therefore, the greatest conceivable being (God) must exist in reality and not merely in the imagination.

Anselm believed that he had the atheist over a barrel on this one (preferably a barrel of Chimay). The atheist must admit that he can at least *conceive* of the idea of God before he can say that God does not really exist. That is, he must say something along the lines of: "Yeah, I know what you're talkin' about – the greatest conceivable being. Sure. But that greatest conceivable being doesn't really exist. It's like Santa Clause – it exists in a childish imagination, but not in the real world."

"Aha!" Anselm can now retort. "Your problem is that you are not really thinking of the greatest conceivable being. *I'm* thinking of a God that exists in the imagination *and* in reality. *You* are thinking of a God that exists *only* in the imagination. Hence my God is better than your God. So, by definition, you are not thinking of God at all. To truly be the 'greatest conceivable being,' God *must* exist!"

Generally when people hear of Anselm's argument for the first time, they are confident that something fishy is going on. The argument, they contend, cannot be correct. But if it is fallacious, where exactly does it go wrong?

One of Anselm's contemporaries, a Benedictine monk named Gaunilo, thought he had the answer. He argued that Anselm was mistaken to think that he, or anyone else, could conceive of "the greatest conceivable being." But Anselm responded by saying that of course we cannot conceive of God in all His unfathomable glory, but the argument doesn't depend on this. It is sufficient that we should understand that God must have certain necessary characteristics. (And if you don't understand even God's most essential characteristics, how can you call yourself a believer?) We can be certain, for example, that the greatest conceivable being is all-powerful, for, if He were not, then a greater being could still be conceived. We can also know that God must be all-knowing, for, if not, a greater being could still be conceived. And, we can know that God must exist in reality, for, if He did not, then a greater being could still be conceived.

Undaunted, Gaunilo offered a second criticism of the argument. This one uses a strategy known as a *reductio ad absurdum*. In essence, he tried to show that Anselm's line of reasoning leads us to patently absurd conclusions. One such conclusion is that a perfect pint of ale exists. Gaunilo reasoned as follows:

Imagine for a moment, an absolutely perfect pint of ale. It is, of course, incredibly delicious and thirst-quenching – so much so that no other ale can compare. And since an ale is better cold, this pint always remains at the perfect temperature, regardless of where you take it, or how long you linger over it. And, given that a pint is always better if it exists in reality and not merely in the imagination, then (since this pint is absolutely perfect), it *must* exist in reality!

No one, Gaunilo argued, would be convinced of the existence of a perfect ale by such a lame argument. Yet the reasoning, he maintained, is exactly parallel to that of Anselm's ontological argument.

As mouth-watering as Gaunilo's counter-argument may be, Anselm didn't buy it. He retorted that existence is a *necessary* feature of God, in much the same way that being 16 fluid ounces is a necessary feature of a pint glass. God *must* exist in order to be the greatest conceivable being, just as a pint glass *must* be 16 fluid ounces in order to be a pint glass. In contrast, he would argue that existence is only a *contingent* feature of ale (perfect or otherwise). No ale *must* exist. Any ale could exist or not, just as any pint glass can be filled with Chimay Bleue or not.

Truth be told

Gaunilo used the example of a *perfect island* in his reply to Anselm – not a *perfect ale*. (But, of course, you know he was really thinking about how nice it would be to have a perfect ale.)

What do you think?

- Does Anselm's ontological argument prove God's existence?
- Is there any significant difference between Anselm's reasoning about God and Gaunilo's reasoning about the perfect ale?
- Is existence a necessary or contingent feature of God?
- Is existence a necessary or contingent feature of the perfect ale?

Did you know?

- "Ontology" pertains to the study and/or theory of existence. Anselm's argument is called *ontological* because it attempts to prove God's existence from the *existence* of the very idea of God.
- Immanuel Kant argued that the problem with Anselm's argument is that "existence" is not a predicate. That is, we can apply predicates

(e.g., qualities such as cold, amber, and delicious) to objects insofar as we can conceive of them as existing, but existence itself is not a quality of an object. Rather it is what makes it an object in the first place.

● The Trappists are a reform branch of the Benedictine Order. Also known as the Order of Cistercians of the Strict Observance, Trappists are well known for their silence (they speak only when necessary), and for their amazing ales.

● St. Arnold is the patron saint of brewing. He spent much of his life teaching peasants about the dangers of drinking water (in the Dark Ages it was often unsafe) and instead suggested that they stick to beer. He is also attributed with the miracle of the "bottomless mug." It is said that he satisfied a tired and thirsty crowd with just one mug of beer.

● If we are going to talk about perfect ales, I have to mention Westvleteren 12. This is like the Holy Grail of beers. It tops Ratebeer.com's list of 100 best beers of 2010 (and has been among the top three for many years running). So why isn't it the pick for the puzzle? It is too hard to find. Very few of these babies are sold outside Belgium. If you do find one, send me a bottle.

Recommended reading

- St. Anselm, *Monologion and Proslogion With the Replies of Gaunilo and Anselm,* trans. Thomas Williams (Indianapolis, IN: Hackett, 1996).
- William Rowe, *Philosophy of Religion: An* Introduction (Belmont, CA: Wadsworth Publishing, 2006).

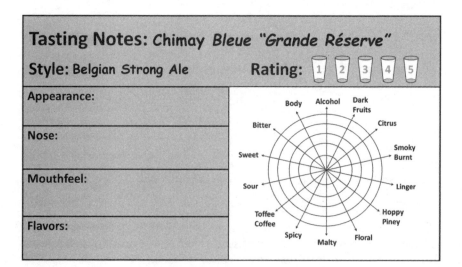

Tasting Notes: Chimay *Bleue "Grande Réserve"*

Style: Belgian Strong Ale   **Rating:** 1 2 3 4 5

| Appearance: |
| Nose: |
| Mouthfeel: |
| Flavors: |

Body · Alcohol · Dark Fruits · Citrus · Bitter · Sweet · Smoky Burnt · Sour · Linger · Toffee · Coffee · Hoppy Piney · Spicy · Malty · Floral

The Problem of Moral Truth

Are moral beliefs ever true?

Pint of the Puzzle: Wasatch *Polygamy Porter*

Is there anything wrong with having two wives? You certainly wouldn't limit yourself to only one beer. But as any married man will tell you, maintaining a good relationship with your beer is infinitely easier than it is with your wife – whether you've got one or many. Reflect on this while you treat yourself to a Polygamy Porter, one of Utah's finest exports.

People make moral claims all the time. We say things like "Slavery is wrong," "Censorship is unjust," and "Brewers have an obligation not to artificially carbonate their beer." But have you ever stopped to think about *what* exactly we are doing when we make such statements? Certainly we are expressing our moral views, but are we saying anything *true*? And, if so, what *makes* them true?

Some philosophers have argued that moral claims can only be true in a belief-dependent way. They contend that morality is *subjective*, suggesting that the truth of moral claims is relative to the beliefs and values of the individual who utters them. According to this view, if you think that polygamy is wrong, then it *is* wrong – for you. But if your neighbor thinks

Philosophy on Tap: Pint-Sized Puzzles for the Pub Philosopher, First Edition. Matt Lawrence
© 2011 Matt Lawrence. Published 2011 by Blackwell Publishing Ltd.

that it is just fine, then it *isn't* wrong – for him. Each of you makes a moral judgment on the basis of your own personal standards. And since there is no truer or higher standard than your own, you're both right.

Another popular position maintains that morality is *culturally relative*. This is to maintain that a culture deeming an act "right" *makes* it right. And when the majority within the culture deems an act wrong that *makes* it wrong. Here the terms "morally right" and "morally wrong" are treated as roughly equivalent to "approved by the culture" and "disapproved by the culture." The cultural relativist believes that there is no higher standard than the cultural consensus. So, since most Western cultures disapprove of polygamy, it *is* wrong – for us. However, in Saudi Arabia, where polygamy is accepted, it *isn't* wrong – for Saudis. According to this view, the beliefs of the individual are pretty much irrelevant. If you are living in New York, it doesn't much matter how you feel about polygamy: since American culture maintains that it is wrong, it is wrong.

A third position is that moral claims are *objective*. This is to say that whether an action is *really* right or wrong depends on the nature of the act itself. According to this position, the moral status of an action has nothing to do with what you or anyone else happens to think about it. As the moral objectivist sees it, there is an objective fact of the matter that exists independently of our opinions, and our job as moral philosophers is to discover it.

You may be inclined to think that moral claims fit into all three categories. That is, some are subjective, some are culturally relative, and others still are objective. But if this is the case, what makes some subjective while others are culturally relative or objective? And isn't it odd that truth claims in other realms don't appear to "cross categories" like this. For example, when it comes to the claims of math, geometry, science (e.g., "$2 + 3 = 5$" or, "The Earth revolves around the Sun"), we tend to think that such claims are objective *across the board*. Similarly, if you are a subjectivist about the judgments of taste in food (e.g., "This is delicious," or "This is awful"), then you probably think that all such claims are subjective. It is not as if the deliciousness of pizza is a subjective matter, but the deliciousness of broccoli is objective. All judgments about deliciousness seem to have the same status. Hence, anyone who takes the position that moral claims occupy all three categories will need an account of *why* this is so.

Ultimately the debate over moral truth comes down to a question of standards. Is it the individual's own beliefs and values that serve as the highest and most relevant standard, or is this trumped by the prevailing beliefs and values of one's culture? Or, is there some objective standard, independent of our personal and cultural beliefs, from which we can distinguish right from wrong?

The way in which you answer these questions has an enormous impact on your moral life. If you think morality is subjective, then you must accept that nobody's moral position is any better than anyone else's. Adolf Hitler's views must be regarded as ultimately no better or worse than your own. If he favors genocide and you oppose it, you may be doing what's right according to your own beliefs and values, but so is he, and there is no higher standard from which to judge your viewpoints. If, on the other hand, you regard morality as culturally relative, then you'll need to accept the idea that your culture can never be wrong. Take the issue of civil rights. Since Dr. Martin Luther King Jr.'s pursuit of civil rights was contrary to the majority American viewpoint at the time, then we would have to conclude that he had an incorrect moral view. Racial segregation was right *at the time*, even though it is wrong *now,* since majority opinion within the culture *makes* an act right or wrong.

For these reasons, many philosophers have found subjectivism and cultural relativism to be rather difficult doctrines to swallow. Moral objectivism, on the other hand, allows you to maintain consistently that Hitler and the racial segregationist have flawed or mistaken moral views. The difficulty, however, is to account for the "objective truth" that such a view requires. Moral claims don't seem to fit the mold of other objective truths, which tend to be statements of simple empirical facts e.g., "The earth is round," "2 + 2 = 4," and "Pilsner is lighter than porter." To say, "Genocide is wrong," or "Racial segregation is unjust," is to express more than an empirical fact; it is to make a value judgment. And non-objectivists will eagerly try to convince you that values, unlike facts, *cannot* be true or false.

What do you think?

- Do you think that moral claims are objective, subjective, or culturally relative? On what do you base your position?
- If you believe that moral claims are objective, on what basis (or by what sort of standard) do you distinguish right from wrong?
- Were Hitler's moral views no better or worse than anyone else's? How would you defend your answer?
- Consider the following (non-moral) statements: "Double IPA's are delicious," "God exists," "It is rude to talk with your mouth full," "Saturn has rings, but Mars does not." Are these statements objective, subjective, or culturally relative? (Consider each claim separately.)

Did you know?

- Martin Luther King Jr. believed in objective moral truth. He maintained that racial segregation was objectively wrong, and that the right thing to do was to fight for civil rights – regardless of majority opinion on the matter.

⊙ Philosophers who rejected the idea of objective moral truth include the Ancient Greek philosopher Protagoras, Friedrich Nietzsche, and Jean-Paul Sartre.

⊙ Two of the most influential accounts of objective moral truth are utilitarianism and Kantianism. Utilitarianism, developed by Jeremy Bentham and John Stuart Mill, maintains that right and wrong are to be understood in terms of the consequences of the action – by looking at the pleasure and pain caused. Kantianism, developed by Immanuel Kant, maintains that we should look to the principle behind the act rather than its consequences.

⊙ Slogans for Wasatch Polygamy Porter include: "Why have just one!" and "Bring some home to the wives."

Recommended reading

- James Rachels, *The Elements of Moral Philosophy* (New York: McGraw-Hill, 1978).
- Martin Luther King Jr. "Letter from Birmingham Jail." Available online through the University of Pennsylvania: http://www.africa.upenn.edu/Articles_Gen/Letter_Birmingham.html.

Tasting Notes: Wasatch *Polygamy Porter*

Style: Porter   **Rating:** [1] [2] [3] [4] [5]

Appearance:	
Nose:	
Mouthfeel:	
Flavors:	

Body   Alcohol   Dark Fruits
Bitter   Citrus
Sweet   Smoky Burnt
Sour   Linger
Toffee Coffee   Hoppy Piney
Spicy   Malty   Floral

25

How to Sew on a Soul

Where do I attach my inner taster?

Pint of the Puzzle: Rogue *Dead Guy Ale*

Do dead guys drink ale? If so, they'd better hope to be more than a mere skeleton – like the one on the Rogue label. If there is life after death, you'll want to bring your "inner taster" with you to the other side, for it will take more than mere bones to appreciate the four varieties of malt and two kinds of hop that create the unique taste of Rogue Brewing's Dead Guy Ale.

According to a 2003 Harris Poll, 84 percent of Americans believe that they have (or are) a soul that will continue to exist after their bodily death. But despite its popular appeal, the idea of an immaterial and eternal soul has long been a contentious matter of debate among philosophers.

One of the more notable defenders of the soul was René Descartes (1596–1650). Like most people, Descartes had been taught to believe in an immortal soul from his early childhood. But as an adult he came to believe that the soul's existence was strongly supported by philosophical reasoning. Descartes's philosophical views on the matter were based largely on the observation that he seemed to have two very different sets of qualities. On the

---

Philosophy on Tap: Pint-Sized Puzzles for the Pub Philosopher, First Edition. Matt Lawrence
© 2011 Matt Lawrence. Published 2011 by Blackwell Publishing Ltd.

one hand, he had a body that could be described in terms of size, shape, location, etc. But on the other, he was a conscious being with thoughts, sensations, emotions, etc. These aspects of himself seemed to have none of the features that we attribute to matter. For example, when Descartes was thinking, "This is an exceptional amber ale," where exactly was that thought? What was its size? How much did it weigh? Or when he experienced the hop-bitterness of a fine IPA, where exactly was that bitter sensation located? Thoughts, sensations, emotions, and all the contents of consciousness seemed to have no location, no size, no shape, no mass, no color. Thus, Descartes concluded that these must be qualities of a substance other than matter – an immaterial substance that he called the "mind" or "soul."

Descartes supposed, as many people do, that the body and soul are constantly interacting with one another. Immaterial events within the soul, (e.g., willing your arm to move), cause material events (such as your arm lifting your pint glass). And similarly, material events within your body (such as a splash of Dead Guy Ale on your tongue) cause immaterial events (such as feelings of delight) within the mind or soul. But the interaction between material and immaterial substances turned out to be quite a puzzle for Descartes, and for all who have entertained this view ever since. For *how* can something immaterial cause changes in something material? And, *how* can something material cause changes in something immaterial?

Causation from one material thing to another is easy enough to understand. For instance, we can see and feel how one object can be used to push or pull another object, and we can describe it in terms of force, momentum, and so on. But how can something immaterial like "thought" or "will" which supposedly lack size, shape, and motion, cause a hunk of matter like your arm to move? Certainly this could not occur by pushing or pulling or by exerting any kind of *physical* force.

Some people are content to simply leave it a mystery – one of the great puzzles of the universe for which only God knows the answer. But philosophers are notorious for wanting to explain *everything*. To maintain that there is an immaterial soul that moves the body, and yet to have no insight into how this could possibly occur, is seen, at minimum, to be a weakness in one's theory, and, at worst, a reason for thinking that the theory is altogether misguided. Descartes therefore felt that it was important to explain the mechanism through which causal interactions between body and soul occur.

He eventually settled upon a solution that focused on the *pineal gland*. Descartes argued that there must be some particular location from which the soul and body interact – a "seat of the soul" – as he sometimes called it. He believed that the pineal gland was the perfect candidate for this because it was centrally located in the brain; it was a single organ (while most were pairs, e.g., eyes, ears, the two hemispheres of the brain, etc.); and because he erroneously thought that it was a gland only found in humans.

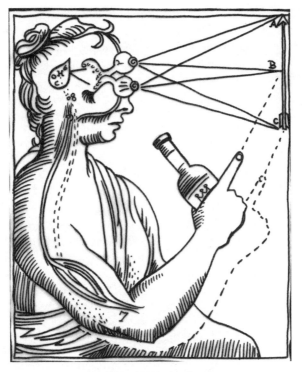

The pineal gland.

Descartes's hypothesis was that information from the body's senses was sent from the sense organs to the pineal gland, where the mind or soul would thus become informed of the world around it. The mind would then create changes in the pineal gland that would be sent to the brain through a series of arteries. Then, through stimulus from the brain, the rest of the body could be moved according to the wishes and whims of the soul.

Today we know that Descartes's biological understanding was well off the mark, but this is true of many of the hypotheses of seventeenth-century biology. What makes Descartes's position interesting is its basic strategy for solving the philosophical puzzle of mind–body interaction. But here too it seems to have failed miserably. For even if the biology had worked out, what we wanted to know was how an immaterial substance could cause changes in a material substance. Descartes's answer really doesn't offer us any help for this problem. For while we can imagine how a pineal gland might affect the body (through the release of chemicals such as melatonin), we are still completely in the dark regarding how an immaterial soul could affect the pineal gland. And it is no easier to understand how an immaterial mind or soul could move a small object like a gland than it is to understand how it could move a larger one like your arm. What Descartes's "seat of the soul" hypothesis failed to provide was an explanation of how something non-physical can exert any influence on the physical whatsoever. Hence, the problem of mind-body interaction remains.

What do you think?

- Do human beings have immaterial souls?
- If so, do our souls causally interact with our bodies?
- Is it helpful to suppose that there is a "seat of the soul" – a specific location at which the soul and body interact?
- Descartes regarded the mind and soul as essentially the same. Do you agree? If not, what is the difference between the mind and the soul?

Did you know?

- Many philosophers and scientists have avoided the problems of mind–body interaction by defending some form of *materialism*. Materialist theories regard the mind as essentially physical. They maintain that the mind simply *is* (or is *caused* by) the functioning of the brain.

- In 1643 Descartes began a philosophically fruitful correspondence with Princess Elizabeth of Bohemia. She raised questions about free will, emotions, and morals, which he had not dealt with in much detail previously. This correspondence eventually inspired Descartes to write *The Passions of the Soul,* published in 1649.

- The Ancient Egyptians were among the first to brew beer, and they treated it with great reverence. Wealthy Egyptians went so far as to put small-scale replicas of breweries inside their tombs. Apparently they wanted to ensure that they could enjoy some homebrew in the afterlife.

- The Dead Guy Ale logo was first created as a private tap sticker to celebrate the Day of the Dead for Casa U Betcha in Portland, Oregon. The Dead Guy design proved so popular that Rogue eventually decided to use it for their Maierbock ale.

Recommended reading

- René Descartes, "Passions of the Soul," in *The Philosophical Works of Descartes,* trans. E. S. Haldane and G. R. T. Ross (Cambridge: Cambridge University Press, 1973).

- George Lakoff and Mark Johnson, *Philosophy in the Flesh: The Embodied Mind and its Challenge to Western Thought* (New York: Basic Books, 1999).

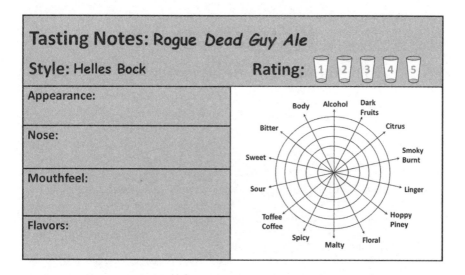

Tasting Notes: Rogue *Dead Guy Ale*

Style: Helles Bock   **Rating:** 1 2 3 4 5

Appearance:

Nose:

Mouthfeel:

Flavors:

Body   Alcohol   Dark Fruits

Bitter   Citrus

Sweet   Smoky Burnt

Sour   Linger

Toffee Coffee   Hoppy Piney

Spicy   Malty   Floral

26

Plato's Forms

Are you tapping into a perfect world?

Pint of the Puzzle: High and Mighty *Purity of Essence Lager*

Have you ever considered what makes beer *beer*? Is there an "essence" to beer – something that we might call "beerness" that all beers have in common regardless of whether they are lagers, ales, or chocolate stouts? And is it still beer if it contains artificial flavors, colors, or carbonation? High and Mighty Brewing's *Purity of Essence* takes you back to the very core of beerness by using only quality malts, Noble hops, yeast, and water, brewed according to the Reinheitsgebot Bavarian purity law, but in a distinctively American, craft brew style.

Have you ever seen a circle? Now I'm not asking if you've seen something that looks kind of like a circle, but, rather, whether you've seen a *real* circle. Before you answer, it might be helpful to look at a specific example.

Philosophy on Tap: Pint-Sized Puzzles for the Pub Philosopher, First Edition. Matt Lawrence.
© 2011 Matt Lawrence. Published 2011 by Blackwell Publishing Ltd.

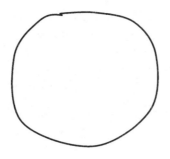

Look at the illustration: is this a circle? Hopefully, you said no. While this shape looks rather like a circle, it is not *really* a circle. To see why, let's refresh our geometrical knowledge with some basic facts about circles:

✓ A circle is a set of points on a plane equally distant from a center point.
✓ The area of any circle will be exactly Pi times its radius squared. (πr^2)
✓ Its circumference will be exactly Pi times its diameter. (πd)

The drawing above fails on all three counts. Not all the points on its circumference are equally distant from the center, and hence its area will not turn out to be exactly πr^2, and its perimeter will not be exactly πd.

What about the rim of your pint glass? Is it a real circle? While this is certainly a better approximation of a circle, the (rather circular) "line" that is made by the rim of your glass has a definite thickness, and hence all points on that line are not equally distant from the center. Points along the outside edge are further from the center than those along the inside edge. Thus it fails to meet even the most basic qualifications of a circle.

So, have you *ever* seen a real circle? I truly doubt it. If someone were to draw a *real* circle, in which every point is equidistant from the center, they would need to draw a curved line that has no thickness at all. (This is why the great geometer Euclid defined a line as *length without breadth*.) But of course it is impossible to draw a line without thickness. Thus no pint glass has ever had a rim that was a true circle, nor have you ever seen a real circle anywhere!

Plato argued this thesis in the fourth century BC. To put the point rather bluntly, he maintained that a real circle must be perfectly round, and perfect roundness simply cannot be found in the material world. If Plato is right about this, then you may begin to wonder if real circles exist at all. But real circles must exist, for we know many things to be true of them. For example, we know that a circle is a set of points equally distant from a center point. We know that circles can be large or small, but they can never have corners, etc. And we can *prove* certain things about them – that their areas *always* equal πr^2, and their circumferences always equal πd, etc.

But if real circles don't exist in the material world, then *where* do they exist? Well, for starters, they exist in the mind. "Circle," is an *Idea* or *Form*. It is grasped by the intellect, but never by the senses. You can't *see* a real circle, but you can *comprehend* one in your mind. And Forms don't only exist in the mind, for if they did, then circles would exist (and have areas of πr^2) only when people were thinking about them. Plato maintained that the Form of Circle has *always* existed. People did not *invent* the idea that the area of a circle equals πr^2 – we *discovered* it. This relation was true long before we ever realized it. It has always been true. So the Form of Circle, Plato argued, must exist in a realm that is both *immaterial* and *independent* of us.

And, if there is a Form of Circle, then of course there must be a Form of Square, a Form of Triangle, and so on. Each is a perfect, immaterial, eternal Idea existing within an immaterial realm. And there is nothing special about geometrical shapes. According to Plato, almost all the things that we see in the physical world are just imperfect copies of their ideal immaterial Forms. Just as you never see perfect circles, you also never see perfect beauty, perfect justice, or a perfect beer (though some come pretty close). Yet these also exist perfectly and eternally in the immaterial realm of Forms.

Think about it. If you've never seen perfect beauty, perfect justice, or a perfect beer, then where did you get the idea of such things? Plato suggests that you must have gotten them by "tapping into" the keg of pure Forms with your mind. That is, your mind accessed the immaterial realm of the Forms without even realizing it. Now, if we could only just find where the Gods are hiding the perfect Form of Beer, we'd really be on to something!

What do you think?

- Do you agree with Plato that immaterial Forms exist?
- If so, do you agree that they exist eternally in an immaterial realm? If not, how do you account for the timeless truths about circles?
- Do you believe that there is such a thing as the "Form of beer" that captures the true essence of beer? And if so, wouldn't there also have to be a Form of Ale, a Form of Pilsner, a Form of IPA? How far can we take this? What about a Form of High and Mighty's Purity of Essence Lager?

Did you know?

- Plato's ambitions for the theory of Forms varied at different points in the development of his thought. In some dialogues, he reserved them for mathematical and geometrical entities. Other times, he extended them to abstract concepts like beauty and justice, and in his more ambitious moments, he extended them to natural kinds like horses and trees, and ultimately even to artifacts like tables and chairs.

- Plato believed that the fact that we have ideas of perfection (e.g., perfect beauty, perfect justice, perfect ale, etc.), even though we've never encountered or experienced them in this life, suggests that we must have known the Forms before our material births.
- Plato was planning to be a poet until Socrates convinced him that philosophy was a more worthwhile pursuit.
- The High and Mighty Brewery takes a religious approach to brewing. They're not just brewers, they're beer evangelists. As they put it, they are the "Clergy of Zymurgy, the Priests of Yeasts, the Joyful Congregation of High Fermentation."

Recommended reading

- Plato, *The Republic*, Bks VI and VII, trans. Benjamin Jowett. Available online through Project Gutenberg: http://www.gutenberg.org/files/1497/1497-h/1497-h.htm.
- Gail Fine, *On Ideas: Aristotle's Criticisms of Plato's Theory of Forms* (Oxford: Oxford University Press, 1993).

Tasting Notes: High and Mighty *Purity of Essence Lager*

Style: American Pale Lager   **Rating:** 1 2 3 4 5

Appearance:	
Nose:	
Mouthfeel:	
Flavors:	

Body   Alcohol   Dark Fruits   Citrus   Smoky Burnt   Linger   Hoppy Piney   Floral   Malty   Spicy   Coffee   Toffee   Sour   Sweet   Bitter

27

Realizing Nirvana

Are you ready to be enlightened?

Pint of the Puzzle: Lhasa *Beer of Tibet*

Since Tibet is the place most commonly associated with the idea of nirvana, I suggest that we pour a pint of Lhasa beer. Brewed in Lhasa, Tibet, at an altitude of 11,975 feet, this is probably the "highest" beer you'll ever drink, and its unique flavor comes from the fact that it is the only beer to use barley that is native to the Tibetan plateau.

When people hear the word "nirvana" they are often not sure what to think (beyond Kurt Cobain and his Seattle grunge rock band). Some suppose that nirvana is something like a heaven for Buddhists. Others equate it with "enlightenment," which is more to the point, but this too can be a pretty vague concept. Based on what the Buddha (Siddhartha Gautama *c.* 563–483 BCE) had to say about it, "enlightenment" is closer to the mark, yet nirvana involves a very specific conception of what it means to be enlightened. Nirvana literally means to "blow out" or "extinguish." But to extinguish what? The Buddha tells us that it is the extinction of craving, of attachment, of illusion. And to put it positively,

---

Philosophy on Tap: Pint-Sized Puzzles for the Pub Philosopher, First Edition. Matt Lawrence
© 2011 Matt Lawrence. Published 2011 by Blackwell Publishing Ltd.

it is liberation, peace, and equanimity. It is the complete liberation from human suffering.

Nirvana is the ultimate aim within Buddhist philosophy. The Buddha even went so far as to say that he only taught four things. He taught that suffering exists, he taught the cause of suffering, he taught that suffering can be overcome, and he taught the path by which suffering can be overcome – the path to nirvana. The Buddha's views on this are put most succinctly in what is commonly referred to as The Four Noble Truths:

1. Life is suffering.
2. Suffering is caused by attachment.
3. Suffering can be overcome.
4. The path is the middle way.

The first Noble Truth is often misunderstood. People sometimes take it to be a rather pessimistic doctrine, suggesting that life is all bad, or more bad than good. The Buddha's point is actually more subtle. He doesn't mean that life is *always* suffering, but, rather, that life as we know it is *intertwined* with suffering. If you are not suffering now, you can be quite sure that sooner or later you will be. When understood in this way, the point is rather uncontroversial. The second Noble Truth, in contrast, should be taken in its extreme sense, that *all* suffering is caused by attachment. The Third Noble Truth, that suffering can be overcome, implies that attachment can be overcome. Remove the cause and you thereby remove the effect. The fourth Noble Truth describes the path to this end as the "middle way" meaning that neither self-indulgence (luxury) nor self-denial (asceticism) can bring a permanent end to suffering. (This explained in much more detail in what is known as the Buddha's *Noble Eightfold Path*.)

The Buddha's teachings on nirvana give rise to three philosophical puzzles. First, is it really true that all suffering is caused by attachment? Second, if it is true, is it humanly possible to overcome all of one's attachment? And third, if it is possible, is it really desirable to give up all attachment?

"Attachment," in the sense that the Buddha had in mind, can be understood as the attempt to try to hold onto things either physically or psychologically. He maintained that wherever pleasure arises, attachment also arises. We become attached to people, to places, to certain beers. We also tend to become extremely attached to things we like about ourselves; to beauty, to youth, to intelligence, and to life itself. But wherever attachment arises, suffering inevitably arises. This is because there is nothing that you can truly hold on to. All these things are impermanent. They will be ripped from your grasp.

It is easy to see that attachments give rise to suffering. (Just remember the last time you spilled your beer – instant suffering.) But does *all* suffering have attachment at its root? The most likely exception seems to be physical pain.

Imagine that your buddies have spiked your pint of Lhasa with hot chili oil. Your mouth and throat are suddenly burning as if they were on fire. On the face of it, it would certainly seem that it is not attachment, but the chili oil, that is making you suffer. Could such brute physical pain actually be the result of attachment? Reflect on this. Is there anything that you are attached to at that moment when your mouth is blazing? The Buddha would contend that your attachment is to certain sorts of sensations. You are attached to the pleasant sensations of your (chili-less) pint of Lhasa, and even to the neutral sensations of your (non-burning) mouth and throat. You wanted to hold on to those sensations, but suddenly they were taken from you and replaced with sensations that you loathe. Suppose that you were to completely abandon your craving for some sensations over others, and allowed all sensations to come and go without attachment. Certainly, the sensations that go along with drinking hot chili oil would continue, but would it still be experienced as suffering?

Some contend that it is impossible not to be attached to pleasure and averse to pain. It is simply human nature, they argue. But many contemporary Buddhists, who have devoted their lives to following this path, seem to offer living examples of the ability to endure great physical pain with peace and equanimity.

Perhaps the most philosophically interesting question is the third. If it is possible to overcome all attachments, should we choose it? Is it really desirable to give up *all* our attachments? Some see this as the proverbial "throwing the baby out with the bathwater." That is to say, "Sure I could lead a life without suffering. All I would have to do is quit caring about anything. But who would want that? It is better to have loved and lost than to never have loved at all."

The issue of love provides a nice focus for this question. Is it possible to truly love without attachment? If not, few of us will be willing to choose the life of non-attachment. Typically, love and attachment go together. When we fall in love, that love is accompanied by the desire that the other *never leave*, and that you will be together *forever*. But does it have to be this way? Isn't it possible to love just as deeply, without such attachments? Consider the following example. Suppose that Grandma has died. At the funeral, we observe her two granddaughters. The elder is totally distraught. She feels like she cannot bear to lose Grandma and she suffers greatly. The younger, on the other hand, had prepared herself for this moment. After all, Grandma was 97, and her health had deteriorated greatly over the past year. She says that she was "ready to let Grandma go," and she seems much more at peace. Now, on the basis of this information, can we conclude that the older granddaughter loved her grandmother more? Or can we only conclude that she is more "attached" to Grandma, and that love and attachment are two very different things?

As you ponder these questions, you might try putting the Buddha's philosophy into practice. Enjoy your beer – even love your beer – but do not become attached to it. Remember, beer, like everything else in this world, is impermanent. Sooner or later your glass will be empty. If you become attached to its fullness, you will surely suffer.

What do you think?

- Is there anything that you can be attached to that won't give rise to suffering?
- The Buddha's position was that attachment offers nothing of value and should therefore be discarded. Do you agree? If not, what good or value does attachment add to your life?
- Is it possible to care about things deeply without becoming attached to them?
- If you were to make it your aim to realize nirvana, what steps would you take to achieve this? For help on this you might research the Buddha's "Noble Eightfold Path."

Did you know?

- The Buddha maintained that even an attachment to attaining nirvana is an obstacle to actually attaining nirvana. *All* attachments must be extinguished.
- The "middle way" that the Buddha describes as the path to overcoming suffering is elaborated upon in detail in a doctrine called *The Noble Eightfold Path*. It involves: (1) Right View, (2) Right Resolve, (3) Right Speech, (4) Right Action, (5) Right Livelihood, (6) Right Effort, (7) Right Mindfulness, and (8) Right Concentration.
- According to armchair philosopher Jack Handy, if you ever reach total enlightenment while drinking beer, it will probably make beer shoot out your nose.
- The Lhasa Brewery is not only dedicated to good beer, but also to good karma. They dedicate 10 percent of their profits to philanthropic efforts to support the health, education, and welfare of the Tibetan people and the preservation of their ancient artistic and cultural heritage

Recommended reading

- Huston Smith and Philip Novak, *Buddhism: A Concise Introduction* (New York: Harper Collins, 2004).

- The Dalai Lama, *The World of Tibetan Buddhism* (Somerville, MA: Wisdom Publications, 1995).

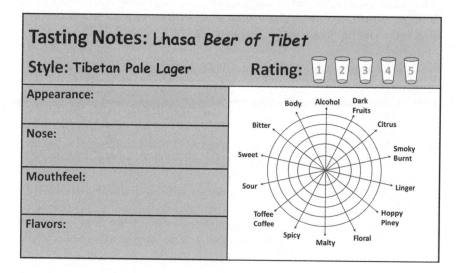

Tasting Notes: Lhasa *Beer of Tibet*

Style: Tibetan Pale Lager   Rating: 1 2 3 4 5

Appearance:

Nose:

Mouthfeel:

Flavors:

Body Alcohol Dark Fruits
Bitter   Citrus
Sweet   Smoky Burnt
Sour   Linger
Toffee Coffee   Hoppy Piney
Spicy   Malty   Floral

28

The Problem of Evil

If God exists, then why are there bad beers?

Pint of the Puzzle: Victory *HopDevil IPA*

Why do good beers go bad? Why do bad beers exist at all? This is a perennial puzzle that is confounded by the assumption that an all-good God exists. Some chock it up to the Devil. They say he's responsible for all the evil in the world. "HopDevil," on the other hand, is a force for good. HopDevil IPA from Victory Brewing of Pennsylvania brings joy and beauty into the lives of beer lovers everywhere.

What's up with all the bad stuff in the world? Earthquakes, famine, genocide, avian flu, skunky beers, the list goes on and on. We could say that the world just sucks in innumerable ways and be done. There is nothing particularly puzzling about badness in and of itself. But bring God into the picture, and a paradox arises. The minute that we suppose that the world was created by an all-good, all-powerful, and all-knowing God, the bad stuff becomes a philosophical problem. In fact, such evils present one of the strongest arguments against the belief in this sort of God.

The paradox only arises on the assumption that God is omnibenevolent (all-good), omniscient (all-knowing), and omnipotent (all-powerful). All

---

Philosophy on Tap: Pint-Sized Puzzles for the Pub Philosopher, First Edition. Matt Lawrence
© 2011 Matt Lawrence. Published 2011 by Blackwell Publishing Ltd.

three characteristics are crucial. If God were not omnibenevolent, then we could explain evil by attributing it to a mean, apathetic, or sadistic streak in the Creator. But if God is perfectly good, why would He allow us to suffer so? We could still explain things by supposing that God just doesn't know about all the disease, disasters, and bad beers. But God's omniscience precludes this. Or, we might suppose that God knows about all these horrors and wants to save us from them, but is simply unable. Perhaps He is just too exhausted from creating the universe, or something like that. But God's omnipotence precludes this possibility as well. This leaves us no room but to suppose that God *knows* that we are suffering, has the *power* to spare us from it, and yet *refuses* to do so. How then, can we regard such a God as completely good? Even your friends (with their limited goodness and compassion) would warn you if you were about to be hit by a bus (or were about to order a bad beer). So how is it that God fails to give us the heads up?

Philosophers and theologians have tried to resolve this paradox in a number of ways. Among the most popular are: (1) The Satan Solution, (2) The Free Will Solution, and (3) The No Unnecessary Evil Solution.

The Satan Solution has to be the weakest of the three. The basic idea is that we can get God off the proverbial hook by blaming the evil on Satan. It's not God's fault that the world is so messed up – its Satan's. Surely this won't work, since it runs afoul of God's omnipotence. If God created everything, then He is responsible for Satan's very existence. And if God is all-powerful, then He could just squash Satan like a grape. So why doesn't He get rid of Satan *and* his skunky beers? The paradox remains.

The Free Will Solution seems to run into similar problems. It tries to get God off the hook by blaming evil on human beings and their free will. But where did we get our free will? From God of course! And, being omniscient, didn't God know all about the evil we would create? And God wouldn't necessarily even have to take away our free will to solve most of our problems. He could have just made us a bit more compassionate, or less selfish and stupid. A second problem with the free will solution is that all the evils in the world aren't attributable to human choices. Consider the majority of diseases, natural disasters, and freak accidents. These aren't the result of our choices, and yet surely an omnipotent God could have prevented them.

The No Unnecessary Evil Solution may have the best chance of resolving the paradox. It maintains that all the bad stuff in the world is there for a reason. God allows it only because its existence is necessary to bring about an even greater good. According to this view, God gave us free will despite the fact that He knew all the horrible things that we would do with it. This is because it is better to allow people to make free choices (good and bad) than it is to create a bunch of "robots" who automatically do the right thing. And similarly, *if* God allows Satan to exist and tempt us, it must be because it is better to do so. Perhaps this is because it gives us an opportunity to resist temptation – which is a glorious thing in God's eyes. But can we really write off all the terrible things in the world as "necessary"? Does it actually make sense to believe that they all contribute to a greater good? The contemporary philosopher of religion, William Rowe, offers up the following problem case:

> Suppose in some distant forest lightning strikes a dead tree, resulting in a forest fire. In the fire a fawn is trapped, horribly burned, and lies in terrible agony for several days before death relieves its suffering. So far as we can see, the fawn's suffering is pointless ... Could an omnipotent, omniscient being have prevented the fawn's apparently pointless suffering? The answer is obvious, as even the theist will insist. An omnipotent omniscient being could have easily prevented the fawn from being horribly burned, or, given the burning, could have spared the fawn the intense suffering by quickly ending its life, rather than allowing the fawn to lie in terrible agony for several days.

Rowe considers the case of a fawn rather than a person because human beings often use their hardships to learn and grow. Their suffering may therefore arguably serve to bring about some greater good. But we don't expect this in the case of the fawn. The fawn's suffering seems completely pointless and unnecessary. If no one even knows about its silent suffering, how could its pain possibly contribute to some greater good? Thus, the paradox remains. Can we make sense of an all-powerful, all-knowing, and all-good God so long as we live in a world of suffering fawns and skunky beers?

What do you think?

- Do you think that any of the three solutions offered can resolve the problem of evil? If not, is there some better solution that has been overlooked?
- Is it possible (or likely) that the fawn's pain serves to bring about some greater good? If so, what good could come from it?
- Pretend, for a moment, that you are God. Is there anything about the world that you would change? Why do you suppose (if God exists) that He does not make such changes?

Did you know?

- William Rowe was playing "devil's advocate" when he came up with the fawn example. He's actually a Christian philosopher.
- The name "The Problem of Evil" is a bit of a misnomer for this paradox. The word "evil" denotes malicious intent, so things like natural disasters, burned fawns, and bad beers aren't technically evil. Nevertheless, they seem to contradict what we might expect from an all-good, powerful, and

knowing God, so they are certainly relevant. It would be more accurate to call this "The Problem of Bad Stuff," but somehow that name just never caught on.

The German philosopher Gottfried Leibniz is one of the more famous advocates of The No Unnecessary Evil Solution. Voltaire poked fun at Leibniz's position in his play *Candide*. Its main character adheres to Leibniz's philosophy and goes about saying that "this is the best of all possible worlds," all the while suffering from one catastrophe after another.

Your best defense against "skunky" (AKA lightstruck) beer is the brown glass bottle. A beer becomes "skunked" when it is exposed to ultraviolet and visible light. The light causes riboflavin to react with and break down isohumulones, a molecule derived from the hops which creates the bitterness of the beer. The result is a chemical similar to that secreted by skunks as a natural defense. Clear and green bottles do nothing to prevent this unfortunate phenomenon. Some beers, such as Miller High Life, avoid this problem by using a hop extract that does not have isohumulones.

HopDevil was named domestic beer of the year by *Malt Advocate Magazine* in 1998, and it won a silver medal in the Australian Beer Awards in 2008.

Recommended reading

- William Rowe, *Philosophy of Religion: An Introduction* (Belmont, CA: Thomson-Wadsworth, 2007).
- Voltaire, *Candide; or The Optimist,* 1759. Available online at: http://www.gutenberg.org/etext/19942.

Tasting Notes: Victory *HopDevil IPA*

Style: India Pale Ale   **Rating:** 1 2 3 4 5

Appearance:	
Nose:	
Mouthfeel:	
Flavors:	

Body Alcohol Dark Fruits
Bitter   Citrus
Sweet   Smoky Burnt
Sour   Linger
Toffee Coffee   Hoppy Piney
Spicy   Malty   Floral

29

Time's Conundrum

Does time exist? What about happy hour?

Do you take time for granted? It wouldn't be surprising. We think about time constantly, but rarely do we pause to think about what time *is*. When you really try to understand it, time becomes a very puzzling thing. Contemplate the nature of time over a La Trappe Quadrupel and you may begin to wonder whether time exists at all.

We typically speak as if there are three aspects to time: the past, the present, and the future. But, as most people understand it, the past is gone – it no longer exists. Similarly, the future doesn't exist, since it is yet to be. It would seem

Philosophy on Tap: Pint-Sized Puzzles for the Pub Philosopher, First Edition. Matt Lawrence
© 2011 Matt Lawrence. Published 2011 by Blackwell Publishing Ltd.

that all that really exists is the present moment – this very instant. But what is an "instant"? Surely it must have no duration (it must take no time) for if it did, then we could divide an instant into several smaller instances, and only one of these could be "this very instant." Thus it begins to seem as if the present moment is just an infinitely small dividing line between two non-existing entities – the past and the future.

This and other theoretical difficulties have inclined many philosophers to suppose that we need to radically rethink our ordinary conception of time. Aristotle, for instance, concluded that time is just the measure of motion. Immanuel Kant maintained that time is not a part of the world, but rather it is an aspect of our mental representation. Time is "in the head," so to speak. But the person to have the biggest impact on contemporary conceptions of time would have to be the eminent physicist Albert Einstein.

Einstein maintained that we should think of time in a way that is similar to how we conceive of space. We regard space as "laid-out" in all directions. Even though we never experience space all at once, we think that all spatial locations are "out-there," existing, whether we presently perceive them or not. For example, I can't see the backside of the moon right now, but I have no doubt it exists all the same, and that if I were to go there I would see it. Einstein suggested that we should think of time in roughly the same way. Imagine all points in time as "laid-out," with the past, present, and future all existing – all equally real. This is generally referred to as the "tenseless" theory of time. From our vantage point in the present moment, we cannot experience the past or the future. All we see is this moment that is right under our noses. But that does not entail that only this moment exists – any more than the fact that your current spatial experience entails that only your current location exists. According to the tenseless theory of time, the past and future exist too, and if you were to go there, you would experience them. In fact, you are traveling into the future right now, moment by moment. If you are wondering what is happening an hour from now, just be patient and soon you will see.

To grasp this picture of reality more fully, we need to quit talking about time and space separately and fuse them into a single entity. Don't think of space as "laid-out" before us, and then time as similarly "laid-out" before us. Instead, imagine that reality is made up of a single space–time continuum. Every object that exists occupies a point in "space–time." For example, you are reading this book at a specific location in space–time (e.g., at the Crow Bar on PCH and McArthur Blvd at 8.22 p.m.). Similarly, you occupied a point on the space–time continuum two hours ago (e.g., at the Goat Hill Tavern on Newport Blvd at 6.22 p.m.) and you will occupy another location on that continuum next Sunday afternoon.

The weird thing about this theory (or about *reality* if the theory is correct) is that facts about the future aren't really any different than the facts about the past or present. They just exist at their own location of space–time. And since these facts exist, there is nothing we can do to change them. Suppose, for example, that it is a fact about the space–time continuum that you will be enjoying a pint of Quadrupel at Brix Brews next Sunday afternoon. If this is the case, then there is nothing you can do to avoid this fact. If you happen to have plans to get married next Sunday afternoon, sorry, but that just isn't going to happen. Sitting on a wooden stool at Brix is (and "always" has been) your location in space–time for next Sunday afternoon, and so there is nothing you can do to change it. We can therefore regard the past, present, and future as much like a book that is already written. You can't *change* how the story ends. All you can do is experience the choices and events that helped to create that ending.

Most people find this theory of time rather unsettling. Our intuitive understanding of time allowed us to believe that while the past is "set," the future is still "open." We typically suppose that there are many possible futures, and which of these becomes real depends upon the paths we choose in the present. But a single space–time continuum does not allow for this. Each person has just one path – a set of locations from birth to death, spread out across space–time. How should we regard such a prospect? Some find it extremely depressing. They hope that tenseless time is "just a theory," because, if true, it would take away the very meaning and purpose of our lives. Others contend that the fact that the future is "set" really doesn't matter, since it is still largely our own choices that *cause* these future events – even if we can't *change* them. After all, if you find yourself at Brix Brews next Sunday afternoon, it is highly unlikely that you are there because someone put a gun to your head. Most likely you are there because you want to be there, at least under the circumstances, whatever they turn out to be.

Truth be told

Quadrupels do not have four times the flavor and alcohol of single ales. It is hard to get an accurate estimate when it comes to flavor (but 4x is surely a stretch) and while the alcohol level varies, your typical single or blonde abbey ale is around 6 percent abv while quadrupels weigh in at 10–12 percent. However, when compared to Bud Light (4.2 percent), a quadrupel can have almost three times the alcohol.

What do you think?

- Would tenseless time take away the meaning and purpose of our lives? Why or why not?
- Do you believe that time "flows" from one moment to the next? Or, is it merely our *experience* of time that is changing?
- If your future is "set," do you find that prospect depressing? If not, why not?

Did you know?

- It was Einstein's theory of *special relativity* that led to the concept of a single space–time continuum. However, the idea of treating space and time as two aspects of a unified whole was actually first articulated by Einstein's teacher Hermann Minkowski in a 1908 essay that built on Einstein's theory. This way of regarding time is also utilized in Einstein's theory of general relativity.
- It follows from the tenseless theory of time that there is no single moment that can be labeled "now" for all observers. As physicist Paul Davies writes: "Questions such as 'What is happening *now* on Mars?' are intended to refer to a particular instant on that planet. But ... a space traveler sweeping past Earth in a rocket who asked the same question at the same instant would be referring to a different moment on Mars. In fact, the range of possible 'nows' on Mars available to an observer near Earth (depending on his motion) actually spans several minutes."
- Abbey ale styles include the dubbel, tripel, and quadrupel, each with increasing intensity.
- The La Trappe brand of beers are brewed by De Koningshoeven Brewery in the Netherlands. It is the only Trappist brewery that is not in Belgium. They make eight beers: blond, dubbel, tripel, quadrupel, witte trappist, bockbier, isid'or, and real trappist.

Recommended reading

- Craig Callender, *Introducing Time* (Cambridge: Totem Books, 2001).
- Paul Davies, *God and the New Physics* (New York: Simon and Schuster, 1983).

Tasting Notes: La Trappe *Quadrupel*

Style: Belgian Abbey Quadrupel   **Rating:** 1 2 3 4 5

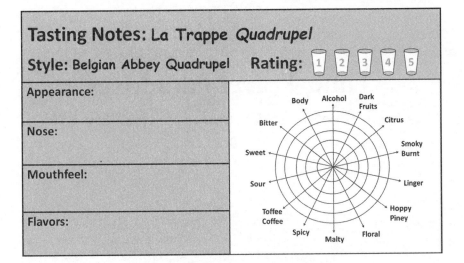

Appearance:

Nose:

Mouthfeel:

Flavors:

30

Time Travel Paradoxes

Is time travel possible? And if so, can I brew the world's first beer?

Pint of the Puzzle: Kronenbourg *1664*

Kronenbourg 1664 is a delicious French lager and it's easily the most popular beer in France. It is named after the year that the Kronenbourg Brewery was established. Coincidentally, this was about the time that Sir Isaac Newton and Gottfried Leibniz developed calculus. If time travel is possible, do you suppose that you could go back in time to prevent calculus from ever being invented? If so, you could be the savior of high school students everywhere!

As we saw in chapter 29, "Time's Conundrum," if Einstein is right, then space and time are "laid out" in a single space–time continuum. Like one huge blanket, the past and future are "out there," existing, despite the fact that we cannot see them from our present spatial-temporal location. But if the past and future are really out there, then it stands to reason that one might be able to travel to them.

Philosophy on Tap: Pint-Sized Puzzles for the Pub Philosopher, First Edition. Matt Lawrence
© 2011 Matt Lawrence. Published 2011 by Blackwell Publishing Ltd.

Time travel is one of the world's best-kept secrets. It always surprises me that so many people still think that it is pure science fiction. But it is a demonstrated reality. Let's start with the less difficult endeavor – forward time travel. For starters, you are proving that forward time travel is possible at this very moment. You are traveling, moment by moment, into the future. Okay, big deal. You knew about that, and you don't find it particularly exciting. To *significantly* achieve forward time travel, a person or object would have to arrive at a future time *before* the rest of us do. Yet this is precisely what scientists have achieved.

According to Einstein's theory of special relativity, time for an object is relative to its motion. The faster an object is moving, the slower time passes for that object. This is called "time dilation." Einstein predicted it, and scientists have since demonstrated it. They have put highly sensitive atomic clocks into jet planes and sent them around the globe at the highest speeds they can muster. When they bring them down, they find that less time has elapsed on these clocks than on synchronized clocks on earth. The trip was "quicker" by a few micro-seconds for the clocks in motion than for the (relatively) stationary clocks on earth. Thus these clocks beat us to the future by a few microseconds.

Now, I know what you are thinking, "A few micro-seconds – you call that time travel?" But the difference between the elapsed time on these clocks is so small only because the speed differential was not that great. If we could send those clocks into orbit at speeds approaching the speed of light, they could beat us to the future by days, weeks, or even years depending on how long they stay in motion. And the important point is that time dilation does not only affect clocks, it affects anything that is in motion. So if a human were in a rocket ship traveling at incredible speeds, time would pass more slowly for them than it would for us, enabling them to beat us to the future.

This is hard to wrap your mind around, so consider an example. Suppose that we have a father (age 40) and a son (age 20). The father has grown tired of being older than the son, so he hops into his ultra-fast rocket and takes what is for him a 10-year space flight. But because time has passed more slowly for him (due to his increased relative motion) than it has on Earth, 40 years have passed for his son. So upon his return, the father is 50 and the son is 60. He beat his son to the future through forward time travel.

As strange as forward time travel may seem, the really crazy phenomenon is backwards time travel. This is something we have yet to pull off, but many physicists believe that it is a real possibility. You may recall from chapter 7, "Lucretius' Spear," that gravity is not an invisible pulling force. Rather, it is the bending of the space–time continuum. Massive objects

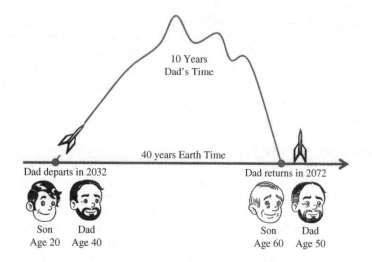

10 Years
Dad's Time

40 years Earth Time

Dad departs in 2032

Son   Dad
Age 20   Age 40

Dad returns in 2072

Son   Dad
Age 60   Age 50

like the Sun bend space–time in such a way that moving objects will be forced to orbit around them. But if an object is incredibly massive, like a black hole, wormhole, or cosmic string, it is possible that space–time can be bent so drastically that it actually folds over onto itself. When this occurs, it may be possible to use that curved space–time trajectory to land your rocket at a point in space–time prior to the point at which you started.

While backward time travel is logically possible within tenseless time, there are many (perhaps insurmountable) physical difficulties. For example, if you could find a suitably curved section of space–time, you would have to have the technology to get there. The nearest black hole, which may not even be a suitable candidate, is more than 10,000 light years away. And while there is scientific evidence to suggest that wormholes and cosmic strings may exist, as of yet none has been discovered. But philosophers are never ones to get bogged down by physical difficulties. So long as we can contemplate the possibility of time travel by means of a thought experiment, we're happy. And when we think about the nature of tenseless time, we can at least come to understand some of the rules that would apply to backward time travel, even if we cannot take the trip ourselves.

Rules of Time Travel in a Tenseless Universe:

1. *You can contribute to the past but you cannot change it.*
   Since the past is "out there," whatever you would do in the past, you've already done. Therefore you cannot go back in time and, say, kill Hitler, because (as we know) you didn't kill Hitler. However, you might show up

at the Munich Hofbähaus in 1913 and spit in Hitler's beer. But you can do this, if and only if your future self did do this back in 1913.

2. *You can contribute to the future but you cannot change it.*
Since the future is also "out there," it contains, for instance, Dad's rocket ride to beat his son to the future. Therefore, whatever he does when he lands in 2072 is what he has "always" done in 2072. His time travel excursion won't *change* the future at all.

3. *Your body can be in two places at the same time.*
For all we know, your future self may have traveled backwards in time to this very day in history and is drinking a pint in a London Pub at this very moment.

4. *You can be at the same space–time at two different points in your life.*
For example, you can go back in time to meet your 5-year-old self. So there you are on the playground at age 5 and age 45. Two bodies at one space–time location. Of course, this is possible only if you *did* meet your older time-traveling self on the playground when you were 5. And, who knows, perhaps you did but don't remember it, because at age 5 you had no idea that this older stranger was actually your future self.

5. *You cannot go back in time and kill your younger self.*
You can't kill your younger self for the same reason that you can't kill Hitler – because you didn't. (This also saves us from the logical inconsistencies that would arise if it were possible to kill your younger self. For then your younger self would never have the opportunity to grow into that older self and hence *couldn't* travel back in time!)

6. *You can cause bizarre causal loops with no causal beginning.*
Suppose that Geronimus Hatt, the founding brewmaster of the Kronenbourg Brewery, were to travel back in time to what is now Kurdistan around 9000 BCE. After a couple of weeks under the hot Middle Eastern sun, he's really thirsty for a beer, but unfortunately it hasn't been invented yet. So Geronimus gathers ingredients from these early farmers and brews a batch of ale. This is the first batch of beer ever brewed in human history. Yet we shouldn't say that he "invented" beer, because he merely followed the recipes handed down to him from his forefathers. Nevertheless, he shares this "original beer" with the native people. Beer catches on, and soon the brewing of beer spreads around the globe. So, who is the original inventor of beer? The answer is *no one*.

What do you think?

● Does the scenario in which beer has no true inventor suggest that backwards time travel is inconsistent and hence impossible? Or, should we find this result to be puzzling, but physically consistent?

⬤ According to tenseless time travel, you can (in principle) go back in time to Munich in 1913. You can buy a gun, and you may be able to walk right up to Hitler. However, you simply *cannot* succeed in killing him. Is it plausible to believe that you cannot succeed? Does this show that the theory itself is implausible? Why/why not?

Did you know?

⬤ The most dramatic evidence for time dilation comes from particle accelerators. Scientists have whirled particles called muons at speeds close to the speed of light, and thereby slowed time for those particles by over 2400 percent. This is seen in their decay rates. Under such conditions they can be "kept alive" for dozens of times longer than they would at otherwise.

⬤ Russian cosmonaut Sergei Krikalyov has traveled forward in time farther than any other human being. By spending 803 days at 17,000 mph, he beat us to the future by 1/48th of a second.

⬤ A wormhole is essentially a tunnel that hypothetically would connect two distant points of space–time. A cosmic string is a hypothesized long thin "defect" in space–time with extremely high gravity thought to have resulted from the big bang. (Cosmic strings are unrelated to "superstrings" or "string theory" in physics.)

⬤ Since gravity warps the space–time continuum, we find that even the earth's gravity causes time dilation. Gravity slows time, so a clock at the top of a tall structure (like the Empire State building) will tick more slowly than a clock on the surface of the earth.

⬤ Kronenbourg 1664 uses a unique hop blend that includes aromatic Strisselspalt hops from France's mountainous region of Alsace.

Recommended reading

• J. Richard Gott III, *Time Travel Through Einstein's Universe: The Physical Possibilities of Time Travel* (New York: First Mariner Books, 2001).
• Matt Lawrence, "How to Really Bake Your Noodle: Time, Fate, and the Problem of Foreknowledge," in *Like a Splinter in Your Mind: The Philosophy Behind the Matrix Trilogy* (Oxford: Blackwell Publishing, 2004), pp. 69–83.

Tasting Notes: Kronenbourg *1664*

Style: French Lager

Rating: 1 2 3 4 5

Appearance:

Nose:

Mouthfeel:

Flavors:

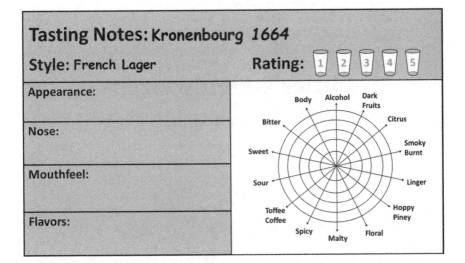

31

Hitler's Hefeweizen

Would you poison Hitler's pint?

Pint of the Puzzle: Hofbräu *Hefeweizen*

If you were to travel back in time and sit face to face with Hitler in an early twentieth-century German beer hall, there's a good chance you'd find him drinking a Hofbräu Hefeweizen. In fact, it was in the Munich Hofbräuhaus beer hall that Hitler proclaimed the 25 theses of the National Socialist program. (Just remember, it's okay to despise Hitler, but please don't take it out on the beer.)

Here's another puzzle dealing with time travel. But for this one, forget about everything that you know about tenseless time and the "rules" of time travel. For the purpose of this thought experiment, let us suppose that time is *not* tenseless, and hence it *is* possible to change the past.

Suppose that you have just traveled back in time to Munich in 1913. Naturally, you decide to check out one of the great German beer halls. So you go down to the Hofbräuhaus for a glass of hefeweizen and a little companionship. Later that evening, by some odd twist of fate, you discover that the guy you've been drinking and chatting with is none other than a young art student named Adolf Hitler. Now, at this point in time he hasn't done

Philosophy on Tap: Pint-Sized Puzzles for the Pub Philosopher, First Edition. Matt Lawrence
© 2011 Matt Lawrence. Published 2011 by Blackwell Publishing Ltd.

anything despicable. He hasn't either killed anyone, or ordered anyone to be killed. He's not spewing hatred – in fact, he seems like a pretty decent guy (though, of course, you barely know him). But since you know the future, your mind is obsessed with one thought: "This is freakin' Hitler!" Once you get over the initial shock of the situation, your mind shifts to your shirt pocket. In it lies the cyanide capsule that you carry just in case your time machine drops you off in the middle of a lion's den or Jeffery Dahmer's basement, or some such horrible thing. So the question naturally arises: Should you kill Hitler?

There are all sorts of reasons why you might decide that you had better not kill Hitler. One personally significant reason is the concern that if you radically change history, your parents will never meet, and you will never be born. Now whether this is a legitimate possibility will depend upon the nature of space–time (for more on this, see chapter 29, "Time's Conundrum"). But let's suppose, for the sake of argument, that this is how time travel works. Change the past, and you'll change the future. Should this reason stop you? (Let's set aside the very real possibility that just by showing up at the Hofbräuhaus you've already affected the future, and perhaps eliminated your own birth.) Many men and women sacrificed their lives to stop Hitler's regime. If you admire them, shouldn't you do the same? Wouldn't it be rather cowardly to let millions of innocent people die just because you may not be born?

Let's take a look at this from a different angle, for there are many important questions to consider. What about the fact that Hitler is (currently) an innocent man? From your conversations, you gather that his highest aspiration is merely to be a successful artist. Becoming the Führer seems to be the farthest thing from his mind. So wouldn't it be wrong to kill him if he hasn't done anything (yet) to deserve it?

There are two general approaches to this sort of question. One is to take a *consequentialist* approach. Consequentialism is the view that the morality of an action is to be judged by its consequences. Looking at the consequences, the end surely justifies the means. By killing Hitler, you achieve a greater good – millions of innocent lives saved. By this reasoning, killing Hitler would be the right thing to do even if you had to blow up the whole Hofbräuhäs, killing everyone inside, including those who would later oppose Hitler. The alternative to consequentialism we can simply call *non-consequentialism*. It is the view that the morality of an action is independent of its consequences. Certain actions – for example, slavery, kidnapping, killing innocent people – are regarded wrong *as a matter of principle*. Such actions are not to be performed – regardless of any good consequences they might produce.

Most of us have strong non-consequentialist leanings. We think, for example, that slavery is wrong independent of whatever good it may produce. It just doesn't matter how much economic prosperity a system of slavery might bring or how many people might be made happy by it. To own slaves is to treat people as objects, to ignore their rights, and to deny them freedom and happiness. This, the non-consequentialist maintains, is inherently wrong.

The thing about the Hitler case is that the consequences of Hitler's life (or death) are so extreme, and so far reaching, that it puts a strain on whatever non-consequentialist leanings one might have. One cannot help but think that by choosing to let Hitler live they would thereby be choosing to let millions of innocent people die. Is a moral principle such as "never kill an innocent person" worth such a cost? Most of the people that I have encountered say no. But here's the rub. If you would be willing to kill an innocent person (or a whole beer hall full of innocent people) to save millions of lives, then, would you do it to save fifty thousand? And, if so, how about two thousand? And, where does it end? The problem we encounter here reminds me of an old joke:

> *He says:* Would you sleep with me for a million dollars?
>
> *She says:* Well, for a MILLION DOLLARS, I would.
>
> *He says:* How about for 20 bucks?
>
> *She says:* Get out of here! What kind of girl do you think I am?
>
> *He says:* Oh, we've already established that. All that remains is to negotiate a final price.

We run into the same sort of problem here. If the numbers can sometimes justify murdering the innocent, then where do you draw the line? And can you avoid the conclusion that *the end always justifies the means?*

Truth be told

If the "tenseless" theory of time is true (see "Time's Conundrum") then even though one might be able to travel to 1913, it would be impossible to kill Hitler. If time is tenseless, you can go to 1913 only if *you were there* in 1913, and you will only do what you "already did" in 1913 (which obviously did not include killing Hitler).

What do you think?

- If you had the opportunity, would you kill Hitler?
- Since we have seen Hitler's future, should we regard his younger self, the 24-year-old art student, as innocent or guilty?

- Are you a consequentialist or a non-consequentialist? Or, does your answer change depending on the particular moral dilemma?
- Are there any other viable options besides murder? What would you think about befriending Hitler in order to encourage his artistic career and steer him away from politics and hateful ideologies?
- If you were to prevent Hitler's rise to power, you would undoubtedly save millions of lives. But, by the same token you would affect millions of lives and thereby prevent almost everyone you know from being born (due to their parents never meeting, etc.). So when you are in 1913, should you feel more of an obligation to those people who already exist, or to those from your own time?

Did you know?

- Utilitarianism is the dominant consequentialist theory of morality. Kantianism, Contractualism, and Virtue Theory are the dominant non-consequentialist theories.
- There are a number of films that explore these sorts of questions. The inspiration for this puzzle came from *The Last Supper*, a relatively unknown, but excellent dark comedy that raises the "Hitler question" and explores the ramifications of a consequentialist moral outlook. Another good one is *Minority Report* starring Tom Cruise. Based on the Philip K. Dick novel, it presents a futuristic world in which "precogs" can see into the future, thereby enabling police to arrest "future criminals" before they commit the crime. This practice drastically reduces violent crime in Washington DC, but it also raises important questions about justice. Stephen King's *The Dead Zone* is also quite interesting. In this story, a man played by Christopher Walken sees into a politician's deadly future.
- The Munich Hofbräuhaus was significant to Hitler long before his rise to power. As a young artist, he painted this beer hall in watercolors.
- Back in the day, weissbier (wheat beer) could only be brewed with permission of the Duke. Hofbräuhaus enjoyed this exclusive right for nearly 200 years, giving it a monopoly on Weissbier in Bavaria.

Recommended reading

- John Stuart Mill, *Utilitarianism*, 1879. Available online through Project Gutenberg: http://www.gutenberg.org/etext/11224.

- Immanuel Kant, *Fundamental Principles of the Metaphysic of Morals*, 1785. Available online through Project Gutenberg: http://www.gutenberg.org/etext/5862.

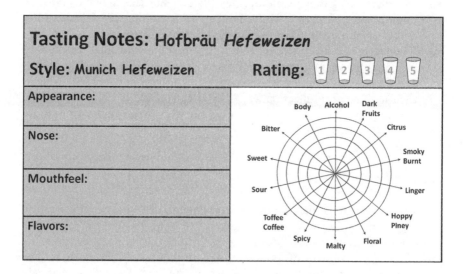

32

The Zen *Kōan*

What is the sound of one glass clinking?

Pint of the Puzzle: Sapporo *Premium Lager*

Sapporo has to be my favorite of the Japanese lagers. If you need a beer to go with a giant platter of sushi, Sapporo is hard to beat. It is also a great beer for contemplating *kōans*, those crazy little Zen mind benders. Is the glass half empty or half full? My meditations on this problem reveal that the only real solution is to top it off with more Sapporo.

What is the sound of one hand clapping? You may have heard this question before. If so, you probably took it to be some kind of joke. But for the student of Zen Buddhism, it is as serious as a question can be. Called a *kōan*, this question is sometimes put to the student by the Roshi (Zen master) as an object of contemplation. A student meditates on the question for days (and sometimes for months or years), and periodically relates an "answer" to the Roshi, who in most instances rejects it as unacceptable.

Philosophy on Tap: Pint-Sized Puzzles for the Pub Philosopher, First Edition. Matt Lawrence
© 2011 Matt Lawrence. Published 2011 by Blackwell Publishing Ltd.

There are thousands of Zen *kōans*. Some of the classics include:

- What was the appearance of your face before your ancestors were born?
- A cow passes by a window. Its head, horns, and the four legs all pass by. Why did not the tail pass by?
- Shuzan held out his short staff and said, "If you call this a short staff, you oppose its reality. If you do not call it a short staff, you ignore the fact. Now what do you wish to call this?"

It should be readily apparent that the common thread that runs through all *kōans* is that they are completely and utterly illogical. They just don't make any sense. But this is precisely the point. The *kōan* is offered to students in order to help them break free of their habitual mind patterns, including logical thinking.

Another classic example is known as the "Mu" *kōan*:

- A monk once asked Master Joshu, "Does a dog have Buddha nature?" To which Joshu replied, "Mu!" [No!]

Master Joshu's reply is paradoxical because, according to Buddhist teachings, *everything* has Buddha nature – even grass and stones. Yet, Master Joshu asserts that a dog does not have Buddha nature. How can this be?

A thirteenth-century monk named Mumon worked on the *Mu kōan* for six straight years, and through this contemplation, he eventually attained enlightenment. Here is his advice for the student working on *Mu*:

> Concentrate your whole self with its 360 bones and joints and 84,000 pores into *mu*, making your whole body a solid lump of doubt. Day and night, without ceasing, keep digging into it. But don't take it as "Nothingness" or as "Being" or as "Non-being." It must be like a red-hot iron ball which you have gulped down and which you try to vomit up, but cannot. You must extinguish all delusive thoughts and feelings you have cherished. After a certain period of such efforts, *mu* will come to fruition, and inside and out will become one naturally. You will then be like a dumb man who has had a dream and then awakens. You will know yourself and for yourself only. Then, all of a sudden, *mu* will break open and astonish the heavens and shake the earth.

Mumon's advice may seem no less bizarre than the *kōan* itself. But he makes it very clear that "solving" the *kōan* is much more than an intellectual enterprise. When thoroughly pursued, the contemplation of the *kōan* becomes an earth-shattering, life-altering experience, ultimately leading to an awakened or enlightened state of consciousness called *satori*.

While those who have experienced satori agree that it cannot adequately be put into words, many have tried to at least point in its direction. For example, the famous Zen scholar D. T. Suzuki (1870–1966) likens it to "grasping reality as a whole," which occurs when the mind "breaks free of the bounds of reason." In this state, all divisions and distinctions, including the distinction between the knower and the known, are obliterated. Over the centuries there have been many people who claim to have experienced satori. Some attained it spontaneously through no obvious cause, others by hearing the sound of a bell or drum or by some other external stimulus, and some have attained it through contemplating a *kōan*.

The best-known *kōan* in the West is that infamous question: "What is the sound of one hand clapping?" in response to which people typically make silly one-handed gestures – clapping their fingers against their palms and so on. What people typically don't realize is that this classic *kōan* was originally about toasting glasses of beer. It is said that Mokurai, a nineteenth-century Zen Master of the Rinzai school, was drinking Sapporo with his best disciples in celebration of the New Year, when a 12-year-old boy named Toyo approached him and asked to become his student. Mokurai's response was to offer the boy a *kōan*. He said:

"Listen to the sound of these two glasses clinking together as we toast the New Year. Now show me the sound of one glass clinking." He then handed an empty glass to Toyo.

Toyo went back to his room and meditated on the problem. "What can the sound of one glass be?" After several hours he happened to hear some water dripping. "I have it," he thought.

When he next appeared before his teacher, he poured some Sapporo from a glass.

"That is the sound of Sapporo dripping, but not the sound of one glass clinking! Try again," Mokurai replied.

In vain Toyo meditated to hear the sound of one glass clinking. He heard the wind howling, but this sound was rejected.

He heard the cry of an owl. This also could not be it.

The sound of one glass clinking was not the locusts.

For more than 10 times Toyo visited Mokurai with different sounds. All were dismissed. For almost a year he pondered what the sound of one glass might be.

At last Toyo entered true meditation and transcended all sounds. "I could collect no more," he explained later, "so I reached the soundless sound."

Toyo had realized the sound of one glass clinking.

Truth be told

As you might have guessed, Mokurai did not develop a "one glass clinking" *kōan* while drinking Sapporo. Instead, he is attributed with the "one hand clapping" *kōan*, and there is no classic Zen *kōan* about one glass clinking – though there certainly could have been, and there probably would have been if Zen monks spent less time meditating and more time drinking. The conversation between Mokurai and Toyo is adapted from the from the *Zen Kōans Database*: http://www.cincinato. org/koans/showone_es.php?koan=the_sound_of_one_hand.txt.

What do you think?

- How would you respond to Master Mokurai's *kōan*?
- Do you think that logic and reason distort or shapes our experience of reality? If so, how?
- Do you believe that it is possible to experience the world without distinctions? Have you ever experienced this?
- What value (if any) do you think there would be in emptying the mind of all thoughts and reasoning?

Did you know?

- "Zen" is the Japanese word for meditation. Zen Buddhism emphasizes meditation as the path to enlightenment.
- D. T. Suzuki first experienced satori at the age of 26 while meditating upon the "Mu" *kōan*. His first words following the experience were "I see. This is it."
- It is said that Master Joshu lived to be 120. At 60 he took a pilgrimage, saying that if he meets a young child who can teach him, he will learn from that child, and if he meets an old man whom he can teach, he'll teach that man.
- Sapporo brewed a limited edition "Space Barley" beer using barley grown from seeds which spent five months on board the International Space Station in 2006. The project was a joint venture with the Russian Academy of Sciences. Six packs were then sold through a lottery system at a price of 10,000 yen.

Recommended reading

- Paul Reps and Nyogen Senzaki, *Zen Flesh, Zen Bones: A Collection of Zen and Pre-Zen Writings* (Boston: Tuttle Publishing, 1998).
- *Zen Buddhism: Selected Writings of D. T. Suzuki*, ed. William Barrett (New York: Three Leaves, 1996).

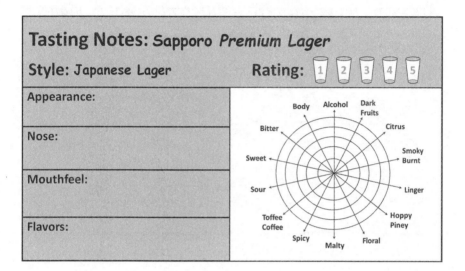

Tasting Notes: Sapporo *Premium Lager*

Style: Japanese Lager   **Rating:** 1 2 3 4 5

| Appearance: |
| Nose: |
| Mouthfeel: |
| Flavors: |

Body · Alcohol · Dark Fruits · Citrus · Bitter · Sweet · Smoky Burnt · Sour · Linger · Toffee Coffee · Hoppy Piney · Spicy · Malty · Floral

33

Sex and Sensibility

Are men and women from different morality planets?

Pint of the Puzzle: His: Anchor *Steam*; Hers: Chardonnay

Okay, I know I'm going to take some flack for this one, so let's be clear. I'm not saying that women don't enjoy a good beer or that they don't drink Anchor Steam. But seriously, when was the last time you saw a woman choose Anchor Steam over chardonnay or an appletini? Now, I'm all for equal rights and sexual equality, but we can't ignore our basic differences.

Many psychological studies suggest that one's gender may profoundly affect how one sees, judges, and relates to the world. This can be seen not only in drink choices and fashion accessories, but also in moral reasoning. Men and women, it seems, approach moral dilemmas differently. The Harvard psychologist Lawrence Kohlberg (1927–1987) pioneered some of the first studies on the psychology of moral reasoning. His initial aim was to understand the stages of moral development in children. Kohlberg did this by presenting school age boys with a variety of moral dilemmas. One of these dilemmas is rather famously known as *The Heinz Dilemma*:

Philosophy on Tap: Pint-Sized Puzzles for the Pub Philosopher, First Edition. Matt Lawrence
© 2011 Matt Lawrence. Published 2011 by Blackwell Publishing Ltd.

In Europe, a woman was near death from a special kind of cancer. There was one drug that the doctors thought might save her. It was a form of radium that a druggist in the same town had recently discovered. The drug was expensive to make, but the druggist was charging ten times what the drug cost him to make. He paid $200 for the radium and charged $2,000 for a small dose of the drug. The sick woman's husband, Heinz, went to everyone he knew to borrow the money, but he could only get together about $1,000, which is half of what it cost. He told the druggist that his wife was dying and asked him to sell it cheaper or let him pay later. But the druggist said: "No, I discovered the drug and I'm going to make money from it." So Heinz got desperate and broke into the man's store to steal the drug for his wife. Should the husband have done that?

Kohlberg's interest was not in *what* the children answered, but in *how* they arrived at their conclusion. On the basis of the responses he received, Kohlberg concluded that moral reasoning follows a clear developmental pattern. He identified six developmental stages within three basic levels:

The Preconventional Level

Stage One: Obedience and Punishment Orientation

Stage Two: Individualism and Exchange

The Conventional Level

Stage Three: Good Interpersonal Relationships

Stage Four: Maintaining the Social Order

The Postconventional Level

Stage Five: Social Contract and Individual Rights

Stage Six: Universal Principles

For our purposes we needn't go into Kohlberg's theory in much detail. The important thing is to notice that the highest developmental stages in Kohlberg's schema are stages four, five, and six. These stages emphasize rules, rights, and abstract principles as the highest forms of moral reasoning. But recall that Kohlberg's study was conducted solely on boys. When girls were later tested, it was found that they were generally less likely to reach these highest stages. Quite often they seemed to get "stuck" at stage three. This seemed to imply that girls are generally less adept at moral reasoning than boys.

These findings soon generated a great deal of controversy. Are girls really morally stunted, or is there something wrong with Kohlberg's methodology? Harvard Psychologist Carol Gilligan argued the latter. Based on her own studies Gilligan agreed that boys and girls (and men and women) tend to take different approaches to moral reasoning. Advanced thought for males tends to revolve around rules, rights, and abstract principles, while advanced thought for females tends to center on interpersonal relationships, compassion, and care. But on what basis should we say that one mode of thinking is "better" or "higher" than the other? Gilligan argued that by supposing that these six stages were *THE* stages of moral development (rather than simply the typical stages of development *for boys)* Kohlberg's theory was male-biased. Gilligan's own position, indicated in part by the title of her book, *In a Different Voice: Psychological Theory and Women's Development,* is that the developmental paths of men and women are different, but not competing.

While it may very well be true that men and women resolve moral issues differently, it is hard to see why these approaches wouldn't compete in at least some instances. After all, they often lead to different conclusions about what ought to be done. And when a "rights approach" yields a different moral conclusion from a "care approach," won't it be necessary to choose between them? And wouldn't this involve making a judgment about which approach was in some sense the "better" way to look at the situation? Alternatively, we could simply reason in whichever way comes to us most naturally. But shouldn't we be concerned that perhaps our own orientation (whether stereotypically male or female) might be deficient, misguided, or somehow inappropriate to the situation at hand?

What do you think?

- In your experience, do men and women think about moral issues differently? And, if so, do you think that this is due to nature or nurture?
- Do you think that there is a "right," "best," or "most developed" way to think about moral issues?
- Might it be the case that both the male and female orientations are biased and that the highest form of moral reason involves a synthesis of the two?
- Is it plausible to regard these two moral outlooks as "separate but equal?" Why or why not?

Did you know?

- Some studies have not supported the claim that there are profound differences in the moral orientations of boys and girls. See, for example, studies by Lawrence J. Walker and Stephen J. Thoma.

- According to Drinkfocus.com, Women comprise only about 25 percent of today's beer market, but they comprise 60 percent of the wine market.
- Kaiser Wilhelm famously remarked, "Give me a woman who loves beer and I will conquer the world."
- Men haven't always dominated the world of beer. According to Patrick Ryan Williams, Curator of Anthropology at the Field Museum, upper-class women were the primary brewers in the pre-Incan societies of Peru over 1,000 years ago.
- Anchor Steam gets its name from the nineteenth century when "steam" was a nickname for beer brewed on the West Coast of America in which lager yeast has been used to drive fermentation at the higher temperatures typically used with ale yeasts. The Anchor Brewing Company of San Francisco has been making steam beer since 1896.

Recommended reading

- Carol Gilligan, *In a Different Voice: Psychological Theory and Women's Development* (Cambridge, MA: Harvard University Press, 1982).
- F. C. Power, A. Higgins, and L. Kohlberg, *Lawrence Kohlberg's Approach to Moral Education* (New York: Columbia University Press, 1989).

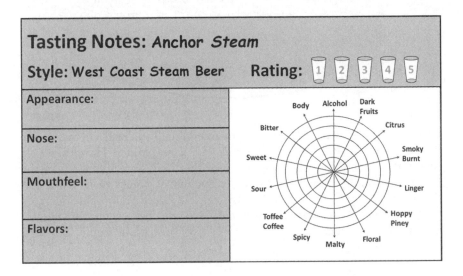

Tasting Notes: Anchor *Steam*

Style: West Coast Steam Beer   **Rating:** 1 2 3 4 5

Appearance:

Nose:

Mouthfeel:

Flavors:

Body   Alcohol   Dark Fruits
Bitter   Citrus
Sweet   Smoky Burnt
Sour   Linger
Toffee   Hoppy Piney
Coffee
Spicy   Malty   Floral

34

Socrates' Virtue

Can you knowingly do wrong?

Pint of the Puzzle: Blue Point *Hoptical Illusion*

Optical illusions abound. For example, the closer an object is, the larger it appears to be. This seems to hold for all physical objects except for beer. Once a pint gets within arm's length, it just gets smaller and smaller until it vanishes altogether – especially when it's a pint of Hoptical Illusion from Blue Point Brewing. It's unique flavor comes from a special strain of hop grown only in Oregon.

Can you knowingly do wrong? Can you intentionally do evil? On the face of it, the answer to these questions seems like a no-brainer. Haven't we all sometimes done things knowing full well that they were wrong? It might be easy to simply dismiss this one, except that it comes to us from one of the greatest intellects of all time – the Ancient Greek philosopher Socrates (*c.* 469–399 BCE). Socrates famously said, "No one does wrong knowingly." When we do things that are wrong, evil, or just plain stupid, Socrates

Philosophy on Tap: Pint-Sized Puzzles for the Pub Philosopher, First Edition. Matt Lawrence
© 2011 Matt Lawrence. Published 2011 by Blackwell Publishing Ltd.

maintained that it is always out of ignorance – we simply didn't know any better.

The impetus behind this unusual claim is Socrates' conviction that people always aim at "the good" as they perceive it. For example, take the person who drank too many pints at the pub last night. They've spent the entire morning with their arms wrapped around the porcelain throne, wondering, "Why, oh why, did I drink so much?" They regret their behavior and castigate themselves, thinking, "I knew better." But if Socrates is right, they didn't know better. Sure they know better *now*, and perhaps they knew better *last Saturday morning* when they found themselves in a similar state. But they didn't know it last night – at least at the moment that they ordered another round. Sure, they may have thought to themselves, "Oh, am I going to regret this!" but they didn't fully believe it. At that very moment, Socrates would contend that they truly believed that the pleasure of one more pint was worth whatever cost the morning might exact.

Socrates accounted for this kind of temporary stupidity by comparing it to an optical illusion. Just as objects appear larger when they are closer to us, so pleasures appear to be better than they are when they are close at hand. Similarly, tomorrow's pains appear to us as smaller or less significant since they are farther away. Now, in the drunkard's case, the phenomenon might be more accurately described as a "hoptical illusion," but, either way, drunk or sober, people are constantly deceived by the nearer pleasures.

If we could avoid being "duped" about what is good, Socrates believed, no one would ever do anything as foolish as drinking themselves sick. Moreover, they would also never do anything immoral. He contended that wrongdoing always makes a person worse off. Or, to put it another way, crime *never* pays. This goes against the common conception. Most people think that wrongdoing *sometimes* pays – at least when you can get away with it. But Socrates argued that immorality damages the soul, and the wealth and power that may result from injustice are trivial in comparison. In *The Apology* he states:

> I spend all my time going about trying to persuade you, young and old, to make your first and chief concern not your bodies, nor your possessions, but for the highest welfare of your souls [virtue] .... Wealth does not bring goodness, but goodness brings wealth and every other blessing, both to the individual and to the state.

Socrates believed that virtue is to the soul as health is to the body. To desire injustice and to perform wrongful actions is to corrupt or infect one's soul. It is the worst thing that a person could do to themselves – let alone to others.

Thus, he maintained that "virtue is knowledge." That is, having a good character (virtue) is essentially the same thing as knowing the truth about what is truly beneficial and truly harmful.

Is virtue your most valuable possession – your highest good? Or, is it sometimes worthwhile to trade away your virtue for material gain? As you think about this, you might try imagining a drug dealer – perhaps the head of a large drug cartel who has incredible wealth, power, and the respect of many people, but who got all of this by lying, stealing, murdering, and fostering the drug addiction of thousands of people. Would you trade your virtue in order to have a life like his? And if not, why would you trade your virtue for monetary gain, or an "A" on an exam?

What do you think?

- Is it true that no one does wrong knowingly?
- If Socrates is right, and people only do wrong because it appears to them as good, do they deserve to be punished for their actions? If so, what sorts of punishments would be appropriate?
- Is it true that crime *never* pays?
- How much is your virtue worth? If the bartender forgot to charge you, would you tell them?

Did you know?

- Socrates was executed for allegedly "corrupting the youth." In his trial he used his hypothesis that "no one does wrong knowingly" in his defense. He argued that if he had in fact corrupted the youth of Athens as his prosecutors charged, then he could not have done so intentionally.
- Virtues are "dispositions" or "states of character" that enable one to be a good human being. The commonly recognized virtues include dispositions such as honesty, justice, wisdom, temperance, courage, generosity, humility, and compassion.
- While Hoptical Illusion is Blue Point Brewing's most hopped-up beer, their flagship brew is their Toasted Lager, which won gold in the 2006 World Beer Cup Awards.

Recommended reading

- Plato, *Apology*. Available online through Project Gutenberg: http://www
  .gutenberg.org/etext/1656.
- Plato, *Protagoras*. Available online through Project Gutenberg: http://www
  .gutenberg.org/etext/1591.

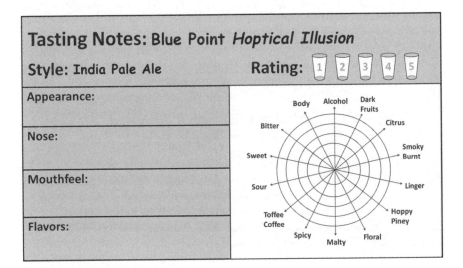

35

Nature Calls

Are human beings inherently good or evil?

Pint of the Puzzle: Stone *Sublimely Self-Righteous Ale* **OR** *Arrogant Bastard Ale*

What is human nature? Are we inherently good, or evil? In either case, the Stone Brewing Company has a beer for you. Sublimely Self-Righteous Ale for you optimists, and Arrogant Bastard for the pessimists. Whichever you choose, rest assured that you'll be drinking a beer with an inherently delicious nature.

People are good and bad, generous and greedy, friendly and fiendish. But what is our inherent nature? Are we naturally kind and generous, but corrupted by outside influences, or are we naturally selfish and mean, but taught to override these inclinations through discipline and training?

These questions were vigorously debated in Ancient Chinese philosophy. Mencius (*c.* 372–289 BCE) took the more optimistic view, arguing that

---

Philosophy on Tap: Pint-Sized Puzzles for the Pub Philosopher, First Edition. Matt Lawrence
© 2011 Matt Lawrence. Published 2011 by Blackwell Publishing Ltd.

goodness flows from our nature. It is only due to unfortunate circumstances and influences that we become bad. In contrast, Xunzi (*c.* 310–220 BCE) regarded humanity as innately selfish, and attributed the virtues almost entirely to the effects of nurture and training.

Mencius maintained that humanity's innate goodness could be seen in people's initial emotional responses to tragedy. For example, if a child falls in a well, anyone's immediate reaction would be one of sympathy and the desire to help. Similarly, he believed that we all have an inherent sense of right and wrong. The first impulse of the beggar who is given food in an insulting manner is to reject the food – even though this could cost him his life. According to Mencius, human goodness is just another aspect of the natural world. A person's desire to act justly and sympathetically toward others is no different than water's tendency to settle toward the lowest point. He tells us:

> By nature we are sublimely self-righteous. There is no human who does not tend toward goodness. There is no water that does not tend downward. Now, by striking water and making it leap up, you can cause it to go past your forehead. If you guide it by damming it, you can cause it to remain on a mountaintop. But is this the nature of water?! It is that way because of the circumstances. That humans can be caused to not be good is due to their natures also being like this.

Xunzi, on the other hand, supported his pessimistic view of human nature by emphasizing the desires and emotions that seem to be within us from birth:

> All people are born arrogant little bastards. Their goodness is a matter of deliberate effort. Now people's nature is such that they are born with a fondness for profit. If they follow along with this, then struggle and contention will arise, and yielding and deference will perish therein. They are born with feelings of hate and dislike. If they follow along with these, then cruelty and villainy will arise, and loyalty and trustworthiness will perish therein .... Thus, if people follow along with their inborn nature and dispositions they are sure to come to struggle and contention, turn to disrupting social divisions and disorder, and end up in violence.

According to Xunzi, we must learn to override our natural impulses. It is only through society's constant and deliberate enforcement of social norms that we become good and responsible citizens. For example, he notes that when we are hungry, our natural inclination is to want to eat before others. It is only because of our parents' diligent training that we patiently wait our turn.

So who is right, Mencius or Xunzi? Or does the truth lie somewhere in between? As we ponder the question of human nature, it quickly becomes apparent that the issue is philosophically problematic. Can we really separate "nature" from "nurture"? The problem is that we always find humans within a social context. We begin to learn from those around us soon after birth, and these experiences significantly shape our personalities and behaviors. And even if we were to find a person who has lived their entire life outside of human society, we couldn't take them as an example of the "natural" human life. For, if we can say anything about human nature, it is surely that we are naturally social. Like wolves, chimpanzees, and many other species, we almost invariably live in groups.

While it may not be possible to reach a definitive answer on the "nature vs. nurture" debate, we all tend to lean one way or the other in our philosophical outlook. It is therefore important to reflect on our views, as they have important ramifications. For those who see things as Mencius did, raising a child to be a good person is rather like the cultivation of a sprout. Meet a child's basic needs, give her a good and supporting environment, and she will develop into a morally good person of her own accord. So long as the child is given the right environment, the parent need not be particularly strict. Instead, freedom for "self-discovery" is what needs to be emphasized. But if you see things as Xunzi did, a more apt metaphor for moral development is that of sharpening a piece of metal. It is only by applying considerable external pressure that you will achieve the desired result. If you hold this view, you are more likely to believe that parents should take a much more strict and authoritarian role in order to instill good tendencies in the child.

Truth be told

The first sentence was added to the passages from Mencius and Xunzi. Most translations don't use the term "arrogant bastards," or speak of the "sublimely self righteous." But, as I'm sure you know, it is difficult to get a literal translation of the Chinese characters into modern English.

What do you think?

- Is there such a thing as "human nature?" And, if so, is it predominantly good or predominantly evil?

- What is the best evidence for settling the issue? Do you think that advances in genetic research will settle it? Why/why not?
- Can we separate "nature" from "nurture?"
- Do you believe in a more, or less, authoritarian style of parenting? Does this reflect your view of human nature?

Did you know?

- Mencius and Xunzi lived in a period of Chinese history known as "the Warring States." During this time (roughly 403–221 BCE), constant battles were waged in the attempt to gain control of all of China. Surprisingly, this was one of the most fertile periods of Chinese philosophy.
- Despite their differences, Mencius and Xunzi both considered themselves disciples of Confucius, and much of their writing elaborated upon the teachings of the master.
- In Western philosophy, Jean-Jacques Rousseau and Thomas Hobbes best epitomize the debate over human nature. Rousseau, like Mencius thought that human nature was inherently good, but corrupted by society. Hobbes thought that human beings were completely egoistic, and only the fear of punishment could adequately keep people in line.
- William Golding's novel *Lord of the Flies* can be interpreted from a Xunzian perspective. It depicts children shipwrecked on a deserted island who soon give way to wickedness when deprived of society's influence and control.
- Stone Brewing describes Arrogant Bastard Ale as follows. "This is an aggressive beer. You probably won't like it. It is doubtful that you have the taste sophistication to be able to appreciate an ale of this quality and depth. We would suggest that you stick to safer and more familiar territory – maybe something with a multi-million dollar ad campaign aimed at convincing you it's made in a little brewery, or one that implies that their tasteless fizzy yellow beer will give you more sex appeal."

Recommended reading

- Phillip J. Ivanhoe and Bryan W. Van Norden, eds., *Readings in Classical Chinese Philosophy* (New York: Seven Bridges Press, 2001).
- William Golding, *Lord of the Flies* (New York: Riverhead Books, 1954).

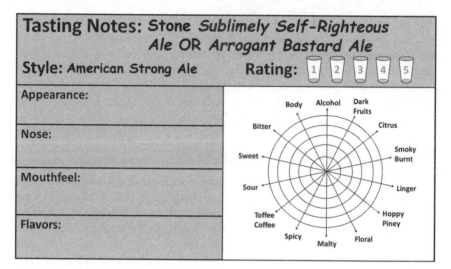

Tasting Notes: Stone *Sublimely Self-Righteous Ale* OR *Arrogant Bastard Ale*

Style: American Strong Ale   **Rating:** 1 2 3 4 5

Appearance:

Nose:

Mouthfeel:

Flavors:

Body Alcohol Dark Fruits
Bitter   Citrus
Sweet   Smoky Burnt
Sour   Linger
Toffee Coffee   Hoppy Piney
Spicy Malty Floral

36

Nietzsche's Eternal Recurrence

Would you choose that beer all over again?
And again? And . . .

Pint of the Puzzle: North Coast *Brother Thelonious Abbey Ale*

"Carpe diem vita brevis" or "Seize the day because life is short" is the slogan on each bottle of Brother Thelonious Belgian Style Abbey Ale from North Coast Brewing. Indeed, life *is* short. But what if your meager life were to repeat itself endlessly? Would that give you more or less reason to seize the day? More, or less reason to buy another round?

What if your entire life, in fact the entire history of the world, were to repeat itself over and over for all eternity? Imagine every pain, every joy, every success, and every mistake to be lived again and again just as it was. This prospect of an *eternal recurrence* was a favorite idea of the German philosopher Friedrich Nietzsche (1844–1900). He called it "the greatest weight," believing that for most people such a fate would be horrifying:

Philosophy on Tap: Pint-Sized Puzzles for the Pub Philosopher, First Edition. Matt Lawrence
© 2011 Matt Lawrence. Published 2011 by Blackwell Publishing Ltd.

> Would you not throw yourself down and gnash your teeth and curse the demon
> who spoke thus? . . . Or how well disposed would you have to become to yourself
> and to life *to crave nothing more fervently* than this ultimate eternal confir-
> mation and seal?

It is one thing to want to relive your favorite moments, but quite another
to embrace, and even wish for, the repetition of one's most embarrassing
and shameful acts. What Nietzsche has in mind is not the sort of recurrence
that was humorously played out in the Bill Murray film *Groundhog Day*,
in which Murray's character had a repeated opportunity to get his day
right. He retained the knowledge of his prior "Groundhog days" so that
he could avoid his previous mistakes. In contrast, what Nietzsche has in
mind is a recurrence where nothing is changed, and hence, nothing is
improved upon.

For Nietzsche, one's attitude toward eternal recurrence reflects one's
attitude toward life itself. And, unfortunately for most of us, the reflection
is not particularly flattering. The prospect of an eternal return brings out two
personalities or "types." One affirms life, and the other has contempt for life.
Nietzsche thought that the person who truly affirms life will say "yes" to it all,
relishing both the good and the bad – choosing it all, not only for today, but
for all eternity. To them, eternal recurrence would be an incredible gift. But to
most people it would be a curse. They constantly wish that things were
different than they are. They don't say "yes" to life as it is; what they affirm
(or cling to) is the possibility of a future "better life" (or an *afterlife*) that
will be radically different from this one.

Nietzsche maintained that the rare individual, the truly exceptional human
being, would be marked by the total affirmation of *this* life. Theirs would be
an attitude of *amor fati* – they would love their fate. They would wish for
"nothing to be different, not forward, not backward, not in all eternity." They
would not try to distance themselves from past suffering or to conceal their
humiliations under the sands of time. Instead, they would *love* and embrace
it all.

But is the prospect of eternal recurrence truly the "greatest weight" as
Nietzsche described it? Would it really be worse than total annihilation?
If, when everything is said and done, one's life has been "worth living,"
then wouldn't it be worth living again, and again? Since most people
seem to long for immortality, why wouldn't recurrence be the next best
thing?

Perhaps the weight of recurrence is to be found in its moral burden. This is
what Milan Kundera suggested in his classic novel, *The Unbearable Lightness
of Being*:

> If every second of our lives recurs an infinite number of times, we are nailed to
> eternity as Jesus Christ was nailed to the cross. It is a terrifying prospect. In the
> world of eternal return the weight of unbearable responsibility lies heavy on
> every move we make.

There is something particularly disturbing about the thought that your
most despicable actions will be replayed, in fact *re-chosen*, over and over. Any
suffering that you have caused would amass toward infinite suffering; any
injustice would eventually be transformed into infinite injustice. Perhaps
this is why Nietzsche maintained that to embrace eternal recurrence
would require freedom from the constraints of morality.

While this way of looking at it may help us to understand why recurrence
would be a terrifying prospect to those with blood on their hands, it is still
not entirely clear that the reasonably good person should dread recurrence.
For although your misdeeds will be magnified with repetition, so too will
your admirable actions. If, from the perspective of a *single* life, we would say
that the goodness of your acts outweighed the bad, then why wouldn't this
hold true if the drama is replayed countless times? While the suffering and
injustice may accrue to infinity, so would your acts of kindness, the joys
you felt, and the love you gave. Is anything then, really made more terrible
by the return?

Another point to consider is how (or whether) the prospect of eternal
recurrence would change your approach to life. Would you act differently if
you knew that everything you do will be repeated endlessly? For instance,
would you be more inclined to quit an unfulfilling job if you faced the thought
of doing it, not just for another 20 years, but for all eternity? Might the
prospect of recurrence even affect the small things, like whether you'd choose
the bargain beer over a well-crafted Belgian style abbey ale? If you were
choosing it not just for today, but all eternity, don't you think that you would
spend a couple of dollars more for a Brother Thelonious? Of course you
would. Who'd want to drink crappy beer ad infinitum? But notice this. If
recurrence is false, shouldn't you still go for quality, whether in work, play,
relationships, or beer? The Schlitz Brewing Company of America popularized
this anti-recurrence thesis back in the 1970s. Their advertising slogan urged
the following:

> You only go around once in life. So grab all the gusto you can.
>
> Even in the beer you drink. Why settle for less?

While recurrence is a motivator, it seems to me that its antithesis, the idea
that you only "go around once," is equally motivating. If you've only got

one shot at life, be it short and fleeting, or endlessly repetitious, shouldn't you "go for the gusto?"

So go ahead. Buy the better beer.

What do you think?

- What is your initial response to eternal recurrence? Is it something that you would welcome or dread?
- If you took the prospect of eternal recurrence seriously, would it change the way that you live your life? If so, how?
- Which personality type best describes you? Are you more "life affirming" or "contemptuous of life?"
- Does the impulse to want to rewrite your past really show contempt for life? Or, is it the appropriate response to the despicable actions of one's past?

Did you know?

- Friedrich Nietzsche is perhaps most widely known for his declaration that "God is dead." Notice that he did not simply suggest that God does not exist. Rather, he contended that God was dead – because we had *killed* Him.
- Arthur Schopenhauer, one of Nietzsche's greatest influences, also maintained that the "thoughtful and honest man" would prefer total annihilation to the prospect of living his life all over again. But Schopenhauer was perhaps the greatest pessimist of all Western philosophy.
- Nietzsche was a staunch social critic – even when it comes to beer. In *Twilight of the Idols*, in an aphorism titled "What Germans Lack," he wrote: "Where does one not find that bland degeneration which beer produces in the spirit?"
- When you buy Brother Thelonious Belgian Style Abbey Ale, you help support the Thelonious Monk Institute of Jazz, whose mission is to offer promising young musicians college-level training from America's jazz masters. They also promote jazz education in public schools around the world.

Recommended reading

- Friedrich Nietzsche, *The Gay Science*, trans. Walter Kaufman (New York: Vintage Books Edition, Random House, 1974).

- Milan Kundera, *The Unbearable Lightness of Being* (New York: Harper and Rowe, 1984).

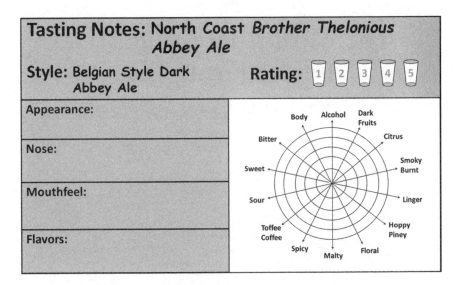

37

The Most Interesting Man
and the Firing Line

Does it matter who pulls the trigger?

Pint of the Puzzle: Dos Equis *Ambar*

If you've seen the commercials for Dos Equis, you're familiar with "The Most Interesting Man in the World." And if you are not, you must be living in Amish country. The guy's reputation precedes him like lightening precedes thunder. His personality is so magnetic that he can't carry credit cards! This is a guy who has it all. Women want to be with him, men want to *be* him, and philosophers want to write about him – as did the Oxford philosopher Bernard Williams in an article that inspired our next puzzle. Stay thirsty my friends!

Sometimes in life we find ourselves in the unfortunate predicament of having to choose between two evils. We may have the best of intentions. yet no matter what we do somebody is going to get hurt. Perhaps the most common strategy for dealing with these situations is to choose the lesser of the two evils – the course of action that will cause the least amount of harm overall. But will this strategy always suffice?

Philosopher Bernard Williams (1929–2003) has offered a scenario that seems to complicate matters:

Philosophy on Tap: Pint-Sized Puzzles for the Pub Philosopher, First Edition. Matt Lawrence
© 2011 Matt Lawrence. Published 2011 by Blackwell Publishing Ltd.

Once I had the incredible opportunity to spend an evening with the most interesting man in the world. I was in holiday in Cordova Spain, having a drink in this quaint little bar. He recognized me and introduced himself as a lover of philosophy. We sat and discussed a variety of topics from Descartes to the nature of the self and swapped a few stories over a couple of pitchers of beer. (By the way, he doesn't always drink beer – but when he does, he prefers Dos Equis.) He told me quite an intriguing story about a predicament he found himself in while traveling through South America. It was back in the 1980s, and he (let's call him "Jim" since his real name is highly confidential) was on a botany expedition with the former Miss Venezuela. They had just driven into the central square of a small village when they saw twenty Indians tied up against a wall. Most were terrified, a few defiant, and in front of them were several armed men in uniform. A heavy man in a sweat-stained khaki shirt turned out to be the captain in charge. He came over to Jim's Land Rover and began to interrogate him. (Police often question him, just because they find him interesting.) The captain, a portly chap named Pedro, then explained that the Indians were a random group of the inhabitants who, after recent acts of protest against the government, were just about to be killed to set an example to future dissidents. However, since Jim was an honoured visitor from another land, the captain was happy to offer him a VIP's privilege of killing one of the Indians himself. If Jim were to accept, then as a special mark of the occasion, the other Indians would be freed. Of course, if Jim were to refuse, then there would be no special occasion, and Pedro would do what he was about to do when Jim arrived, and kill them all.

Now, for most of us, this would be a horrendous experience. What do you do? Kill the one to save the others – or refuse and watch them all die? There were too many guards to play hero. Besides, Jim was unarmed. I figured that Jim was in quite a tight spot, but, as he tells it, he seemed to have been quite amused by the whole situation. (I've since heard that he had an awkward moment only once – just to find out how it feels.) So anyway, Jim told Captain Pedro that he would be honored to oblige, but, as it was quite hot, suggested that they first open a couple of the *Dos Equis* he had in his cooler and toast the occasion. Well, as you might expect, with cold beer and stories of Jim's exploits with Marilyn Monroe while aboard a nuclear submarine, one beer led to another until Pedro (now thoroughly drunk) was so filled with good cheer that he let all the Indians go.

So everything worked out fine in the end. But the point of this story is that, unlike Jim, you are *not* the most interesting man in the world. What works for Jim is not going to work for you. So, what would you do? Would you kill one Indian in order to spare the other 19? What makes this case especially tough is that by choosing the lesser evil, you would have to implicate yourself in that evil. By choosing the death of one over the deaths of 20, you become a murderer. I expect that you'd find this prospect to be quite disturbing. But is it the right choice nonetheless?

On the one hand, if you were to refuse the Captain's offer in order to keep your own hands clean, then haven't you done something despicably selfish? On account of the weight that you put on your own moral purity, 19 additional lives are lost. Surely the Indians would be hoping that you take the Captain up on his offer. But, on the other hand, isn't there something admirable about refusing to take part in evil? If the Captain had received his orders from his superior, we certainly would have liked to see him refuse to comply. After all, aren't we all ultimately responsible only for our *own* actions? As Bernard Williams notes, it only makes sense to say that you (or Jim) would have *caused* the deaths of the 20 Indians if you somehow *cause* Captain Pedro to shoot them. But this is not the case. The Captain shoots as the result of his own choice. If, upon your refusal, he were to say, "You leave me with no alternative," the Captain would be lying. Furthermore, integrity is generally one of the qualities that we admire most in a person. To possess integrity is to stick to your principles. And since the wrongfulness of murder is (presumably) one of your most cherished principles, how could you, as a person of integrity, commit murder?

Truth be told

The passage from Bernard Williams's article "A Critique of Utilitarianism" has been greatly modified. While he did write about Jim, Captain Pedro, and the Indians, he made no reference to The Most Interesting Man in the World, or his cooler full of Dos Equis. But, I'm sure that Professor Williams had sworn himself to secrecy regarding certain details of the event.

What do you think?

- If you were in Jim's shoes, would you have accepted the Captain's offer or refused it?
- If one were to refuse, would they be giving too much weight to their desire to keep their own hands clean?
- Would it affect your decision if you were close friends with one or more of the Indians? If so, how? And *should* your relationship affect your decision?

This dilemma can be seen as a choice between principle (never kill the innocent) and consequences (minimum harm). When you make moral decision do you find that you are influenced more by your commitments to certain principles, or by the consequences of the alternatives available to you?

Did you know?

The following things have been said about the most interesting man in the world:

1. He is the only man to ever ace a Rorschach test.
2. His charm is so contagious that vaccines have been made for it.
3. Even his enemies list him as their emergency contact number.
4. Alien abductors have asked him to probe *them*.
5. He's been known to cure narcolepsy just by walking into a room.
6. He won the same lifetime achievement award twice.
7. He believes that it is never too early to start beefing up your obituary.

The view that we should always choose the action that will yield the best consequences or outcome is called *consequentialism*. The view that we should be guided by principles (without regard to consequences) is called *deontology*.

Before pursuing a career in philosophy, Bernard Williams was a fighter pilot in the British Royal Air Force.

Dos Equis suggests that you think of their Ambar as their Lager's dark, moody, and passionate cousin. It comes in a brown bottle, while their lager comes in green.

Recommended reading

- Bernard Williams, "A Critique of Utilitarianism," in J. J. C. Smart and Bernard Williams, eds., *Utilitarianism for and Against* (Cambridge: Cambridge University Press, 1973).
- Samuel Scheffler, ed., *Consequentialism and Its Critics* (Oxford: Oxford University Press) 1988.

Tasting Notes: Dos Equis *Ambar*

Style: Mexican Amber Lager   **Rating:** 1 2 3 4 5

Appearance:

Nose:

Mouthfeel:

Flavors:

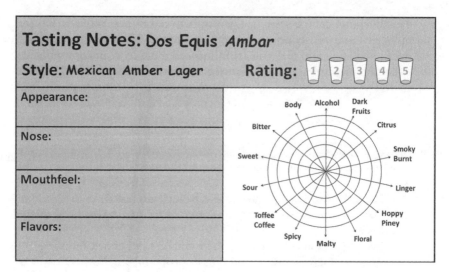

38

Turing's Tasting Machine

Could a computer judge beer?

> ### Pint of the Puzzle: Fuller's *London Pride*
>
> Let's raise our pints to Alan Turing, the English mathematician and computing pioneer. And nothing would be more fitting than an ale from his home town, so let's go with Fuller's *London Pride*. Brewed by the last remaining traditional family brewer in all of London, it will leave you feeling like there are "angels dancing on your tongue."

There's an old saying that goes, "If it walks like a duck and quacks like a duck, then it *is* a duck." Some scientists and philosophers have applied this sort of reasoning to the question of *artificial intelligence*. As they see it, when computers can *act* sufficiently like us, then for most intents and purposes, they will *be* like us. When machines can calculate as well (or better) than the average person, converse on an indefinite range of topics, and respond appropriately to whatever situation confronts them, then we should say that these machines are intelligent, that they believe things, know things, want things, etc.

Philosophy on Tap: Pint-Sized Puzzles for the Pub Philosopher, First Edition. Matt Lawrence
© 2011 Matt Lawrence. Published 2011 by Blackwell Publishing Ltd.

One of the main proponents of this position was Alan Turing (1912–1953). Turing was a pioneer in the computer science field and is perhaps most famous for proposing a test through which we might answer the question: "Can computers think?" He called this test the *Imitation Game* (though it is now widely known as the "Turing Test"). The game requires three players: an interrogator and two subjects, one of which is human, and the other is a computer. The interrogator sits in a room separated from the subjects, and his goal is to try to discern which of the subjects is the human and which is the computer. The goal of both of the subjects is to try to convince him that they are human. The interrogator plays the game by directing questions to each of the players. The interrogator can ask whatever he likes – e.g., "Do you have any hobbies?" "What color is your hair?" etc. The subjects respond with typewritten answers so that voice and handwriting do not come into play. For a computer to win the Imitation Game (or pass the "Turing Test"), it would need to be very sophisticated. For instance, it would have to be prepared to lie. If asked if it was the computer, it would need to say "No." If asked about its favorite beer, it would have to be able to name a beer and describe it accurately.

Turing predicted that by the year 2000 computer technology would be sufficiently advanced for some machines to pass this test. His prediction turned out to be overly optimistic. Today, even our best computers still cannot fool a human interrogator for more than a few questions, but that is partly because there are so many topics that one might bring up. So let's make it a bit easier and limit the parameters to knowledge of beer. Could a machine be a true beer connoisseur? Let's put it to the Turing Test.

Suppose that we hire three judges for the "Silicon Valley Beer Competition." Two are human, while the third is the Brewmaster5000 – a computerized beer tester. Each does their tasting (or data analysis) behind closed doors, and at the end of the day a print-out of their favorites is fed through a slot in the door. Brewers can then interrogate the judges (still behind closed doors) about their choices by typing their questions into a computer interface. Could the Brewmaster5000 fool the brewers into thinking that it is one of the two human judges? Moreover, might the Brewmaster5000 turn out to be the best and most reliable judge? And, perhaps most importantly, if it passes the Turing Test *and* is selected as the most competent judge of beer, would that be sufficient for saying that it truly knows what good beer is all about?

At present we are incapable of creating an adequate computerized beer judge. But the technology may not be that far off. We already know much about the relevant chemistry of taste that would be needed to make transducers that could do the job of human olfactory receptors. Optical sensors could be used to take in the appearance of the beer, and a program could even be written to run simulations of the mouth-feel. Thus we might imagine someday we will have a machine that, when a beer is poured into its "tasting tank," would be able to do a full chemical analysis of the look, aroma, feel, and taste of the beer – discriminating the types and amounts of hops and barley, the strain of yeast, the presence of other ingredients, etc., and produce a "desirability quotient." It would then convert the results into subjective language. Thus, its report might read:

> This beer poured clear, bright, and golden with a very slight swirl of yeast. It had a huge coriander and orange nose – very "Belgian-gone-Californian" – and a wit-yeast aroma that added depth, earthiness, and spice. There was a lingering bitterness and a light warming effect. It had a soft, low to medium body, and a deceptively drinkable mouth-feel. In short, I loved it, and can't wait to have another pint!

Once we get the technology right, it doesn't seem outlandish to suppose that the Brewmaster5000 might pass the Turing Beer Test. That is, there seem to be no problems *in principle* – it is just a matter of overcoming the technical issues. And given such a machine's potential for discriminating small differences in brews through chemical analysis, it would not be altogether surprising if it turned out to be the most reliable judge of great beer. But even if the world's best beer judges were to all concede that the Brewmaster5000 was the most competent judge on the planet, should we go on to conclude that it really "knows" beer? UC Berkeley philosopher John Searle would certainly deny it. For decades he has argued that passing the Turing Test has nothing to do with "knowing" anything. What computers lack, according to Searle, is conscious awareness. And without awareness, the Brewmaster5000 cannot be said to have any idea what beer is, much less know what it tastes like. Searle contends that, as conscious beings, people understand the *meaning* of words and symbols. Computers, on the other hand, merely manipulate them. Searle writes:

> For example, on my pocket calculator if I print "3 × 3 = " the calculator will print "9" but it has no idea that "3" means 3 or that "9" means 9 or that anything means anything. We might put this point by saying that the computer has a *syntax* [grammar] but no *semantics* [meaning].

Almost everyone agrees that pocket calculators aren't conscious and that they don't *know* what information they are presenting on their LCD screens – much less what that information *means*. But Searle's point is that all digital computers work in essentially the same manner – regardless of the complexity of their programming or the expanse of their database. So the Brewmaster5000 may print out a description that says that the beer in question is golden, has a nice head, or an aroma of orange, but this does not entail that it knows what oranges are *or* how they taste. And, it certainly has never experienced the taste of beer. The Brewmaster5000 is a fraud (or at least its designers are if they claim that it *knows* beer). We could say that it *simulates* the taste reactions of normal humans, but this is no more "tasting beer" than a program that simulates hurricanes for the weather service is itself a hurricane!

Searle's opponents contend that he is being unfair to the computer. Why should we say that the Brewmaster5000 doesn't know how oranges taste, or what Irish stout is, or what constitutes a good head? If it can identify a hint of orange with better regularity than most of the rest of us, or can pick out an Irish stout from a line-up of various beers, what's left to know? And if four out of five human beer drinkers can't discern the taste of hops from malted barley, then perhaps it is *they* who don't really know beer.

What do you think?

- Does the Brewmaster5000 really know beer?
- Is the relevant difference between a computer and the human brain solely a matter of complexity?
- If a computer could pass the Turing Test, would you say it is "intelligent?" Why or why not?
- Do you think that computers will ever become "persons" and deserve civil rights?

Did you know?

- Turing's original *Imitation Game* involved determining the gender of two players, A and B. Player A would be a man who tries to trick the interrogator, and player B would be a woman, who answers the questions honestly. Turing then asked, "What will happen when a machine takes part of A [the man] in this game? Will the interrogator decide wrongly as often when the game is played like this as he does when the game is played between a man and a woman? These questions replace our original, 'Can machines think?'"
- Computer programs are subjected to the Turing Test in the annual competition for the Loebner Prize. No program has yet been able to come anywhere close to maintaining a respectable conversation for even a few minutes. Programmers typically don't expect their programs to pass the Turing Test. Instead, they generally aim for the lesser prize of "best entry of the year."

- John Searle does not maintain that it is impossible for "machines" to be conscious. He admits that the human brain is a kind of "biological machine" and it produces consciousness. He simply believes that digital computers are the wrong sort of machine, and that folks in the artificial intelligence community mistakenly disregard the importance of our biology in the production of consciousness.
- Like computers, beer contains silicon. While this may sound disturbing, it is actually good for you. Studies have shown that a high silicon diet helps produce stronger bones and prevent osteoporosis. Dr Jonathan Powell of King's College London estimates that beer may offer the greatest amount of silicon in all foods. Beer's silicon contribution is estimated at 17 percent, while bananas follow at 9.1 percent, and bread and cold cereals offer about 4.5 percent.

Recommended reading

- A.M. Turing, "Computing Machinery and Intelligence," in Alan Ross Anderson, ed., *Minds and Machines* (Englewood Cliffs, NJ: Prentice-Hall, 1964).
- John Searle, "Can Computers Think?" in his *Minds Brains and Science* (Cambridge, MA: Harvard University Press, 1984).

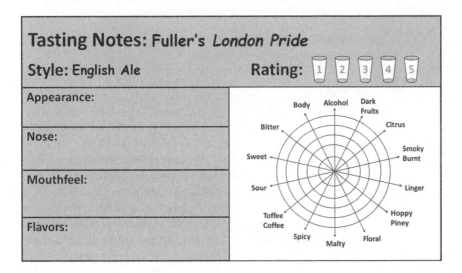

39

Singer's Pond

What do we owe to others? Should we buy them a round?

Pint of the Puzzle: Yuengling *Traditional Lager*

This puzzle deals with economic inequality. While some people on the planet have more money than they know what to do with, others don't have enough to drink. So in consideration of those less fortunate, go for the "happy hour special" and order the cheapest beer you can get. Then you can donate the cash you save to the needy. If you're lucky, you might score a pint of Yuengling Traditional Lager, a relatively inexpensive but high quality American brew. If you're unlucky, you might end up with something that is, God forbid, "light."

We've all come across it. You're walking down the street and someone hits you up for some change, or even a couple of bucks. They say they're hungry, and they probably are, but you tell yourself that they're just going to get a drink with it, and perhaps they will. Nevertheless, if you were on the way to the pub yourself, you might start to wonder about whether it is really fair that you get a beer tonight and they don't. You might also start to wonder whether, in general, we owe anything to other people who are less fortunate than ourselves. Of course, it is a complicated matter. You've worked hard for your

---

Philosophy on Tap: Pint-Sized Puzzles for the Pub Philosopher, First Edition. Matt Lawrence
© 2011 Matt Lawrence. Published 2011 by Blackwell Publishing Ltd.

money – you've sacrificed for it. Maybe the beggar was unwilling to make such sacrifices, or perhaps he is lazy or irresponsible. But certainly this doesn't hold for everyone. To take an easy case, what about the children? Do we owe anything to those starving children whose only mistake is to be born into a famine stricken country? Most people don't give much, if any, of their earnings to the organizations that try to feed and care for these children. The prevailing attitude seems to be that such giving is optional. You don't *have to* give to charities in order to be a morally decent person. While it is praiseworthy to give to such causes, it is generally regarded as going above and beyond your basic moral duties.

Peter Singer, a contemporary Australian philosopher, has tried to challenge the prevailing view about what we owe to others. He asks us to imagine the following sort of case. Suppose that you are on your way to meet some friends at the pub. While walking to your destination, you notice that the recent rains have created a shallow pond in the vacant lot nearby. As you take a closer look, you see a very young child has fallen into this pond, and he appears to be drowning. How do you respond?

Let's consider your options:

1. *Run in and save the child.*
    By taking this course of action you will put yourself in no real danger (as it is a very shallow pond), and it is fairly certain that you will save the child's life. However, your clothes will get extremely muddy, and you'll be late to the pub.
2. *Go find someone else to save the child.*
    The advantage to this strategy is that you can keep your clothes clean. The disadvantage is that the child will most likely die.
3. *Ignore the problem.*
    This way, you'll be sure to make it to the pub on time. However, the child will almost surely die.

Singer supposes that if you are a minimally decent human being, you would undoubtedly choose to run in and save the child. After all, getting your clothes muddy and showing up late to the pub are pretty insignificant compared to the child's life. Singer thinks that we can understand this attitude in terms of a basic moral principle that most people accept:

Basic Moral Principle:
If it is in our power to prevent something bad from happening, without thereby sacrificing anything of comparable moral importance, we ought, morally, to do it.

But the problem, Singer thinks, is that most people are pretty inconsistent when it comes to putting this principle into practice. Sure, most of us would run in and save the child. And sure, most of us do so in part because we believe that we *ought* to prevent very bad things from happening when it would involve only a small sacrifice from us. But we tend to fail miserably when it comes to applying this standard to the problem of world hunger. UNICEF reports that approximately 90 million children worldwide are severely food-deprived. All these children suffer greatly, and many will die of malnutrition and starvation. And what are we doing about it? Not nearly enough, according to Singer. Anytime we spend our money on luxury items such as video games, designer clothes, craft beers, etc., we are acting as if these things are more important than a starving child's life. But surely these are trivial in comparison. Thus Singer argues that those who spend their money on such things are really no different from the person who ignores the drowning child because he doesn't want to get his clothes muddy.

Of course we don't think about our choices in these terms, but nevertheless we know full well that these starving children exist, and that if we all made just a few small sacrifices (rather than spoil ourselves with unnecessary luxuries) we could save a great many of these dying children. Are we making a fundamental moral mistake by living as we do? And if so, do we have a moral obligation to drink only the bargain beer tonight – or to drink water instead?

Truth be told

Singer's original thought experiment involving the drowning child made no reference to a pub. But I, for one, refuse to take seriously any thought experiment in which I am walking by a shallow pond for no apparent reason.

What do you think?

- If moderately wealthy people never give to charity, are they really no better than the person who would ignore the drowning child? And, if there is a significant difference, what is it?
- What if there was not just one, but 1,000 drowning children. Would that increase or decrease your obligation to help – or is it irrelevant?

- Why do you suppose that so many people seem to feel no strong moral obligation to make sacrifices to end world hunger?
- How much should one be willing to sacrifice for those who are less fortunate?

Did you know?

- Peter Singer currently teaches at Princeton University and the University of Melbourne. His appointment at Princeton prompted a number of protests because of his controversial moral views – especially his belief that euthanasia is sometimes justified for severely disabled newborn babies.
- In 1970 the United Nations General Assembly set a target of 0.7 percent of GNP (gross national product) for wealthy nations to contribute to development assistance for impoverished countries. Over the past 35 years, all rich nations have consistently failed to reach their agreed obligations, with contributions averaging between 0.2 and 0.4 percent. The United States has generally been among the smallest contributors by this standard.
- Yuengling is the oldest brewery in the United States. It was founded in Pottsville Pennsylvania in 1829.
- In 2000, students at Oberlin College conducted "The Cheap Beer Challenge" in order to determine the best cheap beer. Their top five picks were: (1) Schaefer, (2) Genny Cream Ale, (3) Miller High Life, (4) Black Label, (5) Pabst Blue Ribbon

Recommended reading

- Peter Singer, "Famine, Affluence and Morality," *Philosophy and Public Affairs*, 1 (1972).
- Biologist Garrett Hardin offers a sharply contrasting view of how we ought to think about famine relief in "Lifeboat Ethics: The Case Against Helping the Poor," *Psychology Today*, 8 (1974): 38–43.

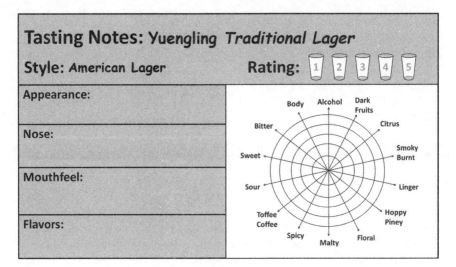

Tasting Notes: Yuengling *Traditional Lager*

Style: American Lager

Rating: 1 2 3 4 5

Appearance:

Nose:

Mouthfeel:

Flavors:

Body   Alcohol   Dark Fruits

Bitter   Citrus

Sweet   Smoky Burnt

Sour   Linger

Toffee Coffee   Hoppy Piney

Spicy   Malty   Floral

40

The Wisest One of All

Can ignorance be wisdom?

Pint of the Puzzle: Elysian *The Wise ESB*

Each sip of Elysian Brewing's The Wise ESB (Extra Special Bitter) reminds us that wisdom can be bitter-sweet. Take, for instance, the life of Socrates. Although Socrates was arguably the wisest man of his day, he was nevertheless executed for his "corrupting influence" (or perhaps we should say, his "bitter truths"). So let us raise our glasses to the Grandfather of Western philosophy. May he find peace, truth, and good conversation amidst the *Elysian Fields*.

In Ancient Greece, at the Temple of Apollo, there was a dark cavern that emitted noxious fumes from its depths. At the entrance of this cavern sat the Oracle of Delphi. The Oracle was famous throughout the Greek world for her cryptic, yet seemingly unerring, prophecies. People would come from miles around to ask her questions. When Socrates' friend Chaerephon paid her a visit, he had a specific question in mind. "Is there anyone wiser than Socrates?" he asked. Her astounding reply was that "No man is wiser."

When Socrates (*c.* 470–399 BCE) heard the news, he was flabbergasted. He couldn't believe that there was no one wiser than himself, because he himself knew so very little. Whenever Socrates considered the big questions

Philosophy on Tap: Pint-Sized Puzzles for the Pub Philosopher, First Edition. Matt Lawrence
© 2011 Matt Lawrence. Published 2011 by Blackwell Publishing Ltd.

of life (What is truth? What is justice? What is courage? etc.) he could never come up with an answer that was completely satisfying. So Socrates concluded that the Oracle must have been mistaken. From then on, he made it his life's mission to find a person who was wiser than himself.

Socrates asked these "big questions" of everyone he met – especially of the most prominent citizens of Athens and the traveling teachers or "sophists," who often claimed to know such things. But every time, these conversations took a similar course. Socrates would ask his question – for example, "What is justice?" – and his interlocutor would rather pompously claim to have all the answers. He might say: "Justice is benefiting your friends and harming your enemies," or, "It is speaking the truth and paying your debts." But with additional questioning, Socrates would always find flaws in their answers. For example, to the latter definition, Socrates replied:

> Take this matter of doing right: can we say that it really consists in nothing more or less than telling the truth and paying back anything we have received? Are not these very actions sometimes right and sometimes wrong? Suppose, for example, a friend who had lent us a weapon were to go mad and then ask for it back, surely anyone would say that we ought not to return it. It would not be "right" to do so; nor yet to tell the truth without reserve to a madman.

Through questions and counter-examples such as these, Socrates would always manage to show that the definition that had been offered was at odds with what both parties believed to be true.

As you might imagine, Socrates created a number of enemies through this kind of questioning. People do not like to be proven wrong – especially the pompous know-it-alls. And, of course, they hate it all the more when they are shown the bitter truth of their ignorance in front of a large crowd (and Socrates' discussions would often draw a crowd). Eventually, Socrates' questioning annoyed enough powerful people that he was put on trial for corrupting the youth.

At his trial Socrates told the jury that he had finally come to appreciate the Oracle's prophecy. Maybe she had been right all along and he *was* the wisest person around. For while others mistakenly took themselves to know things about which they were ignorant, at least he *knew* that he did not know – putting him "one-up" over the rest.

What do you think?

- Might the wisest people among us be those who simply realize that they know very little?
- Do most people take themselves to know much more than they really do? If so, why?

- Do you believe that the Oracle at Delphi had supernatural (or highly unusual) powers?
- How would you define justice?

Did you know?

- Socrates was ultimately convicted and sentenced to death. And although he had ample opportunity to escape, he chose to accept his sentence and drink poison hemlock. If you are into bitter drinks (but don't have a death-wish) you might also try *Hemlock Bitter,* from Nottingham's Castle Rock Brewery.
- Plato was Socrates' student, and he had his own take on wisdom. He is noted for saying: "He is a wise man who invented beer."
- The Delphic Oracle or "Pythia" was a position, rather than a particular person. The position was held by a number of women during a period that spanned more than 1,000 years.
- The Elysian Fields were a section of the underworld that was reserved for heroes and the virtuous. It is also the inspiration behind the naming of the Elysian Brewing Company of Seattle.

Recommended reading

- Plato, *Apology*. Available online through Project Gutenberg: http://www.gutenberg.org/etext/1656.
- Plato, *The Republic*. Available online through Project Gutenberg: http://www.gutenberg.org/etext/1497.

Tasting Notes: Elysian *The Wise ESB*

Style: Extra Special Bitter   **Rating:** 1 2 3 4 5

Appearance:	
Nose:	
Mouthfeel:	
Flavors:	

Body   Alcohol   Dark Fruits
Bitter   Citrus
Sweet   Smoky Burnt
Sour   Linger
Toffee Coffee   Hoppy Piney
Spicy   Malty   Floral

41

Enter the Matrix

Is your pilsner merely electrical signals in your brain?

Pint of the Puzzle: Moonlight Brewing
Reality Czeck Pilsner

Appearances can be deceiving. So every now and then it is a good idea to "question reality." And what better way to do it than with a Reality Czeck pilsner from the Moonlight Brewing Company. Can real Czech pilsner be brewed in California? I'll let you be the judge of that. Unfortunately Reality Czeck is only available in kegs and at select Northern California brewpubs – anybody for a road trip?

What if the entire world was an illusion – a computer generated dream-world? This was the premise of the 1999 film *The Matrix*. Millions of people living out their lives in a "virtual world" – a digital replica of our planet and culture as it was at the end of the twentieth century. For all intents and purposes, these peoples' lives were just like ours. They went to work, paid their taxes, fell in love, and swapped stories at the pub. But, in reality, they were encased in slime filled cocoons with electrodes plugged into their brains.

Philosophy on Tap: Pint-Sized Puzzles for the Pub Philosopher, First Edition. Matt Lawrence
© 2011 Matt Lawrence. Published 2011 by Blackwell Publishing Ltd.

The basic idea behind *The Matrix* was that all of a person's experiences can be generated by artificially stimulating their brain. As Morpheus puts it: "What is real? How do you define real? If real is what you can feel, smell, taste and see, then real is simply electrical signals interpreted by your brain."

Typically, these electrical signals are the product of sensory stimulation; your eyes see the golden effervescent pint of Reality Czeck sitting on the bar, you smell the tantalizing aroma of a fresh baguette, your tongue feels the tingling bubbles and tastes the sweet biscuity malts and Saaz hops. But there is no reason why the same experience couldn't be achieved by stimulating the brain directly. And with the sophisticated computer technology of the future, we might be able to create a whole virtual world in which millions of people could live out their lives.

Such a "matrix" or "simulation" could be crude, and look no more real than the video games of today, or it could be quite sophisticated – perhaps so much so that it is literally indistinguishable from the natural world. To come up with such a "perfect simulation" would be quite a programming achievement, but it is within the realm of possibility. So consider this. Might you be in a matrix at this very moment? You probably don't take such a prospect very seriously, since we don't currently have the technology to create a convincing matrix. But this is to assume that you are living in the early twenty-first-century. Perhaps you are not. Perhaps the year is really 2199 and you are plugged into a simulation of early twenty-first-century-Earth.

If high-quality matrices are possible, then there is really no way to be sure that you are not in a matrix right now. But even those who admit this point of logic don't tend to find it very disconcerting. For even if we could be in a matrix, they think that the odds of it are close to zero. Oxford philosopher and futurist Nick Bostrom disagrees. He has argued that the odds of being in a matrix are actually quite high. As he sees it, there are three basic possibilities:

> The first possibility is that the human species will almost certainly go extinct before becoming technologically mature. The second possibility is that almost no technologically mature civilization is interested in building matrices. The third possibility is that we are almost certainly living in a Matrix.

Bostrom concedes that it is difficult to predict whether the human species will thrive long enough to reach technological maturity. There are so many variables (nuclear war, disease, environmental catastrophe, etc.) to consider. But should humanity make it to technological maturity (the point at which they could create an unlimited number of high-quality simulations), it seems rather likely that they *would* do so. There are numerous motives for making matrices. Historians might build them to recreate the past, or to explore counterfactual historical scenarios – e.g., what would be the course of human history if there had never been hops or barley? Artists might create aesthetically interesting matrices for people to live in, or to observe from the outside. Think of the possibilities for psychology, anthropology, evolutionary biology, and (especially) tourism.

So Bostrom supposes that if we don't go extinct, and we continue to have reasons to build matrices, advanced societies will likely build thousands – perhaps millions of them – each with billions of people inhabiting them. Under these conditions, he believes that *we are almost certainly in a matrix* simply because most of the lives ever lived will have been lived inside matrices. The vast majority of the people inside these matrices, of course, would not be biologically human. They would be sentient programs – artificially intelligent, entirely digital people. That would be the only way to populate so many worlds. So consider this: not only could that be a simulated beer you are holding, you could be a simulated human!

Since we don't know if any society will ever reach technological maturity or if such a society would want to build matrices, we cannot conclude that we are almost certainly in a matrix. Nevertheless, Bostrom thinks that the odds are still pretty good. Personally, he believes that there is about a 20 percent chance that we are living in a matrix.

If we are in a matrix, at least we can be grateful that the programmers made a pretty good simulation of beer. But then again, can we even be sure about that? As the character "Mouse" puts it in *The Matrix*:

> Maybe they got it wrong. Maybe what I think beer tastes like actually tastes like oatmeal, or tuna fish. It makes you wonder about a lot of things. Take chicken for example. Maybe they couldn't figure out what to make chicken taste like – which is why chicken tastes like everything.

As you can see, once you let the possibility of a matrix into your consciousness, questions and doubts tend to multiply like "splinters in your mind."

Truth be told

The quote from Mouse actually referenced a cereal called "Tastee Wheat" rather than beer. The argument, of course, pertains equally well to beer.

What do you think?

- Is it possible that you could be in a matrix at this very moment?
- Is Bostrom right to think that if a society were to reach technological maturity and have an interest in building matrices then we are almost certainly living in a matrix?
- If you were to find out that we are living in a matrix, would that make your life less meaningful?
- What if a future society made our simulated world because there was no beer (or ingredients to make beer) left in the natural world. Would you want to "wake up" to that reality, or would you prefer to stay in this hoppy dreamworld?

Did you know?

- Plato's "Allegory of the Cave" in *The Republic* describes the world's first matrix, *c.* 350 BCE. In this tale, prisoners are tricked into thinking there is no other reality than the shadows cast upon the cave wall.
- While Bostrom suggests that most of the inhabitants of matrices would be programs, not all of them would need to be "conscious." As a labor-saving device, many might be "zombies" in the sense that they *act like* they think and feel things, but in actuality they have no conscious "inner life." (For more about Zombies, see chapter 45, "Fear of Zombies.")
- Moonlight Brewing is housed in the Abbey de St. Humulus in Santa Rosa, California. It may be the first and only abbey brewery in the US, though it doesn't actually brew any of the European abbey styles and is in no way affiliated with the Trappist monasteries.
- If you can't get your hands on a bottle of Reality Czeck, let me suggest Pilsner Urquell as an alternate. Pilsner Urquell is the original pilsner, first brewed in 1842, whose style has been simulated by brewers (and matrix architects) ever since.

Recommended reading

- Nick Bostrom, "Why Make a Matrix? And Why You Might Be In One," in William Irwin, ed., *More Matrix and Philosophy: Revolutions and Reloaded Decoded* (Chicago: Open Court, 2005).
- Matt Lawrence, *Like a Splinter in Your Mind: The Philosophy Behind the Matrix Trilogy* (Oxford: Blackwell 2004).

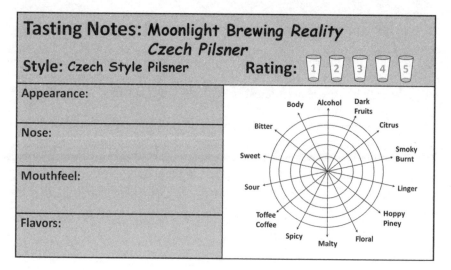

Tasting Notes: Moonlight Brewing *Reality Czech Pilsner*

Style: Czech Style Pilsner   **Rating:** 1 2 3 4 5

Appearance:

Nose:

Mouthfeel:

Flavors:

A Case of Bad Faith

Are you responsible for everything you do?

As most people tell it, they rarely get to do what they want to do. Instead, the bulk of their time is spent on the things that they *have to do*. They *have to* go to school, or they *have to* go to work, and then they *have to* kiss up to their idiot boss, and so on. You're probably no different. How many times today have you either said, or thought to yourself, that you *have to* do this or you *have to* do that?

If you stop and think about it, aren't you lying to yourself? Do you really *have to* go to work? People call in sick every day. People quit their jobs every day. You don't *have to* go in. Now, sure, if you don't go to work then you won't get paid. But you don't *have to* get paid – and for that matter, you don't

Philosophy on Tap: Pint-Sized Puzzles for the Pub Philosopher, First Edition. Matt Lawrence
© 2011 Matt Lawrence. Published 2011 by Blackwell Publishing Ltd.

have to make your car payment. People skip out on their payments all the time. The point here is that going to work isn't something that you *have to* do. Rather, it is a choice. There are millions of things that you could have done with your day. You just happen to *choose* going to work. So again, I ask, what do you really *have to* do? "Eat," you say? Do you really *have to* eat? Gandhi didn't eat; Caesar Chavez didn't eat. Both men went weeks without eating. They realized that eating was a choice. So is there anything at all that you really *have to* do? According to the French existentialist philosopher Jean-Paul Sartre (1905–1980), there is only one thing that you truly *have to* do, and that is to make choices. As Sartre rather famously said, "man is condemned to be free."

To put it this way makes freedom sound like a bad thing – like you are a prisoner sitting on death row. This is quite intentional. In certain respects you *are* like the prisoner. For example:

1. *You didn't choose your freedom.*
   You didn't ask for it, you were just born with it.
2. *You cannot escape from your freedom.*
   Try as you might, you cannot avoid making choices.
3. *You really wish you could.*
   Most people seem to want nothing more than to escape their freedom.

The most interesting point is the third. It goes against the common conception. Ask anyone and they'll tell you that they love freedom. They'll readily claim that freedom is one of the most important things in life. But Sartre believed that our actions indicate otherwise. As we've already seen, we lie to ourselves constantly about our freedom. We try to convince ourselves, and anyone who'll listen, that we *have to* do the things that we do, despite knowing deep down that we *choose* them.

Sartre calls this phenomenon of lying to oneself "bad faith." And most peoples' favorite lie is that they are not free. So why do we do it? It all comes down to responsibility. Think about it. If you don't *have to* go to your lousy job and kiss up to your moronic boss, and in fact, there were millions of better things to do, then whose fault is it that this is how you spent your day? Suddenly you're forced to realize that it is not simply your job that sucks. Rather, you suck. You make lousy choices. So long as you have options (and Sartre contends that you *always* have options) then there is no one but yourself to blame. You are "left alone, without excuse."

This is where Sartre's existentialist view of freedom really gets controversial. For he thinks that one *never* has a legitimate excuse for the things one does. This also runs counter to the common view. We tend to think that there are all sorts of excuses, from childhood trauma to manic depression. In fact, the American Psychiatric Association has recently ruled that binge-eating and gambling should be diagnosed as psychological disorders (though it failed to do the same for obesity, internet addiction, or sex addiction, as many psychiatrists had wanted). If someone has a bona fide disorder, we generally cut them some slack. We don't blame them so much as we blame their "condition." But consider the binge-eater, for example. I once read about a man who said that he became obese on purpose. He said, "Of course it was on purpose. I never put anything into my mouth on accident." Sartre would agree wholeheartedly with his analysis. The binge-eater doesn't *have to* eat, just as the alcoholic doesn't *have to* drink, and the gambler doesn't *have to* gamble. One always has options (e.g., put the cookie down), and thus there is no one and nothing to blame but oneself. So if you feel *compelled* to pour another Pissenlit Saison, just realize that you are making a choice – and quite a tasty one at that!

Truth be told

Earlier I implied that if you wet the bed after too many Pissenlit Saisons, you've got "no excuse" from Sartre's point of view. This statement requires some qualification. Sartre maintains that you are responsible for your decisions and actions (as well as your emotions). But wetting the bed isn't really an action. It is not something that you *do*; rather it is something that *happens* to you. The person with a bladder dysfunction is therefore not responsible for their incontinence. By the same token, neither is the young child who wets the bed. In contrast, the over-indulging Saison drinkers are at least responsible for putting themselves in a situation where wetting the bed becomes more likely. And for this reason, I believe that Sartre would agree that they are "left alone without excuse."

What do you think?

- Is Sartre correct to maintain that we never have an excuse for the decisions we make?
- Do you live your life in bad faith? Under what sorts of circumstances do you most often lie to yourself?
- Why do people so often live in bad faith? Does it always come down to an attempt to shirk the responsibility for our actions?

Did you know?

- It is always better to have a case of Belgian Saison than a case of bad faith.
- The opposite of bad faith is what Sartre calls "authenticity." To live authentically is to be honest and true to yourself. It is to live in full awareness of your freedom and responsibility.
- Sartre's long-time friend and lover Simone de Beauvoir used existentialist ideas to analyze gender and the subjugation of women in her book *The Second Sex*.
- Jean-Paul Sartre served in the French army as a meteorologist. He was eventually captured by the Nazi's and spent nine months as a prisoner of war. This experience had a profound impact on Sartre's later philosophical views.
- Saison ales were traditionally brewed in the autumn or winter for consumption during the late summer harvest for farm workers who were typically entitled to five liters during the workday. Today, many Saisons are brewed with rather high alcohol content (Pissenlit Saison is 8 percent abv), but originally they were generally less than 3 percent abv, in order to refresh a thirsty workforce.

Recommended reading

- Jean Paul Sartre, *Existentialism and Human Emotions* (New York: Citadel, 2000).
- Jean Paul Sartre, *Being and Nothingness* (London, Routledge Classics, 2003).

Tasting Notes: Fantôme *Pissenlit Saison*

Style: Saison with Dandelion   **Rating:** 1 2 3 4 5

Appearance:	
Nose:	
Mouthfeel:	
Flavors:	

(Tasting wheel with axes: Body, Alcohol, Dark Fruits, Citrus, Smoky Burnt, Linger, Hoppy, Piney, Floral, Malty, Spicy, Coffee, Toffee, Sour, Sweet, Bitter)

43

Cask and Cleaver

Are you a speciesist?

Pint of the Puzzle: Laughing Dog
Alpha Dog Imperial IPA

Is there anything wrong with grabbing a burger to go with that ale? Most people think nothing of it. After all, isn't that one of the perks of sitting at the top of the food chain? Aren't we the "Alpha Dogs" in this dog-eat-dog world? Well, at least enjoy an Alpha Dog Imperial IPA from the Laughing Dog Brewing Company while Peter Singer tries to knock you off your high horse.

This puzzle pertains to our treatment of animals in general, and meat-eating in particular. Surely there is no easier way to make enemies than to question a person's God-given right to a juicy steak. So let's start by discussing something that we are more likely to agree about – like the moral wrongness of racism. Let's define racism as follows:

Racism: A prejudice or attitude of bias toward the interests of members of one's own race and against the interests of members of other races.

Philosophy on Tap: Pint-Sized Puzzles for the Pub Philosopher, First Edition. Matt Lawrence
© 2011 Matt Lawrence. Published 2011 by Blackwell Publishing Ltd.

This definition seems to me to capture the essence of racism. The slave owner, for example, valued white people's freedom, happiness, and economic prosperity, but seemed to see little to no value in the black slave's interest in such things. Yet there simply was no legitimate reason to favor the interests of whites over blacks. To do so was sheer prejudice and bias.

We find a similar situation regarding sexism:

Sexism: A prejudice or attitude of bias toward the interests of members of one's own sex and against the interests of members of the other sex.

To deny women the right to vote, to drive cars, or to have a choice about whom they marry is again to disvalue their interests. Yet these are the exact same interests that men unwaveringly value for themselves.

The Australian philosopher Peter Singer has argued that the moral wrong behind racism and sexism is essentially the same. Both violate a basic moral principle that he calls the *Principle of Equality*. This is the idea that similar interests ought to carry similar weight, and differences in treatment must be justified in terms of relevant differences in the beings themselves. According to Singer, if you find racism and sexism to be morally wrong, it is because you (rightly) care about the Principle of Equality.

Now consider a third parallel phenomenon.

Speciesism: A prejudice or attitude of bias toward the interests of members of one's own species and against those of members of other species.

Singer contends that speciesism is wrong for the exact same reason that racism and sexism are wrong – it violates the Principle of Equality. It is precisely the same sort of phenomenon. Only the target group has changed.

Are you a speciesist? Most people are, and here's why. If you reflect upon your strongest or most important interests and an animal's strongest or most important interests, you will find something like the following:

Top Human Interests	*Top Animal Interests*
Life	Life
Liberty	Liberty
Freedom from pain	Freedom from pain
Family	Family
Friendship	Companionship
Sex	Sex
Accomplishment	Tasty food

This is by no means a complete list or exact ordering. You probably have thousands of interests including things like furthering your education, expanding your philosophical horizons, or discovering a great Imperial IPA. Animals, on the other hand, are generally more limited in terms of the number of interests they have. But notice that their top interests are quite similar to ours. Things like life, liberty, and freedom from suffering are important to them in much the same way that they are to us. So where in your list of interests would "eating juicy steaks" (or burgers, or babyback ribs, etc.) fall? Although enjoyable, I'm guessing that eating meat is not one of your most fundamental interests. So when you order a steak, aren't you acting as if one of your more trivial interests outweighs *all* of the animal's most fundamental interests? And isn't this precisely the same sort of thing that the racists and sexists do?

Opponents of Singer's speciesism argument contend that species matters in a way that one's race and sex do not. Generally it comes down to the fact that animals are far less intelligent, and this, they contend, is a *relevant* reason for treating them differently. But on this point, Singer agrees. Animals should be treated differently (as should humans) when there are relevant differences involved. For example, pigs should not be given the right to vote – but neither should 4-year-old humans or the clinically insane. Intelligence is certainly relevant to some things, like voting rights, access to higher education, and issuing driver's licenses. But is lower intelligence a legitimate reason for discounting another being's suffering? The severely retarded person hates pain in pretty much the same way as the rocket scientist, the cow, and the pig. How smart you are seems to make little difference to the weight that we should give to one's physical pain. As the famous Utilitarian philosopher Jeremy Bentham put it: "The question is not can they talk, or can they reason, but can they suffer?"

Singer admits that the range and number of human interests (due to our advanced intelligence) can give us non-speciesist reasons for regarding human lives as more valuable than animal lives. However, given the loss of freedom and tremendous suffering imposed on animals through modern techniques of animal agriculture and factory farms, he contends that meat eating cannot be justified. Beer and carrot sticks anyone?

What do you think?

- Is speciesism on a moral par with racism and sexism?
- Do you agree with Singer's analysis that the problem with racism and sexism is that they violate the principle of equality? If so, does speciesism do the same?
- If you disagree with Singer's argument, where does he go wrong?
- Does the fact that we are at the top of the food chain give us the right to eat animals?
- If we are justified in eating meat, can we also justify the horrendous suffering that factory farming inflicts upon farm animals?

- If omnivorous aliens far more advanced than us were to land on earth looking for a meal, are there any legitimate reasons why they shouldn't eat us?

Did you know?

- Vegetarians tend to have a lower incidence of heart disease, lower rates of high blood pressure and Type 2 diabetes, less colon cancer, and a longer life expectancy than the general population.
- Peter Singer's specisism argument was the central premise of his book *Animal Liberation*, which sold more than 1.5 million copies and jump-started the modern animal rights movement.
- Almost as heinous as racism and sexism is *lagerism*. Lagerism is a prejudice or attitude of bias in favor of all lager beers and against all ales, stouts, and porters. It is a common attitude – even in some of the most free-thinking nations. So remember, friends don't let friends become lagerists.
- Laughing Dog Brewery hales from Sandpoint Idaho. Their Alpha Dog is a real hop bomb. They use hops from Columbus and Mt. Hood for a piney hop flavor and serious bitterness.

Recommended reading

- Peter Singer, *Animal Liberation: A New Ethics for Our Treatment of Animals* (New York: Avon, 1975).
- Carl Cohen, "Do Animals have Rights?" *Ethics and Behavior* 7, no. 2 (1997).

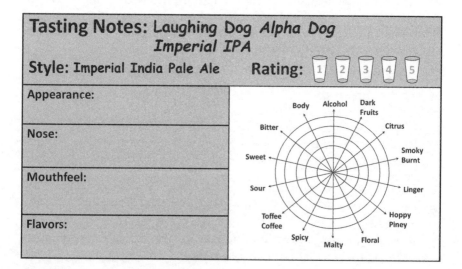

Tasting Notes: Laughing Dog *Alpha Dog Imperial IPA*

Style: Imperial India Pale Ale   **Rating:** 1 2 3 4 5

Appearance:	
Nose:	
Mouthfeel:	
Flavors:	

(Radar chart axes: Body, Alcohol, Dark Fruits, Citrus, Smoky Burnt, Linger, Hoppy Piney, Floral, Malty, Spicy, Toffee Coffee, Sour, Sweet, Bitter)

44

Flirting with Disaster

When does flirtation become harassment?

Pint of the Puzzle: St. Pauli Girl *Lager*

Have you ever caught one of your friends fondling their beer bottle? If so, it was probably a bottle of St. Pauli Girl Lager – the beer most likely to generate "love at first sight." As the slogan goes, "You never forget your first girl." But you have to wonder, was she being valued for her own sake, or merely treated as an object to be used and then discarded?

The label of the St. Pauli Girl brand of beers is arguably one of the most iconic in the beer industry. Its depiction of a beautiful busty blonde barmaid seems to hit the main interests of its intended demographic.

As one internet blogger put it, "Boobs and beer, what more could we want?" Of course the "St. Pauli Girl" is smiling as she carries out those cold lagers – she's only too happy to serve you. But one might surmise by her smile that she is just beginning her shift. In a few hours, it is unlikely that she'd look so happy and fresh – not because carrying large mugs of beer is exhausting (though of course it is), but because she will be the object of endless flirtations and advances by a wide variety of, often unseemly, patrons.

Philosophy on Tap: Pint-Sized Puzzles for the Pub Philosopher, First Edition. Matt Lawrence
© 2011 Matt Lawrence. Published 2011 by Blackwell Publishing Ltd.

Men always have, and always will, flirt with beautiful barmaids, wait-resses, and the like. Sometimes it is perfectly harmless and is enjoyed by both parties. But quite often it is unwelcome or simply goes too far. What may (or may not) be intended as "harmless fun" can quickly turn into sexual harassment. But what exactly constitutes sexual harassment? Where is that invisible line between innocent flirtation, playful banter, and wrongful harassment?

Catherine Mackinnon, a feminist philosopher and lawyer, who argued some of the first sexual harassment cases in the 1970s, offers the following definition of sexual harassment:

> In its broadest definition, it is sexual pressure that you are not in a position to refuse. In its verbal form, it includes a working environment that is saturated with sexual innuendoes, propositions, and advances. Other forms include leering, for example, at a woman's breasts while she talks, or staring up her skirt while she is bending over to get files. In its physical form, it includes unwanted sexual touching.

Consider how this definition might apply to a waitress, whether the mythical St. Pauli Girl, or a real-life waitress at your local pub. Many bars and pubs are certainly saturated with sexual innuendoes, proposi-tions, and advances – a good deal of which are directed at the waitresses. And then there is the leering and staring, etc. One might hope that it rarely moves beyond this to unwanted sexual touching, but on occasion it surely does. The question then becomes whether the waitress is in a position to refuse. Of course she can always walk away, deny service, or (in extreme circumstances) pour a drink in the offender's lap. But such actions may have severe consequences for her job security. So while she can refuse, she may nevertheless feel considerable pressure to put up with it. In that case, she seems to be a victim of what women's studies professor Rosemary Tong describes as *coercive sexual harassment*. This occurs when someone is compelled to do (or put up with) something that she would not normally do, because the coercer has adversely changed her options.

Most instances of coercive sexual harassment at the workplace involve a manager and subordinate, since the manager tends to have the power to most effectively limit the subordinate's options. But at the pub it is often the customer who regularly wields direct financial leverage upon the waitress, since the majority of her wage comes from tips, and her job security often depends significantly upon customer satisfaction.

While the pub patron is well situated to engage in coercive sexual harassment, there is still the matter of distinguishing between innocent flirtations and injurious harassment. Many would argue that Mackinnon's definition includes too much. Social philosopher Ellen Frankel Paul warns against taking the notion of sexual harassment too far:

> Cases have reached the courts based on everything from off-color jokes to unwanted, persistent sexual advances by co-workers. ... Do we really want legislators and judges delving into our most intimate private lives, deciding when a look is a leer, and when a leer is a Civil Rights Act offense?

But there are two aspects to the harassment issue. One is legal, and concerns the limits of legitimate prosecution. The other is moral, and concerns whether or not one has done something wrong (regardless of the legal ramifications of the action). Frankel Paul contends that we need an *objective standard* from which to judge sexually charged behavior. And while her point was made in the context of law, it seems to be relevant to the moral realm as well. She believes that we are on dangerous ground when we allow the alleged victim's *subjective perception* of the act to rule the day. Her recommendation is that the behavior would have to be offensive to the proverbial "reasonable man" of tort law in order to qualify as sexual harassment.

But some feminists have argued that a "reasonable man standard" is part of the problem, not the solution. Women's studies professor Barbara Gutek reports that women and men differ in their perceptions and attitudes regarding sexual harassment. For instance, Gutek's research showed that 84 percent of women, but only 59 percent of men regarded sexual touching at work to be harassment. Other studies suggest that men and women often disagree about what constitutes "friendly" sexual behaviors, and men are more likely to fail to realize that certain behaviors are unwelcome if they believe that the woman is behaving in a sexual manner.

Catherine Mackinnon attacks a similar standard, that of the "average person applying contemporary community standards" in her writings on pornography:

> Feminism doubts whether the average person, gender-neutral exists; has more questions about the content and process of defining what community standards are than it does about deviations from them ... and questions why a body of law that has not in practice been able to tell rape from intercourse should, without further guidance, be entrusted with telling pornography [and we might add harassment] from anything else.

This general line of thinking has led some judges to adopt a "reasonable *woman* standard." For example, in *Ellison v. Brady,* the Ninth Circuit Court of Appeals argued that "a sex-blind reasonable person standard tends to be male-biased and tends to systematically ignore the experiences of women."

Frankel Paul disagrees. She contends that women cannot demand equality when convenient, and then expect special dispensations when the going gets tough. "Equality has its price," she argues, "and that price may include unwelcome sexual advances, irritating and even intimidating sexual jests from lewd and obnoxious drunken idiots." And this is the critical issue. Is a "reasonable woman standard" a special dispensation for women? The Ninth Circuit Court of Appeals argued that it is not:

> The reasonable woman standard does not establish a higher level of protection for women than men …. Instead, a gender-conscious examination of sexual harassment enables women to participate in the workplace on an equal footing with men.

So the next time you come across the St. Pauli Girl and are ready to unload your brilliant come-on, try to appreciate the complexity of this issue. Don't just *assume* that your flirtatious advances are as charming as you think.

Truth be told

The last quotation from Ellen Frankel Paul originally referred to "obnoxious colleagues" rather than "obnoxious drunken idiots."

What do you think?

- Where do you draw the line between flirtation and harassment? Do you find Mackinnon's definition satisfactory?
- Should we judge harassment from a gender-neutral standpoint, or from a "reasonable woman" standpoint?
- Since pub patrons have financial power over the waitress, should their actions be held to a standard similar to that of workplace managers? Why or why not?

Did you know?

- While there have been numerous cases of workplace sexual harassment in the courts, the vast majority deal with issues involving managers and subordinates or between co-workers. While some cases exist, it has been much more difficult to successfully prosecute customers on charges of sexual harassment.

- Camille Paglia, a self-described "dissident feminist" and author of *Sexual Personae: Art and Decadence from Nefertiti to Emily Dickenson*, is critical of feminist outlooks like Mackinnon's. She contends that we need "a new kind of feminism, one that stresses personal responsibility and is open to art and sex in all their dark, unconsoling mysteries." She maintains that "the sizzle of sex comes from the danger of sex. You can be overpowered."
- St. Pauli Girl updated their label in 2006. On the new label the St. Pauli Girl lets her hair down after years of keeping it in a bun. This is not as big a change as the prior revision in which she seems to have undergone breast augmentation surgery. In 1999 St. Pauli Brauerei began using *Playboy* magazine playmates to represent the St. Pauli girl in magazine ads, television commercials, and live appearances.
- There seems to be an underlying message that the St. Pauli Girl may be more than a just a waitress. While the St. Pauli Brauerei was built upon St. Paul's Monastery, the name choice also seems to allude to Hamburg's famous St. Pauli red light district.

Recommended reading

- Catherine Mackinnon, *Sexual Harassment of Working Women: A Case of Sex Discrimination* (New Haven CT: Yale University Press, 1979).
- Ellen Frankel Paul, "Bare Buttocks and Federal Cases," in James Sterba, ed., *Morality in Practice*, 7th edn. (Belmont, CA: Thomson Wadsworth, 2004).

Tasting Notes: St. Pauli Girl *Lager*

Style: German Lager   **Rating:** 1 2 3 4 5

Appearance:	
Nose:	
Mouthfeel:	
Flavors:	

Body Alcohol Dark Fruits
Bitter   Citrus
Sweet   Smoky Burnt
Sour   Linger
Toffee   Hoppy
Coffee   Piney
Spicy Malty Floral

45

Fear of Zombies

Are you tasting what I'm tasting? Are you tasting anything at all?

Pint of the Puzzle: Alesmith *Old Numbskull Barleywine*

This puzzle invokes the notion of a zombie, not in the Hollywood sense of the flesh-eating undead, but in the philosophical sense of a person who has no phenomenal experience – no "inner life." The philosophical zombie is a "numb skull" in the most literal sense. So grab a pint of Old Numbskull West Coast-style barleywine from Alesmith Brewing. It won't turn you into a zombie, but it will certainly take the "edge" off your phenomenal experience.

If you think about it, you really have no direct evidence of anyone's conscious experience but your own. Your friends *act* as if they have conscious experiences similar to yours, but can you really be sure? For example, you and a friend each hold up your glasses of Old Numbskull and comment on its beautiful amber hue. Does this mean that you are experiencing the same sensation of color? Isn't it quite possible that while you see amber, your friend sees a shade of green? He only calls it "amber" because that is what he has been taught. "Amber," he's been told, is the color of honey, of beer, and of fossilized tree resin. Yet, if you could pull a Freaky Friday and get inside his

Philosophy on Tap: Pint-Sized Puzzles for the Pub Philosopher, First Edition. Matt Lawrence
© 2011 Matt Lawrence. Published 2011 by Blackwell Publishing Ltd.

head, it would become quite evident that the color he sees for all of these objects is green. And if you then go out and check the color of the front lawn, sure enough, it is brilliant shade of amber when seen through his eyes.

This sort of case is called an *inverted spectrum*. Since there is no way of getting inside your friend's mind, there is no way of being sure that his visual spectrum is not inverted. And, more disturbingly, it may well be *you* who has the inverted spectrum. What you call "amber" everyone else might call green (if they could see it as you do). The same point holds for flavor. You both may comment on the toffee flavors in your pints of Old Numbskull, but "toffee" to him might well taste like "licorice," for example, to you. (And licorice to you may taste the way toffee tastes to him.)

Generally we think that such inversion cases are highly unlikely. Science has shown us that all human beings have very similar biology, and it is our biology that accounts for our sensations of color, taste, and so on. And since your eyes, nervous system, and brain are doing very similar things to what your friend's eyes, nervous system, and brain are doing when you each observe your beer, we conclude that you must both be experiencing pretty much the same thing. But what we must remember is that while scientists can observe and measure the states of your body, they have no access to your phenomenal experience. While you can report that you are having sensations of "amber hues," scientists can't know if the way that "amber" seems to you is how it seems to the rest of us (or to any of us). The only access to conscious states that anyone has ever had is their own. So when we assume that others are experiencing things roughly as we do, we are generalizing to all of humanity based upon just one case – our own!

If you really have no evidence about *what* your friend is feeling, then how do you know your friend is actually feeling anything at all? Of course he tells you that he's worried about finding a job, or is excited about tonight's game. But this is just external behavior. How do you know that this behavior is accompanied by inner experience? That is, how do you know that your friend is not a *zombie* – someone who has no phenomenal experience whatsoever? A zombie in this philosophical sense is just like you or me, except without the experience of sensations, thoughts, desires, moods, or feelings. David Chalmers, a contemporary philosopher of mind, describes the notion of a zombie by positing his own "zombie twin":

> What is going on in my zombie twin? ... He will certainly be identical to me *functionally*: he will be processing the same sort of information, reacting in a similar way to inputs, with his internal configurations being modified appropriately and with indistinguishable behavior resulting. ... He will even be "conscious" in the functional senses described earlier – he will be awake, able to report the contents of his internal states, able to focus attention in various places, and so on. It is just that none of this functioning will be accompanied by

any real conscious experience. There will be no phenomenal feel. There is nothing it is like to be a zombie.

The basic concept here is not so outlandish. Many people have wondered how far down the evolutionary scale conscious experience extends. For example, do cockroaches have an "inner life"? What about snails, or amoebas? Perhaps cockroaches have only a kind of "functional psychology" that enables them to seek food, avoid danger, mate, and so on, without the need for conscious experiences. If this is the case, then cockroaches would be zombies of a rather primitive sort. If your friend is a zombie, he's certainly a more sophisticated one. He does more than merely seek out beer; he can observe and discuss its beautiful amber hue, or its delicious toffee flavors. But if he's a zombie, then he doesn't have a sensation of "amber" or the twinge of "awe" that accompanies such a beautiful sight for us. He can speak of toffee flavors and say that it reminds him of his childhood, but he has no sensation of "toffee" or feeling of "nostalgia" going on in his mind.

Although Chalmers doesn't think it is very likely that your friend is a zombie, he believes that the notion of a zombie (or even a whole world of zombies) is conceptually coherent. It is at least logically possible. For the faint-hearted, the prospect of zombies around every corner can be somewhat frightening. But at least there is some good news wrapped up in all of this. While your best friend, husband, or wife could be a zombie, there is no need for you to stress over the idea that *you* might be one. If you have conscious experiences, then you generally know that you have them. Insofar as you are capable of fearing zombies, you can rest assured that you are not one of them.

What do you think?

- Is it possible that one of your friends could be a zombie? Could all of them be zombies?
- Do you think that it is very likely that some lower life forms are zombies?
- Supposing that no humans are zombies, would this suggest that evolution favors consciousness? And if so, why? If zombies could eat, reproduce, and even create technologies, what is the additional advantage of possessing conscious mental states?
- Is it possible that you might have an inverted spectrum? Is there any strong evidence to suggest the contrary?

Did you know?

- The first philosopher to expressly raise the notion of a zombie was most likely Robert Kirk in "Zombies vs. Materialists" in the journal *Mind* in

1974. However, René Descartes also seemed to hold a rather zombie-like view of non-human animals.

- David Chalmers has a web page devoted to zombies and philosophical zombie literature. You can find it at: http://consc.net/zombies.html.
- Some philosophers, like Daniel Dennett, think that the idea of a zombie is self-contradictory. See his "The Zombic Hunch" (below).
- *Old Numbskull* has won a number of awards, including Gold in its category at the Chicago Real Ales Festival and Silver for Best-of-Show. The Alesmith Brewing Company is located in San Diego, California.

Recommended reading

- David Chalmers, *The Conscious Mind: In Search of a Fundamental Theory* (Oxford: Oxford University Press, 1996).
- Daniel Dennett, "The Zombic Hunch: Extinction of an Intuition," Royal Institute of Philosophy Millennial Lecture, 1999. Available online through New York University: http://www.nyu.edu/gsas/dept/philo/courses/consciousness/papers/DD-zombie.html.

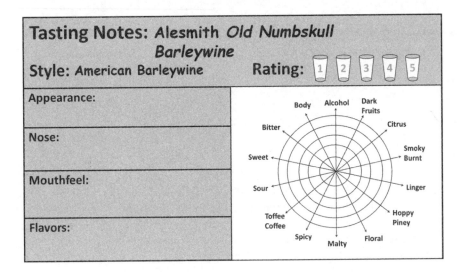

Tasting Notes: Alesmith *Old Numbskull Barleywine*
Style: American Barleywine   Rating: 1 2 3 4 5

Appearance:	
Nose:	
Mouthfeel:	
Flavors:	

(Flavor wheel axes: Body, Alcohol, Dark Fruits, Citrus, Smoky Burnt, Linger, Hoppy Piney, Floral, Malty, Spicy, Coffee, Toffee, Sour, Sweet, Bitter)

46

Lao Tzu's Empty Mug

What good is emptiness?

Pint of the Puzzle: Tsingtao *Lager*

Few things in life are worse than an empty mug. But if Lao Tzu was right, nothing is more necessary. As you dip into the Ancient Chinese puzzle of "emptiness," pop open one of China's best exports, Tsingtao Lager. By the time your glass is empty and you've finished the puzzle, I'm sure that you'll be more enlightened *and* more confused.

The great Taoist sage Lao Tzu (*c.* 500 BCE) unraveled the mysteries of the universe while drinking a beer. Well, actually, it was only after his beer was finished and he was staring at his empty mug that the insight struck. He had been pondering the nature of the universe and wondering about the source of all things. He realized that the ultimate source (which he referred to as the *Tao*) could not itself be a thing, for it too would then require a source. But if it wasn't a thing, then what was it? Nothing at all? And then it hit him. Non-being ("non-thingness" or "non-stuff") is distinct

Philosophy on Tap: Pint-Sized Puzzles for the Pub Philosopher, First Edition. Matt Lawrence
© 2011 Matt Lawrence. Published 2011 by Blackwell Publishing Ltd.

from absolute nothingness. It has power. It can do things. Non-being is creative and useful. As he put it in his most famous work, *The Tao Te Ching*:

> The Tao is like an empty mug;
>
> used but never used up.
>
> It is like the eternal void;
>
> filled with infinite possibilities.

He realized that the universe is composed of two ultimate essences, *Being* and *Non-being*. *Being* is associated with what we call matter. It can take many forms, just as a mug can be made of glass, clay, or wood. *Non-being*, in contrast, is akin to the empty space created by the mug. This is the very reason that you want the mug in the first place. When thirsty, you aren't so concerned about what your mug is made out of. What matters is that it has an empty space to hold your beer. Non-being, Lao Tzu realized, is a wonderful thing – you couldn't drink your beer without it. And one of the best things about non-being is that, while it can be used, it can never be used up. You may fill your mug a thousand times, but it can always hold another beer. This is because emptiness is used but not *consumed*.

Lao Tzu began to see the significance of non-being all around him:

> Thirty spokes are united around the hub to make a wheel,
>
> but it is on the Non-being that the utility of the carriage depends.
>
> Doors and windows are cut out to make a room,
>
> but it is on its non-being that the utility of the room depends.
>
> Clay is hollowed to make a mug,
>
> but it is its non-being that our beer depends.

In the study of Reality, the philosopher's focus is typically on Being. But Lao Tzu saw that Non-being was every bit as important. In fact, Being and Non-being were interdependent complimentary opposites. They were the core duo behind the myriad of opposite pairs (referred to as *yin/yang*) that comprise the universe.

> Being and Non-being create each other.
>
> Difficult and easy support each other.
>
> Long and short define each other.

High and low depend on each other.

Before and after follow each other.

Hops and barley balance each other.

Lao Tzu maintained that it was the interaction between Being and Non-Being that created the dance and flow of life. And, it is the (generally neglected) aspect of Non-being that governs those interactions. As Lao Tzu rather cryptically put it:

The Tao never does anything,

yet through it all things are done.

How can that which is not a thing, do anything? Lao Tzu's answer is *wu wei* – the action of non-action. We can get a glimpse of this phenomenon by analyzing the name of our Tsingtao Chinese Lager:

TSINGTAO

If we start by considering the Being or "stuff" of the word above we find that it is composed of ink. Now try this thought experiment. Suppose that I could lift the ink off of the paper and hold it in my hand. Then, I throw it back onto the paper and it lands like this:

ONGITAST

We no longer have TSINGTAO, but it is the very same ink (the very same *Being*). So what has changed? Obviously, the difference is in the *order* of the letters, that is, in the *relationship* that each letter has to those in front of and behind it. And what exactly are these relationships made of? Nothing. Relationships are not "stuff." They are what happens *between* the stuff – and this is the essence of Non-being. Hence, Lao Tzu maintains that Non-being makes things happen. It gives meaning to the world. And it is not so much the stuff, but the processes and relationships that make life worthwhile. What are love and friendship? Not hunks of matter, but relationships. And what is your beer if not a cosmic dance of hops, barley and yeast expressing just the right relationships to give you a delicious brew? Thus Lao Tzu concluded that Non-being lies at the very heart of any great beer.

Empty yet inexhaustible,

it gives birth to infinite beers.

Truth be told

Okay, so I changed most of the passages from the *Tao Te Ching* to include beer. In the second, I added the part about the mug. In the third, I added the hops and barley, and in the last Lao Tzu wrote that the Tao gives birth to "infinite worlds" rather than to *infinite beers* – but the philosophical point is largely the same. And, since nothing is certain about Lao Tzu's biography (scholars debate about whether there really was a single author of the *Tao Te Ching*), I took some liberty in assuming that his beer mug was the inspiration behind his insights. (Though I've got a strong hunch that he first contemplated the puzzle of Non-being at the bottom of a beer.)

What do you think?

- Does Non-being really exist? Can it really do things?
- Can processes and relationships be adequately described in terms of matter, or is Lao Tzu right to attribute them to Non-being?
- Try to imagine a world without Non-being. Is it even conceivable?

Did you know?

- In addition to its reflections upon the source and nature of the universe, other central themes in the *Tao Te Ching* include *ethics* (how one should live) and *political philosophy* (how people should be governed). It is the most influential text of the Taoist philosophical tradition.
- Bruce Lee was a student of Taoist philosophy. He valued *wu wei* and relied heavily on this "action of non-action" in his Kung Fu style. He wrote about its influence in his philosophical notebook, now published as: *Striking Thoughts: Bruce Lee's Wisdom for Daily Living*.
- According to physicist Lawrence Krauss, 70 percent of the energy in the universe is contained in empty space.
- Most people are familiar with the concept of yin/yang from its symbol ☯. Traditional examples of yin/yang (interdependent opposites pairs) include: female/male, cold/hot, moon/sun, water/stone, valley/mountain, soft/hard, receptive/active.

⊕ Tsingtsao used to be touted as the beer that was "brewed with mineral water from the Laoshan Spring," which was said to contribute to its unique flavor. Today this only applies to Tsingtao that is brewed in the province of Qingdao.

Recommended reading

- Lao Tzu, *Tao Te Ching*, trans. Stephen Mitchell (San Francisco: First Perennial Classics, 2000).
- Bruce Lee, *Striking Thoughts: Bruce Lee's Wisdom for Daily Living* (Boston: Tuttle, 2000).

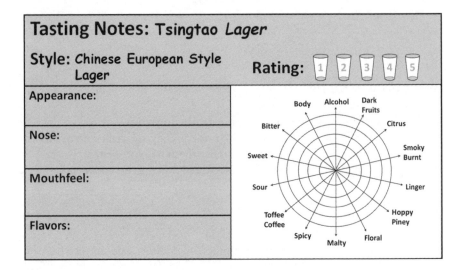

Tasting Notes: Tsingtao *Lager*

Style: Chinese European Style Lager

Rating: 1 2 3 4 5

Appearance:

Nose:

Mouthfeel:

Flavors:

Body · Alcohol · Dark Fruits · Bitter · Citrus · Sweet · Smoky Burnt · Sour · Linger · Toffee Coffee · Hoppy Piney · Spicy · Malty · Floral

Beer and the Meaning of Life

Does life have meaning? Does it mean that I should have another beer?

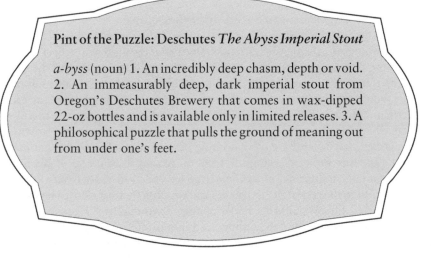

Pint of the Puzzle: Deschutes *The Abyss Imperial Stout*

a-byss (noun) 1. An incredibly deep chasm, depth or void. 2. An immeasurably deep, dark imperial stout from Oregon's Deschutes Brewery that comes in wax-dipped 22-oz bottles and is available only in limited releases. 3. A philosophical puzzle that pulls the ground of meaning out from under one's feet.

When you are deep into a pint of The Abyss, it is easy to lose sight of the meaning of life – or to begin to wonder if you had ever really seen it in the first place. Two threats seem to bubble up from the darkness: space and time – each attempting to steal away the significance of our lives.

To seriously consider the expanse of space is at once awe-inspiring and unnerving. What we normally regard as immense – our planet, or even the whole solar system – turns out to be quite small in the grand scheme of things. Our sun is just one of millions of suns in our galaxy, and our galaxy is merely one in one hundred million or so galaxies that light up the observable

Philosophy on Tap: Pint-Sized Puzzles for the Pub Philosopher, First Edition. Matt Lawrence
© 2011 Matt Lawrence. Published 2011 by Blackwell Publishing Ltd.

universe. The universe itself, as far as we can determine, is at least 93 billion light years across. The enormity of it all boggles the mind. When viewed from this perspective, we realize that our planet is little more than a speck of dust. And if a speck of dust can have miniscule specks of dust upon it, well, that would be us. On this cosmic scale, our actions seem to be utterly insignificant.

Our lives fare no better when viewed through the lens of time. Even if you live for 100 years, this is nothing but an instant in the history of the universe. If you are lucky, perhaps some of your achievements will continue after your death. Maybe you'll even be remembered for generations. But this too amounts to practically nothing from the temporal perspective. In fact, the whole of human history has been but a flicker. If you were to divide the history of the Earth into a 24-hour day, from its early formation to the present moment, then humans would have appeared on the scene at roughly one second before midnight. On such a scale, the duration of any individual person's achievements would scarcely be measurable.

So at first glance, the enormity of space and time seem to diminish, if not totally obliterate, the significance of our lives. But the more you reflect on this, the more puzzling it becomes. After all, why should size matter? If the Gods were to cut away and obliterate the outer 90 billion light years of the universe, how would that make our lives any more meaningful? It is said that the great German philosopher Immanuel Kant never left his native town of Königsberg. If the entire universe were nothing more than the town of Königsberg itself – if there were nothing beyond it at all – would that make Kant's life any more meaningful? I see no reason to think so. If his life is significant, its significance must come from how he lived it, not from its spatial proportion to the rest of the universe. And suppose that we were to be blessed with eternal life. Would this really change anything? If 80 years of life is meaningless, how would extending it ad infinitum give meaning to it?

So maybe time and space aren't the problem at all. Perhaps what dissolved life's meaning was not so much space and time themselves, but the fact that, by looking at life in this way, we were taking an utterly objective, *external* perspective – what the contemporary philosopher Thomas Nagel calls "the view from nowhere." In contrast, from a subjective, personal, or *internal* perspective, life seems quite naturally filled with meaning. Typically, meaning pops up almost everywhere we look – from the sports scores to the price of beer. The universe itself may not care about such things, but we certainly do. For most of us, it is only in the rare moments of our darkest moods (if even then) that we fail to find meaning in life. This is why the existentialist psychologist Victor Frankel famously asked his new patients: "Why do you not commit suicide?" Anyone who is still around to answer the question must obviously have found some meaning in life – something that keeps them going.

The skeptic can still press the point that perhaps we are fooling ourselves about meaning. Haven't we all taken certain events to be quite important, only to believe later that we were foolish to do so? We can easily imagine even the person who achieves something incredible, such as climbing Mount Everest, being left with the feeling: "Is that all there is?" Whether such achievements are meaningful or not seems to depend, at least in part, on one's *finding* them meaningful, and this is never absolutely necessary. For anything we do, it is always possible to ask, "Was it really worthwhile?"

Many people look to God for the meaning of life. Some think that if God did not exist, then life *would* be meaningless. But with God in the picture humanity has a point or purpose – presumably to fulfill God's divine plan. I find this reasoning difficult to fathom. Why do God's plans matter but not ours? Even when it comes to the Divine Plan, can't we still wonder, "What's the point of that?" Can't we still ask: "Is *that* really worthwhile?" And if what ultimately justifies God's plan is that it leads to a "greater good," i.e., ultimate justice, happiness, and so on, then cannot our own lives be similarly justified through the goodness of our actions – the amount of justice, love, and happiness that we bring to the world?

What do you think?

- Does the enormity of time and space have any effect upon the significance of our lives?
- Does life have meaning only from a subjective or "internal" perspective?
- Do we create or invent the meaning in our lives? Can we mistakenly regard something as significant when really it is not?
- Does life have meaning only if God exists? If so, how does God bring meaning to our lives?

Did you know?

- Some people find meaning by helping others. As armchair philosopher Jack Handey puts it: "Sometimes when I reflect back on all the beer I drink I feel ashamed. Then I look into the glass and think about the workers in the brewery and all of their hopes and dreams. If I didn't drink this beer, they might be out of work and their dreams would be shattered. Then I say to myself, 'It is better that I drink this beer and let their dreams come true than be selfish and worry about my liver'."
- The French novelist Anais Nin suggested that "There is not one big cosmic meaning for all, there is only the meaning we each give to our life, an individual meaning, an individual plot, like an individual novel, a book for each person."

(!) Friedrich Nietzsche observed that human beings can live with suffering (in fact they seek it out. What they cannot live with is *meaningless* suffering—suffering for no reason at all. See *The Genealogy of Morals* III: 28.

(!) The effects upon the drinker of The Abyss Imperial Stout vary with the individual and circumstance. Be advised that not everyone experiences a crisis of meaning with this beer. Quite to the contrary, many Abyss drinkers have reported that this dark elixir gave new meaning to their lives. Others claim to have experienced true love for the first time upon drinking this beer. I suppose that, as they said in the 1960s, "You take the *trip* that you are already on."

Recommended reading

- Thomas Nagel, *The View From Nowhere* (Oxford: Oxford University Press, 1989).
- Victor Frankel, *Man's Search for Meaning* (New York: Washington Square Press, 1984).

Tasting Notes: Deschutes *The Abyss Imperial Stout*

Style: Imperial Stout   **Rating:** 1 2 3 4 5

Appearance:	
Nose:	
Mouthfeel:	
Flavors:	

Flavor wheel axes: Body, Alcohol, Dark Fruits, Citrus, Smoky Burnt, Linger, Hoppy Piney, Floral, Malty, Spicy, Coffee, Toffee, Sour, Sweet, Bitter

The Case for Temperance

To drink or not to drink? That is the question.

Pint of the Puzzle: O'Doul's *Original Premium*
Non-alcoholic Beer

For this puzzle we're going with a non-alcoholic beer or "non-beer," as some would say. The call is O'Doul's. Now, to be quite honest, I did not subject myself to the pain of tasting a variety of these pseudo brews in order to find you the very best. Since I've never met anyone who truly enjoyed any of the non-alcoholic beers on the market, I decided that there was no reason to put myself through it. Since O'Doul's fared better than most in *some* published taste tests, I imagine that it is as good a choice as any.

This is a book for people who appreciate beer. Why, then, would it end with arguments against beer drinking? Has all the preceding been a ploy to lure you in, so that you can now be lambasted with some kind of guilt trip? Of course not. The thing to remember is that this book is first and foremost an exercise in philosophy, and the task of the philosopher is to examine the tough questions. And while some questions are tough because of their conceptual complexity, others are tough because we just don't want to look at them very closely.

Philosophy on Tap: Pint-Sized Puzzles for the Pub Philosopher, First Edition. Matt Lawrence
© 2011 Matt Lawrence. Published 2011 by Blackwell Publishing Ltd.

One of the most visible problems that stems from drinking beer or any other alcoholic beverage is drunk-driving. According to the Center of Disease Control and Prevention, every day in the United States roughly 32 people die in crashes involving an alcohol-impaired driver. This amounts to one death every 45 minutes. On average, drunk drivers cause an injury to someone every single minute. Now, of course, one needn't give up drinking altogether to solve this problem. All you have to do is avoid driving while intoxicated. But this is apparently easier said than done. We wouldn't find these horrible statistics if all those who said that they would never drive drunk (or would never do it again) actually kept their word. Alcohol undeniably impairs one's judgment – including one's judgment about whether they are fit to drive. This leads us to another very telling statistic: roughly 1.46 million drivers in the US were arrested for driving under the influence of alcohol or narcotics in 2006. Of those who were guilty, none of them was a person who *never* drinks or does drugs. Clearly, the most certain way to ensure that you never drive drunk is simply not to drink.

Even if you are the sort of person that can be counted on never to get behind the wheel while intoxicated, there may be sufficient reason to quit drinking all the same. Consider for a moment the effects of your action on others. Might the fact that you invited your friends out to the pub inadvertently lead to one of them driving when they really shouldn't – perhaps hours after you've gone home? We tend to shrug such things off saying that we can only be responsible for our own actions. But I suspect that the matter would look different to you if the next morning you were to find out that your friend veered out of his lane on his drive home, killing an unsuspecting family in another car. The Buddhist monk Thich Nhat Hanh takes this point even further. He encourages us to consider the influences of our actions, not just on ourselves and our friends, but on society at large. He contends that we *are* the world. Every thought and every action creates the society that we live in, and that will shape the lives of our children. Don't all drinkers contribute (directly or indirectly) to a social climate in which alcoholism, drunk-driving, drunken brawls, and drunken sex (leading to unwanted children and the spread of STDs) are commonplace? Every dollar spent on alcohol contributes to advertising budgets that will recruit a new generation of drinkers – many of whom will drink irresponsibly. Given the countless lives that have been destroyed by alcohol, shouldn't we take our indirect contributions to the problem more seriously?

The gist of these sorts of argument is essentially utilitarian. The basic idea is that whatever good that comes from drinking cannot outweigh the horrible consequences that arise from it. Indeed, it is difficult to imagine how much happiness something would have to bring about in order to justify thousands of innocent deaths each year. But notice that we seem to think that some things can. For example, if we were to set the speed limit to no more than 30 mph on all roads and highways, countless lives would be saved. But very few people would support such a measure. Quite frankly, we would rather accept all these foreseeable deaths if it means that we can arrive at our destinations more quickly. Perhaps similarly, all the good that comes from beer might outweigh its evils – at least in many people's decision calculus.

Arguably, there are significant goods that stem from beer. The most obvious is the simple pleasure of tasting a well-crafted brew, or of relaxing with a cold lager on a hot summer's day. But also, and perhaps most importantly, we should consider beer drinking's social ramifications. Plutarch, the Ancient Greek historian, famously noted that the proper end of drinking is to "nourish and increase friendship." This view has been argued more recently by the contemporary philosopher Jason Kawall. He writes:

> We could say that drinking a beer together is not merely drinking a beer together: it is talking, planning, reminiscing, joking, advising, encouraging, and so on. It is a much richer overall ritual, in the same way that for many people a morning cup of coffee is not merely a method of obtaining caffeine – it is the smell of the coffee, the time spent reading the newspaper, and so on.

So why not simply get together with friends for coffee? While that may also have its place, any beer drinker knows that it is just not the same. Beer is the pre-eminently social drink and has been so for centuries. This is probably due to beer's unique "metaphysical" properties as well as the social framework within which beer is consumed. Unlike coffee drinking, beer drinking is an activity that is reserved for late in the day or evening – after the work is done and one is prepared to truly relax. And it is a beverage that, by its very nature, encourages reflection and sharing. As Kawall notes, drinking beer among friends generally increases self-disclosure: "We share aspects of ourselves which reveal more of our character and lives to our friends – and in turn, our friends disclose aspects of themselves to us." By engaging in such mutual self-disclosure, he rightly contends, we become better friends to our friends, and our relationships deepen.

If deep and lasting friendships are among the greatest goods that life has to offer, then perhaps the good of beer might outweigh its evils. The fear, of course, is that, as we turn to our final summation of the issue, our love of beer will incline us to "stack the deck" by overestimating the virtues of beer drinking while slighting its often disastrous side effects. For this reason, if your analysis has (thankfully) come down in favor of beer, it may be prudent to revisit the issue occasionally to re-examine your reasoning. Better yet, you might discuss it with a couple of friends over a pint.

What do you think?

- When you really take a hard look at it, do you find that the benefits of beer drinking outweigh its negative consequences?
- If your analysis led you to believe that the costs of beer drinking outweighed its benefits, would you give it up?
- Should we take any responsibility for how our actions may influence other people?
- Is it true that beer drinking enhances friendships? And if so, is there any better beverage on the planet in that regard?

Did you know?

- There are numerous health reasons for drinking beer – *in moderation*. DrinkingBeer.Net cites the following, most of which are supported by legitimate medical studies. (1) Beer reduces stress. (2) Beer is good for the heart. (3) Beer improves circulation. (4) Beer has lots of fiber. (5) Beer is high in B vitamins and minerals. (6) Beer helps to prevent strokes. (7) Beer keeps your brain young. (8) Beer is good for your liver. (9) Beer cures insomnia. (10) Beer protects against gallstones.
- Jason Kawall crunches the "happiness" numbers on beer friendships as follows: "Suppose drinking a beer provides 5 units of happiness (whatever these amount to), while spending time with a friend provides 10 units of happiness. The proposal is that sharing a beer with a friend might produce 20 units of happiness (say), rather than just 15. The conversation with the friend flows that much more freely; you can share observations about the beer you are drinking, and so on ..."
- Aristotle famously surmised, "No one would choose to live without friends, even if he had all other goods."
- An appreciation for the unique virtues of beer goes back almost as far as recorded history. As an Egyptian proverb from *c.* 2000 BCE puts it, "The mouth of a perfectly contented man is filled with beer."

Recommended reading

- Jason Kawall, "Another Pitcher? On Beer Friendship and Character," in Steven D. Hales, ed., *Beer and Philosophy: The Unexamined Beer isn't Worth Drinking* (Oxford: Blackwell, 2007).
- Thich Nhat Hanh, *The Path of Emancipation* (Berkeley: Parallax Press, 2000).

Tasting Notes: O'Doul's *Original Premium Non-alcoholic Beer*

Style: Non-alcoholic Lager

Rating: 1 2 3 4 5

Appearance:	
Nose:	
Mouthfeel:	
Flavors:	

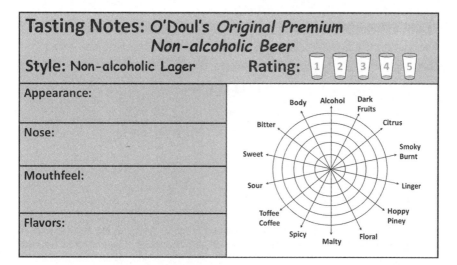

Notes

1 Transporter Troubles

- For more on the physics of teleportation and other Star Trek technologies, see Rick Stembach and Michael Okuda's *Star Trek: The Next Generation Technical Manual* (New York: Pocket Books, 1991). Stembach and Okuda were technical advisors to the television series. For a more philosophical look at the series, see Richard Hanley's *The Metaphysics of Star Trek* (New York: Basic Books, 1997).
- Derek Parfit's teleportation thought experiment, upon which my story is loosely based, appears in *Reasons and Persons* (Oxford: Clarendon Press, 1984), p. 199.

2 Zeno's Hand to Mouth Paradox

- Zeno's original paradoxes of motion can be found in Aristotle's *Physics* 239b 5–18. Available online through the Massachusetts Institute of Technology: http://classics.mit.edu/Aristotle/physics.html.

3 If a Pint Spills in the Forest

- The quote from Berkeley comes from section 4 of his *A Treatise Concerning the Principles of Human Knowledge*. Available online through Oregon State University: http://oregonstate.edu/instruct/phl302/texts/berkeley/principles_contents.html.

4 The Beer Goggles Paradox

- Dennett's analysis of the "first sip of beer" comes from his *Consciousness Explained* (Boston: Little Brown, 1991), pp. 395–396.

Philosophy on Tap: Pint-Sized Puzzles for the Pub Philosopher, First Edition. Matt Lawrence
© 2011 Matt Lawrence. Published 2011 by Blackwell Publishing Ltd.

5   Pascal's Wager

- Pascal's "wager argument" can be found in his *Pensées*, 1660. See primarily Section III, "On the Necessity of the Wager," especially §233. Available online at Project Gutenberg: http://www.gutenberg.org/etext/18269.

6   The Experience Machine

- The (modified) quote from Robert Nozick comes from his *Anarchy, State, and Utopia*, (New York: Basic Books, 1974), pp. 42–45. It is also reprinted in Steven M. Chan and Christine Vitrano, eds., *Happiness: Classic and Contemporary Readings in Philosophy* (Oxford: Oxford University Press, 2007).
- The University of Michigan study on chocolate's effects on the brain was reported in "Brain Effects Chocolate." Available online at: http://www.brainhealthandpuzzles .com/brain_effects_chocolate.html.

7   Lucretius' Spear

- Lucretius' reflections on the bounds of the universe can be found in the latter half of Book I of his *On the Nature of Things*. Available online through the Massachusetts Institute of Technology: http://classics.mit.edu/Carus/nature_things.1.i.html.
- Physicist Lawrence Krauss discusses the implications of a flat, infinite universe in his lecture "A Universe From Nothing," AAI 2009. Available online through Youtube: http://www.youtube.com/watch?v=7ImvlS8PLIo.
- For more about recent discoveries concerning the size and shape of the universe, see the NASA website: http://map.gsfc.nasa.gov/universe/uni_shape.html.

8   The Omnipotence Dilemma

- A similar strategy (distinguishing two senses of *omniscience*) is often used to escape another divine dilemma, the problem of freedom and divine foreknowledge, as we will see in #12, "The Foreknowledge Paradox."

9   What Mary Didn't Know About Lager

- The quote from Frank Jackson in the "Did You Know?" section appears in his article, "Mind and Illusion," in Anthony O'Hear, ed., *Minds and Persons* (Cambridge: Cambridge University Press, 2003), pp. 251–271.

10   Malcolm X and the Whites Only Bar

- Charles Lawrence III's argument that "race" is better conceived as a verb than a noun can be found in his "If He Hollers Let Him Go: Regulating Racist Speech on Campus," *Duke University Law Review* (1990).

11   Untangling Taste

- The (modified) quote from Virgil Aldrich appears in his "Beauty as a Feeling," *Kenyon Review*, 1 (1939).
- Ludwig Wittgenstein's remark about "rubbing his stomach" can be found in his *Lectures and Conversations on Aesthetics, Psychology, and Religious Beliefs*, ed. C. Barrett (Oxford: Blackwell, 1966).
- The (modified) passage from Kant's *Critique of Judgment* can be found in the Second Moment §7. Available online through the University of Adelaide: http://ebooks.adelaide.edu.au/k/kant/immanuel/k16j/.

12   The Foreknowledge Paradox

- Another way that some have tried to escape the paradox is by denying that free will requires alternate possibilities. Harry Frankfurt offers an interesting account of this "compatibilist" view of free will in his "Alternate Possibilities and Moral Responsibility," reprinted in J. Feinberg and R. Shafer-Landau, eds., *Reason and Responsibility* 14th edn. (Belmont CA: Wadsworth, 2011).

13   The Buddha's Missing Self

- While most cells in the human body live less than 10 years, notable exceptions include bone cells, which live more than 10 years, intestinal cells, which average more than 15 years, and brain cells. Some brain cells do not appear to regenerate at all. See "Life Span of Human Cells Defined: Most Cells are Younger than the Individual." Available on *Times Higher Education Website* (August 12, 2005): http://www.timeshighereducation.co.uk/story.asp?storycode=198208.
- The Buddha's instruction to his son Rahula comes from a collection of his teachings called the *Sanyutta-nikaya* [*The Book of Kindred* Sayings] XVII, 2, 22, trans. C. A. F. Rhys Davids and F. L. Woodward. See Bart Gruzalski, *On The Buddha* (Belmont CA: Wadsworth, 2000), p. 24.
- The quote from David Hume in the "Did you know?" section comes from his *A Treatise of Human Nature* (1739–1740), (London: Dent and Dutton, 1966), vol. I, Book I, Part IV, 6, p. 239.

14   The Blind Men and the Black and Tan

- John Hick's analysis of the story of the blind men and the elephant (analogous to my story of the blind men and the black and tan) can be found in his "Do All Religions Worship the Same God?" in Steven Cahn and David Shatz, eds., *Questions about God* (Oxford: Oxford University Press, 2002).
- Hick's utilization of the duck-rabbit appears in "The Pluralistic Hypothesis," in David Stewart, ed., *Exploring the Philosophy of Religion*, 7th edn. (Upper Saddle River, NJ: Prentice Hall, 2010), p. 43. The cartography example appears in the same essay on pp. 46–47.

15   Liar's Paradox

- Roy Pitz Brewery's claim that it is "America's Freshest Brewery" appears on their website, http://www.roypitz.com/wp/welcome-to-roypitz-com/ (accessed June 5, 2010). While it is a bold claim (which explains the scare-quotes), they do seem obsessed with using the freshest ingredients available.
- The quote from Mark Ruffalo appears in Jess Lebow, *The Beer Devotional: A Daily Celebration of the World's Most Inspiring Beers* (Massachusetts: Adams Media, 2010).
- We do not have Eubulides' commentary on the paradox – only the fact that he included it among a list of seven puzzles.
- The crocodile version of the liar's paradox is attributed to the Stoics *c.* 280 BCE.

16   Paley's Cask

- The (modified) quote from William Paley appears in his *Natural Theology*, 1809. Reprinted in Steven Cahn, ed., *Exploring Philosophy of Religion: An Introductory Anthology* (Oxford: Oxford University Press, 2009), p. 74.

17   Chuang Tzu's Butterfly

- The (modified) quote from Chuang Tzu can be found in Philip Novak, ed., *The World's Wisdom: Sacred Texts of the World's Religions* (New York: HarperCollins, 1995), p. 166.

18   Descartes' Doubt

- The (modified) passage from Descartes appears in Meditation I, Section 12 of his *Meditations on First Philosophy*. Available online through Oregon State University: http://oregonstate.edu/instruct/phl302/texts/descartes/meditations/meditations.html.

19   God's Command

- A common objection to the argument against the Divine Command Theory is that it seems to put reason prior to God. Yet, if God is eternal, nothing can be prior to God. But the argument need not involve a claim about temporal priority. Rather, the issue is really about what is explanatorily fundamental.

20   Mill's Drunkard

- The (modified) quotes from Mill both come from ch. 2, paragraphs 3 and 6, in *Utilitarianism*, available online at Project Gutenberg: http://www.gutenberg .org/etext/11224.

21   The Myth of Gyges

- The (extremely modified) quote from Glaucon comes from Bk. II 359d–360e of Plato's *Republic*. Available online at Project Gutenberg: http://www.gutenberg.org/ etext/1497.

22   Laplace's Superscientist

- For more on Libet's research on decision-making, see his *Mind Time: The Temporal Factor in Consciousness* (Cambridge, MA: Harvard University Press, 2004).
- *Old Fezziwig Ale* is a seasonal brew for the winter months. The guys at Sam Adams describe it as "a big Christmas cookie of a beer, bursting with spices of the season." If you really want to surprise someone, pull out one of these on a hot July afternoon.

23   Gaunilo's Perfect Ale

- Aquinas' ontological argument appears in ch. 2 of his *Proslogium*. Available online through Fordham University's *Medieval Sourcebook*: http://www.fordham.edu/ halsall/basis/anselm-proslogium.html.
- Gaunilo's "perfect island" reply can be found in his *In Behalf of the Fool*. Available online through Fordham University's *Medieval Sourcebook*: http://www.fordham .edu/halsall/basis/anselm-gaunilo.html.

24   The Problem of Moral Truth

- There is a fourth position on the issue of moral truth that was not covered in the puzzle. This is the view that it makes the most sense to simply claim that moral claims are *never* true. This position is known as *moral nihilism*.

25   How to Sew on a Soul

- The Harris Poll mentioned at the start of the essay can be found at: http://www.harrisinteractive.com/vault/Harris-Interactive-Poll-Research-The-Religious-and-Other-Beliefs-of-Americans-2003-2003-02.pdf. In addition to finding that 84% of Americans believe in an immortal soul, the survey found that 27% of Americans believe in reincarnation, and 69% believe in hell.
- For Descartes' account of mind–body interaction, see his "Passions of the Soul," sect. 31, *The Philosophical Works of Descartes*, trans. E. S. Haldane and G. R. T. Ross (Cambridge: Cambridge University Press, 1973), pp. 345–346.

26   Plato's Forms

- Plato also held that all Forms resemble a highest Form – the Form of the Good. For more on this, see Gerasimos Santas, "The Form of the Good in Plato's Republic," in Gail Fine, ed., *Plato I: Metaphysics and Epistemology* (Oxford: Oxford University Press, 1999).

27   Realizing Nirvana

- The Buddha's Noble Eightfold Path can be found online through the Buddha Dharma Education Association: http://www.buddhanet.net/wings_h.htm.

28   The Problem of Evil

- The "no unnecessary evil solution" is also called the "harmony solution." For an interesting literary analysis, see "Rebellion," Bk V, ch. IV of Fyodor Dostoyevsky's *The Brothers Karamazov*. Available online through Project Gutenberg: http://www.gutenberg.org/etext/28054.
- The quote from William Rowe appears in his "The Problem of Evil and Some Varieties of Atheism," *American Philosophical Quarterly* 16 (Oct. 1979), p. 337. See also his *Philosophy of Religion: An Introduction* (Belmont, CA: Thomson-Wadsworth, 2007), p. 120.
- For more information regarding how beers get "skunked," see P. S. Hughes and E. D. Baxter, *Beer Quality and Safety* (Cambridge: The Royal Society of Chemistry, 2001).

29   Time's Conundrum

- The quote from Paul Davies appears in his *God and the New Physics* (New York: Simon and Schuster, 1983), p. 124.

30 Time Travel Paradoxes

- The idea of an invention without an inventor is explored in the *Terminator* film series. In *Terminator 2: Judgment Day* we find that humans created the first artificially intelligent machine based upon technology from the terminator arm they discovered – which had been created many years in the future.

31 Hitler's Hefeweizen

- The classic joke that appears at the end of this puzzle can be found, along with a plethora of other philosophical jokes, in Thomas Cathcart and Daniel Klein's *Plato and a Platypus Walk into a Bar ... Understanding Philosophy Through Jokes* (New York: Penguin Books, 2008), p. 83.

32 The Zen Koan

- The passage from Mumon on the Mu Koan appears in *Gateless Gate: The Classic Book of Zen Kōans*, trans. Koun Yamada (Somerville, MA: Wisdom Publications, 2004), pp. 11–12.
- The other *kōans* can also be found in *The Gateless Gate*.
- The (modified) story of Toyo and the soundless sound comes from Paul Reps and Nyogen Senzaki, eds. *Zen Flesh, Zen Bones: A Collection of Zen and Pre-Zen Writings* (Boston: Shambhala, 1994), pp. 43–45.
- The quotes from D. T. Suzuki appear in his "The Meaning of Satori," in Kit R. Christensen ed., *Philosophy and Choice: Selected Readings from Around the World* (Mountain View CA: Mayfield Publishing, 1999).

33 Sex and Sensibility

- "The Heinz Dilemma" comes from Lawrence Kohlberg's "A Cognitive-Developmental Analysis of Children's Sex-Role Concepts and Attitudes," as quoted in W. C. Crain, *Theories of Development* (Upper Saddle River, NJ: Prentice-Hall, 1985), p. 118.

34 Socrates' Virtue

- Socrates' thesis that no one does wrong knowingly appears in many of Plato's dialogues. See, for example, *Apology* 25e. Available online through Project Gutenberg: http://www.gutenberg.org/etext/1656.

- Socrates' comparison of wrongdoing to optical illusions appears in Plato's *Protagoras* 356c–e. Available online through Project Gutenberg: http://www.gutenberg.org/etext/1591.
- The passage from Plato's *Apology* appears in sect. 30b of Hugh Trednnick's translation, reprinted in Edith Hamilton and Huntington Cairns, eds., *Plato: The Collected Dialogues* (Princeton, NJ: Princeton University Press, 1987).

35 Nature Calls

- The (modified) passage from Mencius appear in "Mengzi" 6A2 as translated by B. W. Van Norden, in P. J. Ivanhoe and B. W. Van Norden, eds., *Readings in Classical Chinese Philosophy*, (New York: Seven Bridges, 2001).
- The (modified) passage from Xunzi appears in the same text on p. 284.

36 Nietzsche's Eternal Recurrence

- The passage from Friedrich Nietzsche appears in sect. 341 of his *The Gay Science*, trans. Walter Kaufman, Vintage Books Edition (New York: Random House, 1974).
- The passage from Milan Kundera comes from Part I, ch. 2, para 1 of *The Unbearable Lightness of Being* (New York: Harper and Rowe, 1984).
- Nietzsche's remark about beer and the German spirit comes from aphorism 2 in his *Twilight of the Idols: Or How to Philosophize with a Hammer*, trans Duncan Large (Oxford: Oxford University Press, 2008).

37 The Most Interesting Man and the Firing Line

- The (greatly modified) story of Jim and the Indians comes from Bernard Williams, "A Critique of Utilitarianism," reprinted in Christina Hoff Summers, ed., *Right and Wrong* (New York: Harcourt, Brace, Jovanovich, 1986) p. 95.

38 Turing's Tasting Machine

- The suggestion that *Fuller's London Pride* is similar to "angels dancing on your tongue" comes from beer reviewer Stephen Cox, as quoted on Beerpal.com: http://www.beerpal.com/Fullers-London-Pride--Beer/709/.
- The beer review that was attributed to the Brewmaster5000 was an adaptation of the remarks of Lee Chase, the Head Brewer at Stone Brewing, taken from his "tasting notes" on a six-month-old *Vertical Epic Ale,* as published on the Stone Brewery website: http://www.stonebrew.com/timeline/020202/notes/020809.html.

- The passage from John Searle appears on page 2 of his "The Myth of the Computer," a review of *The Mind's I: Fantasies and Reflections on Self and Soul*, composed and arranged by Douglas R. Hofstadter, by Daniel C. Dennett, for the *New York Times*, April 29, 1982. Available online through the *New York Times Review of Books*: http://www.nybooks.com/articles/archives/1982/apr/29/the-myth-of-the-computer/.

39   Singer's Pond

- Singer's "Basic Moral Principle" appears in the sixth paragraph of his "Famine, Affluence, and Morality." Available online through Utilitarian.net: http://www.utilitarian.net/singer/by/1972----.htm.

40   The Wisest One of All

- The passage containing Socrates' reflections on justice appears in Plato, *The Republic*, Bk I, 331d. Available online through Project Gutenberg: http://www.gutenberg.org/etext/1497.

41   Enter the Matrix

- The quote from Morpheus and the (modified) quote from Mouse both appear in *The Matrix*, Warner Bros. 1999.
- The quote from Nick Bostrom appears in his, "Why Make a Matrix? And Why You Might Be In One," William Irwin, ed., *More Matrix and Philosophy: Revolutions and Reloaded Decoded* (Chicago: Open Court, 2005), p. 83.

42   A Case of Bad Faith

- Sartre's claims that "Man is condemned to be free," and "We are left alone, without excuse" appear in Walter Kaufmann, ed., *Existentialism From Dostoevsky to Sartre* (New York: Penguin 1975) p. 353.

43   Cask and Cleaver

- Singer's definition of speciesism appears in his *Animal Liberation: A New Ethics for Our Treatment of Animals* (New York: Avon, 1975), p. 7.
- The quote from Jeremy Bentham appears in his *Principles of Morals and Legislation* (Amherst, NY: Prometheus Books, 1988), ch. 17.

44 *Flirting with Disaster*

- Catherine Mackinnon's definition of sexual harassment comes from a 1991 interview with Peggy Brawley for *People Magazine*, vol. 36, no. 16 (October 28, 1991). Available online through the *People Magazine Archive*: http://www.people.com/people/archive/article/0,,20111140,00.html.
- Both quotes (the latter of which has been modified) from Ellen Frankel Paul appear in her "Exaggerating the Extent of Sexual Harassment" in James Sterba, ed., *Morality in Practice*, 7th edn. (Belmont, CA: Thomson-Wadsworth, 2004).
- Barbara Gutek's research on gender differences in attitudes regarding sexual behavior appears in "Understanding Sexual Harassment at Work," in James Sterba, ed., *Morality in Practice*, 7th edn. (Belmont, CA: Thomson-Wadsworth, 2004).
- The passage in which Mackinnon attacks the "average person" standard appears in her "Pornography, Civil Rights, and Speech" in Judith Boss, ed., *Analyzing Moral Issues*, 5th edn. (New York: McGraw-Hill, 2010).
- The two quotes from Ellison *v.* Brady (1991) appear on pp. 3 and 4 of the decision. Available online through the Columbia University Law School: http://www2.law.columbia.edu/faculty_franke/Torts/ellison.pdf.
- The quote from Camille Paglia appears in the Introduction to her *Sex, Art and American Culture* (New York: Vintage Books, 1992).

45 *Fear of Zombies*

- David Chalmers' account of his Zombie Twin appears on p. 95 of his *The Conscious Mind: In Search of a Fundamental Theory* (Oxford: Oxford University Press, 1996).

46 *Lao Tzu's Empty Mug*

- The (modified) quotes from Lao Tzu appear in *Tao Te Ching*, trans. Stephen Mitchell (San Francisco: First Perennial Classics, 2000). The passages quoted include nos. 4, 11, 2, 37, 6.

47 *Beer and the Meaning of Life*

- Victor Frankel's question about suicide appears in the Preface of his *Man's Search for Meaning* (New York: Washington Square Press, 1984).
- The quote from Jack Handey (originally a character on NBC's *Saturday Night Live*) appears in many internet sources, but without citation. Jack Handey has several books of enlightening aphorisms. See, e.g., *Deep Thoughts: Inspiration for the Uninspired* (New York: Berkeley Books, 1992).

- The quote from Anais Nin comes from Gunther Stuhlmann, ed., *The Diary of Anais Nin*, vol. 2 (New York: Harcourt, 1966), Preface.

48　The Case for Temperance

- The statistics associated with drunk driving come from the Center of Disease Control and Prevention: http://www.cdc.gov/MotorVehicleSafety/Impaired_ Driving/impaired-drv_factsheet.html.
- All quotes in the body of the essay from Jason Kawall appear in "Another Pitcher? On Beer, Friendship, and Character," in Steven D. Hales, ed., *Beer and Philosophy: The Unexamined Beer Isn't Worth Drinking* (Oxford: Blackwell, 2007), pp. 126–128.
- The health reasons for drinking beer come from DrinkingBeer.net: http://www. drinkingbeer.net/BeerArticles/Top_10_Reasons_Beer_is_Good_for_your_Health .php5.
- Aristotle's claim that "No one would choose to live without friends, even if he had all other goods," appears at the opening of Bk. VIII of his *Nicomachean Ethics*. Available online through the University of Adelaide: http://ebooks.adelaide.edu .au/a/aristotle/nicomachean/.

Glossary of Beer and Philosophical Terms

Abbey ale: A strong ale traditionally brewed by Trappist monks in Belgian abbeys. They are top-fermented and bottle-conditioned. The term also applies to any beer that is brewed in the Trappist style. (Try Pint of the Puzzle 23, Chimay *Bleue*; Pint of the Puzzle 29, La Trappe *Quadrupel*; and Pint of the Puzzle 36, North Coast *Brother Thelonius Abbey Ale*.)

Aesthetics: The branch of philosophy that studies beauty and art. (See Puzzle 11, "Untangling Taste.")

Aesthetic objectivism: The view that at least some aesthetic judgments (judgments about what is beautiful or artistic) are objective. That is, some aesthetic judgments are true independently of the beliefs and feelings of the person or group who makes the judgment. (See Puzzle 11, "Untangling Taste.")

Aesthetic subjectivism: The view that aesthetic judgments (judgments about what is beautiful or artistic) are purely subjective. That is, the truth of aesthetic judgments is entirely dependent upon, or relative to, the beliefs and feelings of the person who makes the judgment. (See Puzzle 11 "Untangling Taste.")

Alcohol by volume (ABV): The worldwide standard for measuring the alcohol content in beer. It pertains to the amount of space that the alcohol takes up as a percentage of total volume of the beer. Most beers range from 4% to 8% ABV, though many stouts and strong ales will top 10%.

Ale: Beer made with "top-fermenting" strains of yeast (i.e., yeast that ferments at the top of the fermentation tank). Ales can be fermented at warmer temperatures than lagers, which use bottom-fermenting yeasts. (Try Pint of the Puzzle 15, Roy Pitz *Truly Honest Ale*, and Pint of the Puzzle 25, Rogue *Dead Guy Ale*.)

Anatta: The Buddhist doctrine of no-self. It is the view that there is no permanent, self-sufficient, or independent "Self" or "soul" that persists over time. (See Puzzle 13, "The Buddha's Missing Self.")

Philosophy on Tap: Pint-Sized Puzzles for the Pub Philosopher, First Edition. Matt Lawrence © 2011 Matt Lawrence. Published 2011 by Blackwell Publishing Ltd.

Argument by analogy: To argue that since two things are similar in certain relevant respects, similar conclusions can be drawn about them. (See Puzzle 14, "The Blind Men and the Black and Tan"; Puzzle 23, "Gaunilo's Perfect Ale"; and Puzzle 39, "Singer's Pond.")

Argument to the best explanation: To argue that a conclusion, although not proven, is the best explanation for the phenomena in question. (See Puzzle 16, "Paley's Cask.")

Aromatic hops: Hops that are added late in the brewing cycle and are chosen for their aroma contribution to the beer. Examples include Cascade, Crystal, and Saaz hops.

Bad faith: A term used by the French existentialist Jean-Paul Sartre to refer to the phenomenon of lying to oneself about one's freedom. The attempt to see oneself as unfree or without options when one knows this to be false. (See Puzzle 42, "A Case of Bad Faith.")

Barley: A cereal grain of the genus *Hordeum*. There are two varieties, two-row and six-row, classified according to the number of rows of seeds on the head of the plant. Barley is heated (kilned) to create malt, one of the main ingredients in beer.

Barleywine: A style of strong ale that is as potent as wine – generally 10–15% ABV. (Try Pint of the Puzzle 4, Flying Dog *Horn Dog Barleywine*.)

Beer: One of the oldest alcoholic beverages, dating back to about 3000 BCE. Beer is made by brewing and fermenting grains (usually malted barley), with the addition of hops as a flavoring agent.

Beer goggles paradox (10@2 paradox): The paradoxical phenomenon in which another person seems to become more beautiful in correlation with the amount of beer that the observer consumes. Also known as the 10@2 paradox, because a person might rate a "2" at 10.00 p.m. and yet become a "10" by 2.00 a.m. – after one has consumed a sufficient quantity of beer. (See Puzzle 4, "The Beer Goggles Paradox.")

Bittering hops: These are hops that are added early in the brewing cycle for their contribution to the bitterness of the beer. Examples include Chinook, Magnum, and Newport hops.

Black hole: 1. A region of space from which nothing, including light, can escape. It is the result of the deformation of the space–time continuum caused by a very compact mass such as when a star collapses under its own weight. (See Puzzle 30 "Time Travel Paradoxes.") 2. *Black Hole Old Ale* from Weyerbacher Brewing of Pennsylvania.

Black lager (*Schwarzbier*): Black lager, known in Germany as *schwarzbier*, is a dark beer brewed in the lager style. It is milder tasting than stouts and porters, due to the use of lager yeast rather than ale yeast. Its dark color comes from the use of particularly dark malts in the brewing process. (Try Brew Dog *Zeitgeist Black Lager*.)

Blonde: The French and Belgian name for golden beer. (Try *Leffe Blonde*.)

Bock (*bockbier*): Bock is the German word for *strong*. Bock beer (*bockbier*) tends to be stonger, darker, and sweeter than "regular" beer. Variations include the even stronger *doppelbock*. Bock was originally used to celebrate the end of the brewing season, and is traditionally served in autumn, late winter, and spring. (Try *Sprecher Maibock*.)

Body (mouthfeel): The density of the beer as felt by the mouth when tasting.

Bottle conditioning: Refers to the secondary fermentation that occurs when yeast and sugars are added to the beer right before bottling. This extends storage life and allows the flavor to continue to develop over time.

Brown ale: Ale made with dark or brown malt; the roasted malt produces caramel and chocolate flavors. The basic style originated in London and has since evolved into a variety of styles. (Try Pint of the Puzzle 11, Big Sky *Moose Drool Brown Ale*, and Pint of the Puzzle 16, Newcastle *Brown Ale*.)

Cartesian theater model of the mind: A view of conscious experience that is akin to imagining a tiny theater in the brain where a homunculus (tiny person) observes all the sensory data as if it were projected on a screen. (See Puzzle 4, "The Beer Goggles Paradox.")

Cask: The British term for a barrel-shaped container for holding beer. (See Puzzle 16, "Paley's Cask.")

Causal determinism: The view that (a) every event has a cause and (b) prior causes determine the characteristics of each event in every precise detail. If causal determinism is true, then every event occurs exactly as it must occur – due to the prior causal conditions. (See Puzzle 22, "Laplace's Superscientist.")

Chocolate malt: Dark brown roasted malt. Although it can provide chocolatey flavors, it contains no chocolate.

Cold filtering: An alternative to pasteurizing beer by passing it through a very fine filter that removes the yeast and ends the fermentation process.

Compatibilism: The view that free will is compatible with causal determinism. This view maintains that "alternate possibilities" are not required for free will. (See Puzzle 22, "Laplace's Superscientist," and Puzzle 12, "The Foreknowledge Paradox.")

Consequentialism: Any ethical theory that maintains that an action is "right" if it produces the best overall consequences. The most notable example is utilitarianism. (See Puzzle 31, "Hitler's Hefeweizen," and Puzzle 37, "The Most Interesting Man and the Firing Line.")

Cosmic strings: Slender strands (skinnier than a proton) of very concentrated mass-energy. A piece of cosmic string 1.6 kilometers long would weigh more than the earth. It has been hypothesized that cosmic strings could stretch the length of the universe and might be utilized to travel backwards in time. (See Puzzle 30 "Time Travel Paradoxes.")

Craft beer: This term is used rather loosely, generally to refer to beer that comes from artisanal brewers who work exclusively with natural ingredients, in small batches, and with no automation. Sometimes it is used to refer to any beer of high quality.

Cream ale: Cream ale is an American style of very pale ale. Typically it is a blend of half lager and half golden ale. (Try Anderson Valley's *Summer Solstice Cerveza Crema*.)

Crystal malt (caramel malt): A specially processed type of malt that is used to add body, color, and flavor to dark and amber beers.

Cultural relativism (ethics): The view that the truth of moral claims (e.g., slavery is wrong), depends upon or is entirely relative to the beliefs and/or feelings of one's culture. (See Puzzle 24, "The Problem of Moral Truth.")

Dilemma: A choice that is limited to two options, both of which are unfavorable. (See Puzzle 8, "The Omnipotence Dilemma," and Puzzle 19, "God's Command.")

Divine command theory: A theory of morality that maintains that actions are right if and only if God commands (or wills) them. Actions are wrong if and only if God forbids (or wills against) them. (See Puzzle 19, "God's Command.")

Dopplebock (double bock): Dopplebock is German for an extra-strong beer – typically 7.5% ABV or higher. It is a bottom-fermented beer, dark brown in color. It is a spring specialty beer that originated in southern Germany, traditionally brewed in March and April. (Try Spaten *Optimator*)

Dubbel: An abbey-style beer that uses up to double the amount of malt of a "simple" or blonde abbey-style beer. (Try Pint of the Puzzle 36, North Coast *Brother Thelonious Abbey Ale*.)

Dunkel (dunkler bock): *Dunkel* means "dark" in German, and dunkels are dark lager beers. Dunkler bock is a bock-strength (strong) dark lager. (Try Ayinger *Altbairisch Dunkel*.)

Dunklweizen: A dark version of a wheat beer. (In German, *dunkel* means dark and *weizen* refers to wheat.) (Try New Belgium *Lips of Faith Dunkelweiss 30°*)

Draft (draught): Beer drawn from a keg. "Draught" is the British spelling of "draft" and has the same pronunciation. "Genuine draft," when applied to bottled beer, implies that it is unpasteurized (as is keg beer). Generally such beers are sterile filtered for longer shelf life.

Dry hopping: The addition of dry hops during fermentation to increase the hop aroma without adding bitterness.

Elysian: 1. In Greek mythology the Elysian Fields were the final resting place for the souls of the virtuous and heroic. 2. The Elysian Brewing Company of Seattle, Washington, makers of *The Wise ESB*, *The Immortal IPA* and *Perseus Porter*. (See Puzzle 40, "The Wisest One of All.")

Epistemology: The study and/or theory of knowledge. Epistemological questions include: What is knowledge? How is knowledge attained? Can we know what is real? (See Puzzle 17, "Chuang Tzu's Butterfly," and Puzzle 18, "Descartes' Doubt.")

ESB (extra special bitter or extra strong bitter): A bitter beer style (but generally not as bitter as the name suggests). ESBs tend to be medium bodied and copper to amber in color with hoppy aromas and flavor. (Try Pint of the Puzzle 40, Elysian *The Wise ESB*.)

Esters: Flavor compounds naturally created during fermentation that can add fruity, flowery, and spice flavors to beer.

Eternal recurrence: German philosopher Friedrich Nietzsche's hypothesis (or thought experiment) that one's life will recur over and over without change.

Ethics: The study and/or theory of morality. Ethical questions include: What makes an action right or wrong? Is anything really right or wrong? What would be right in this situation? (See Puzzles 19, 21, 24, 31, 33, 34, 39, 43, 44.)

Existentialism: A school of philosophical thought that emphasizes subjectivity, freedom, and personal responsibility. Major existentialists include: Søren Kierkegaard, Martin Heidegger, Jean Paul Sartre, and Simone de Beauvoir. (See Puzzle 42, "A Case of Bad Faith.")

Fermentation: The process of converting sugars into alcohol and CO_2 by the activity of yeast.

Functionalism: A theory within the philosophy of mind that maintains that what makes something a mental state of a particular type is not its internal constitution, but, rather, the function that it plays within the system that it is a part. "Believing X" or "Feeling Y" is a matter of instantiating a particular input–process–output relationship. (See Puzzle 38, "Turing's Tasting Machine," and Puzzle 45, "Fear of Zombies.")

Game theory: The study of strategic interactions among rational agents by analyzing the outcomes of available choices with respect to the preferences of those agents. (See Puzzle 5, "Pascal's Wager.)

Gravity: 1. The fundamental force by which objects with mass attract one another, caused by the curvature of the space–time continuum. (See Puzzle 7, "Lucretius' Spear.") 2. A brewer's term for the weight of beer. The "original gravity" is the weight of beer before fermentation. The "final gravity" is the weight of a beer after fermentation.

Growler: A half-gallon glass jug used to transport draft beer from the pub or brewery. Some 32-ounce growlers are now available.

Head: The layer of foam that lies on top of a beer. It is recommended that you pour your beer straight into the center of the glass in order to create an adequate head.

Hedonism: The view that pleasure is the only intrinsic good. All other things are regarded as good only as a means to, or as a part of one's pleasure. (See Puzzle 6, "The Experience Machine" and Puzzle 20, "Mill's Drunkard.")

Hefe: German for yeast.

Hefeweizen: *Hefe* is German for "yeast," while *weizen* is German for "wheat." Hefeweizen is wheat beer in the German style, also called Hefeweisse, Hefeweissbier, and Weissbier. (Try Pint of the Puzzle 31, Hofbräu *Hefeweizen*.)

Hell (Helles): 1. A place of punishment after death typically believed to involve eternal suffering. 2. The German word for "pale" used to refer to golden beers. (Try Pint of the Puzzle 12, Aktien's *Hell Lager*.)

Hops: The dried blossom of the female hop plant, a climbing vine of the *Cannabacinae* family. Hops are responsible for the bitterness in beer, as well as other flavors and aromas.

IBU (international bittering units): A standard scale that measures the bitterness of beer. Most beers range from 10 to 100 IBUs. The higher the number the more bitter the beer. While there is no real gauge beyond 100, some beers are rated even higher. (Try Pint of the Puzzle 43, Laughing Dog *Alpha Dog Imperial IPA*, rated at 127 IBU's.)

Idealism (metaphysical idealism): The view made famous by Bishop George Berkeley, that all that exists are minds and the ideas of minds (including thoughts, feelings, perceptions, etc.) According to idealism, matter (i.e., substance that exists outside of and independently of minds) does not exist. (See Puzzle 3, "If a Pint Spills in the Forest …")

IPA (Indian pale ale): A robust, heavily hopped ale. In the eighteenth century IPAs were exported to India from Britain because most beer could not hold up under the long journey by ship. IPA's higher level of hops (which act as a preservative) and high level of alcohol (generally 7–8%) enabled it to withstand the warm voyage. (Try Pint of the Puzzle 28 *Hopdevil IPA*, and Pint of the Puzzle 43, Laughing Dog *Alpha Dog Imperial IPA*.)

Kantianism: The moral theory of Immanuel Kant. Kant argued that right and wrong were to be determined through *the categorical imperative* which states: "Act only on that maxim whereby you can at the same time will that it should become a universal law." This view contrasts sharply with Utilitarianism. (See Puzzle 31, "Hitler's Hefeweizen.")

Karma: 1. The law of karma is the law of causality within Hindu and Buddhist philosophy. An individual's karma is the total effect of their actions and conduct that determines the content of their present and future. (See Puzzle 27, "Realizing Nirvana.") 2. *Karma Ale* from Avery Brewing.

Kas: The Ancient Sumerian word for beer. Its literal meaning: "What the mouth desires."

Kellerbier: "Cellar beer" in German. Kellerbier is unfiltered lager with a high hop content and low carbonation. (Try Voodoo Brewing *Pilzilla*.)

Kōan: A paradoxical puzzle used as an object of meditation in Zen Buddhism. (See Puzzle 32, "The Zen Kōan.")

Kriek: A tart cherry beer that is usually based on lambic. (Try Selins Grove *The Phoenix Kriek*.)

Lager: From the German word "lagern" which means "to store." Lagers are made with "bottom-fermenting" strains of yeast, and are brewed for longer periods of time than ales and at colder temperatures, resulting in a lighter, crisper beer.

Lambic: Beers fermented by wild airborne yeasts in a style unique to breweries of the Payottenland region of Belgium. Lambic tends to be naturally dry, acidic, and effervescent. (Try Lindeman's *Framboise*.)

Malts (malted barley): Barley which has been steeped in water, allowed to germinate, and then heat dried. The type of barley, the level of germination, and the temperature of drying all influence the resulting flavor.

Mash: The mixture of ground malt and boiled grits that break down into fermentable sugars in the beer-making process.

Materialism (metaphysical materialism): The view that matter is the only substance in the universe. If materialism is true, everything that exists is composed of matter. (See Puzzle 3, "If a Pint Spills in the Forest . . .," and Puzzle 9, "What Mary Didn't Know About Foster's Lager.")

Microbrewery: A small brewery produces fewer than 15,000 barrels annually.

Mind–body dualism: The view that human beings are composed of two distinct substances – one material (the body) and the other immaterial (the mind, spirit, or soul). (See Puzzle 25, "How to Sew on a Soul.")

Mind–body materialism: The view that human beings are composed of only a single substance: matter. The mind is therefore regarded as the brain or a phenomenon of the brain. According to the mind–body materialist, there is no immaterial soul. (See Puzzle 25, "How to Sew on a Soul," and Puzzle 9 "What Mary Didn't Know About Lager.")

Mind–body problem: The problem of determining how the mind is related to the body. (See Puzzle 25 "How to Sew on a Soul," and Puzzle 9 "What Mary Didn't Know About Lager.")

Moral egoism: The view that the morally right action is that which maximizes one's own interests. (See Puzzle 21, "The Myth of Gyges.")

Moral objectivism: The view that some moral claims (e.g., slavery is wrong) are objectively true. That is, their truth or falsity is not relative to the beliefs or feelings of the individual or culture. (See Puzzle 24, "The Problem of Moral Truth.")

Moral relativism (cultural relativism): The view that moral claims are relative to the beliefs or feelings of one's culture. There is no "objective" right or wrong that exists independently of the cultural outlook. (See Puzzle 24, "The Problem of Moral Truth.")

Moral Subjectivism: The view that moral claims are relative to the beliefs or feelings of the individual. There is no "objective" right or wrong that exists independently of the moral outlooks of people. (See Puzzle 24 "The Problem of Moral Truth.")

Mouthfeel: See Body.

Ninkasi: 1. The Ancient Sumerian Goddess of fermentation. Much of what we know of her comes from the *Hymn to Ninkasi,* a poem of praise written onto a clay tablet circa 1800 BCE. 2. Ninkasi Brewing Company of Eugene Oregon.

Nirvana: The Buddhist term for enlightenment, characterized by peace, equanimity and the complete cessation of suffering. (See Puzzle 27, "Realizing Nirvana.")

Noble hops: The term "noble hops" refers to four high-aroma varieties that originated in central Europe: Tettnanger, Hallertauer Mittelfrueh, Spalter, and Saaz. This strain of hops provides the traditional aroma and flavor of many classic styles including Pilsner, Dunkel, and Oktoberfest.

Ontological argument: The attempt to prove God's existence from the mere idea, or definition of God. (See Puzzle 23, "Gaunilo's Perfect Ale.")

Pasteurization: The process of heating of beer to 60–79 °C/140–174°F in order to increase its shelf-life.

Pale ale: A bronze- or copper-colored ale with bitterness, flavor, and aroma dominated by hops. Pale ales have medium body and low to medium maltiness. (Try Pint of the Puzzle 3, Sierra Nevada *Pale Ale*.)

Paradox of bisection: The puzzle that arises out of the (apparent) fact that a finite distance can be bisected an infinite number of times, and therefore into an infinite number of discrete distances. (See Puzzle 2, "Zeno's Hand to Mouth Paradox.")

Philosophy: The area of study devoted to the systematic examination of basic concepts such as truth, existence, reality, knowledge, and morality.

Philosophy of mind: The philosophical study of the mind. Central questions include: Is the mind just the brain? Can computers become conscious? Is there free will? (See Puzzles 1, 4, 9, 11, 13, 21, 22, 25, 38, 45.)

Pilsner (Pils): A style of very clean, crisp lager. Pilsner is the most popular lager in the world today. The first Pilsner was brewed at the Bürgerlisches Brauhaus in Plzen, Czechoslovakia in 1842, using a special yeast smuggled from Germany by a Czech monk. (Try Pint of the Puzzle 41, Moonlight Brewing *Reality Czech Pilsner*.)

Principle of bivalence: The principle that any meaningful statement must be true or false. (See Puzzle 15, "Liar's Paradox.")

Principle of equality: The moral principle that maintains that similar interests ought to carry similar weight, and differences in treatment must be justified in terms of relevant differences in the beings affected by the action. (See Puzzle 43, "Cask and Cleaver.")

Plato: 1. The student of Socrates and teacher of Aristotle, best known for his masterwork *The Republic,* and for his theory of Forms. (See Puzzle 26, "Plato's Forms.") 2. A scale of measurement used to determine the density of beer wort. It was developed by Bohemian scientist Karl Balling and later improved by Fritz Plato.

Pliny the Elder: 1. A stoic philosopher and naturalist 23–79 CE, Pliny and his contemporaries are responsible for the botanical name for hops, *lupus Salictarius*, which means "wolf among scrubs." 2. *Pliny the Elder* Double IPA from the Russian River Brewery.

Pliny the Younger: 1. An ancient Roman lawyer and scientist; nephew of Pliny the Elder. 2. *Pliny the Younger* Triple IPA from the Russian River Brewery.

Porter: A strong, dark malty style of ale, full bodied, but less heavy than stout. Porter was named after the porters who hauled goods from wagons to the stands in the open-air markets common to England in the eighteenth century. (Try Pint of the Puzzle 24, Wasatch *Polygamy Porter*.)

Problem of evil: The paradox that arises when one assumes that there is an all-good, all-knowing, and all-powerful God, *and* that the world is full of moral and natural evils. (See Puzzle 28, "The Problem of Evil.")

Problem of freedom and divine foreknowledge: The paradox that arises when one assumes that there is a God who knows all (including people's future actions) *and* that people have free will. (See Puzzle 12, "The Foreknowledge Paradox.")

Problem of personal identity: The problem of determining what makes someone the "same" person over time. (See Puzzle 1 "Transporter Troubles," and Puzzle 13 "The Buddha's Missing Self.")

Problem of other minds: The problem of knowing the content of another person's consciousness – or whether they are truly conscious at all. (See Puzzle 9, "What Mary Didn't Know about Foster's Lager," and Puzzle 45, "Fear of Zombies.")

Psychological egoism: The thesis that people only act for their own self-interest. There is no purely unselfish act. (See Puzzle 21, "The Myth of Gyges.")

Quadrupel: The strongest of the Belgian abbey ale styles, more intense than a Dubbel or Tripel. (Try Pint of the Puzzle 29, La Trappe *Quadrupel*.)

Qualia: The subjective qualitative properties of mental states, such as sights, sounds, smells, etc. (See Puzzle 9, "What Mary Didn't Know About Foster's Lager" and Puzzle 45, "Fear of Zombies.")

Rasputin: 1. Grigori Yefimovich Rasputin was a Russian mystic and faith healer (some would argue a charlatan), who influenced the latter days of the Russian Tsar Nicholas II and his wife Tsaritsa Alexandra. 2. *Old Rasputin* Russian Imperial Stout from North Coast Brewing.

Religious pluralism: The view that many religions can all be true, despite points of opposition or contradiction. No religion represents the whole truth, since ultimate religious truths cannot be put into human concepts without some inevitable distortion. (See Puzzle 14, "The Blind Men and the Black and Tan.")

Rheinheitsgebot: Pronounced *rhine-heights-geh·bot*, this is the German Purity Law of 1516 that specifies that beer can only be made with three ingredients: barley, hops, and water. At the time no one knew that the yeast in the air was involved in the process. It was later approved as the fourth approved ingredient.

Saison: French for "season," this is the name originally given to low-alcohol pale ales brewed seasonally in farmhouses in Wallonia, Belgium, for the refreshment of the farm workers. This Belgian style is now replicated by breweries around the globe. (Try Pint of the Puzzle 42, Fantôme *Pissenlit Saison*.)

Scotch ale: A very strong malty style of ale developed in Scotland. (Try Pint of the Puzzle 8, Belhaven *Wee Heavy Scotch Ale*.)

Shiva: 1. A Hindu God responsible for the destruction of the illusory world. 2. *Shiva India Pale Ale* from the Asheville Brewing.

Skunkiness: A foul aroma that can come from beer if it has been "lightstruck." When bright light strikes the hops in beer for an extended period of time, a chemical reaction occurs which causes the beer to skunk (i.e., stink). Clear and green bottles do nothing to prevent skunking. Brown bottles are much more, though not completely, effective at preventing skunking.

Social construction: Something is "socially constructed" if it is created by society. The contrasting concept would be something that is a "natural or biological fact." Many philosophers have argued that race and gender are social constructions. (See Puzzle 10, "Malcolm X and the Whites only Bar," and Puzzle 33, "Sex and Sensibility.")

Sour ale: A very sour beer produced with wild yeasts and other micro-organisms. (Try Russian River *Consecration.*)

Skepticism: Philosophical views are typically classed as *skeptical* when they involve doubting claims that are generally taken for granted. (See Puzzle 18, "Descartes' Doubt".)

Steam: Considered the only classic American beer style, steam beers tend to have a deep amber color, a sharp flavor, and high carbonation. Steam was invented in California during the Gold Rush when lager yeast was used to drive fermentation at the higher temperatures typically used with ale yeasts. (Try (His) Pint of the Puzzle 33, *Anchor Steam.*)

Stout: The darkest and heaviest of beers. Stout is top fermented, but differs from regular ale by its brown-black color, chocolate-coffee flavors, and fuller body. This is achieved by brewing with barley that has been dark-roasted to the point of charring. (Try Pint of the Puzzle 1, Guinness *Extra Stout.*) **Chocolate Stout** is a sub-category that uses different malts for an even more pronounced chocolate flavor. Some brewers add actual chocolate or chocolate extract into the brew. (Try Pint of the Puzzle 6, Young's *Double Chocolate Stout.*) **Coffee Stout** uses dark roasted malts to add a bitter coffee flavor and often ground coffee beans as well. (Try Pint of the Puzzle 17, Great Divide *Espresso Oak Aged Yeti.*) **Cream Stout** or milk stout is a variation made sweeter with milk sugar. (Try St. Peter's *Cream Stout.*) **Imperial Stout or Russian Stout** is an extra strong, high alcohol variation, so named because of its popularity with the Imperial Court of Russia's Catherine II. (Try Pint of the Puzzle 47, Deschutes *The Abyss Imperial Stout.*) **Oatmeal Stout** adds oatmeal to the mash to provide smoothness and creaminess. It has more restrained flavors and less alcohol than imperial stout. (Try Pint of the Puzzle 20, Samuel Smith's *Oatmeal Stout.*)

Subjectivism: See Aesthetic subjectivism and Moral subjectivism.

Taoism: A principal philosophy and system of religion of China based on the teachings of Lao-tzu as expressed in the *Tao Te Ching.* (See Puzzle 46, "Lao Tzu's Empty Mug.")

Tap: A valve for controlling the release of beer from a cask or keg. When a beer is "on tap" it is available on draft – its freshest means of delivery. When philosophy is "on tap" it is available in the freshest possible form and should be enjoyed with a fine beer.

Trappist: The Order of Cistercians of the Strict Observance, or "Trappists," is a Roman Catholic religious order of contemplative monks who follow the Rule of St. Benedict. Trappist monks are famous for their abbey ales, produced in five breweries in Belgium and one in the Netherlands. They have exclusive rights to use the term "Trappist" in the marketing and packaging of their beer. (Try Pint of the Puzzle 33, *Chimay Bleue.*)

Tripel: A style of Belgian beer in which up to three times the amount of malt is used than in a standard "simple" or blonde abbey style beer. (Try Pint of the Puzzle 7, *La Fin du Monde,* and Pint of the Puzzle 33, Chimay *Bleue "Grande Réserve."*)

Utilitarianism: A moral philosophy developed by Jeremy Bentham and John Stuart Mill that defines right actions as those which yield the greatest happiness for the greatest number. (See Puzzle 20, "Mill's Drunkard," and Puzzle 31, "Hitler's Hefeweizen.")

Weisse (Weisbier, Wit, Witbier, Wheat Beer): *Weissbier* is the German word for white beer, a pale beer made from wheat. The Dutch/Flemish (Belgian) term for Weissbier is *witbier.* Belgian witbieren are often brewed with spices such as coriander, or fruits such as orange peel. (Try Pint of the Puzzle 10, Avery's *White Rascal Ale.*)

Wormhole: A hypothetical topological feature of space–time that would serve as a shortcut through space–time. In much the same way that a worm might take a "shortcut" to the other side of an apple by eating through it, as opposed to navigating around the apple's skin, a wormhole might enable space–time travelers to arrive at their destination much more quickly than those who take the conventional route. (See Puzzle 30 "Time Travel Paradoxes.")

Wort: The liquid that is extracted from the mashing process during the brewing of beer. This is then fermented in order to break down the sugars to produce alcohol.

Yeast: Single celled organisms of the fungus family that are responsible for converting the sugars contained in malt into alcohol and carbon dioxide. Yeast also imparts flavor and can be used to give a fruity taste to beer. It is a traditional slogan of brewers that: "We make the wort, the yeast makes the beer."

Yin/yang: In Chinese philosophy yin/yang refers to the balance of interdependent opposites. Yin represents the passive and receptive polarity (dark, cool, soft, moist, etc.) and yang represents the aggressive and active polarity (light, heat, hard, dry, etc.). (See Puzzle 46, "Lao Tzu's Empty Mug.")

Zombie: 1. The philosophical term for a person (or creature) who has no phenomenal experience, i.e., no thoughts, desires, moods, or feelings. 2. The Hollywood term for the living-dead who want to eat your brain. (See Puzzle 45, "Fear of Zombies.")

Zymurgy: The science of fermentation.